D0929842

THE GREAT ESCAPE

THE GREAT ESCAPE

THE FULL DRAMATIC STORY
WITH CONTRIBUTIONS FROM
SURVIVORS AND THEIR FAMILIES

ANTON GILL

review

Concept and programme material © 2001 Granada Media Group Limited
Text copyright © 2002 Anton Gill/Granada Media Group Limited

The right of Anton Gill to be identified as the Author of
the Work has been asserted by him in accordance with the
Copyright, Designs and Patents Act 1988.

First published in 2002 by
REVIEW

An imprint of Headline Book Publishing

10 9 8 7 6 5 4 3 2 1

This book accompanies the television film produced by United Productions
for ITV and first broadcast in 2001.
Producer/director: Steven Clarke
Assistant producer: Louise Osborne
Production manager: Liz Stevens

Cataloguing in Publication Data is available from the British Library

ISBN 0 7553 1037 3

Map by ML Design

Designed by Ben Cracknell Studios

Typeset by Palimpsest Book Production Limited, Polmont, Stirlingshire

Printed and bound in Great Britain by
Mackays of Chatham plc, Chatham, Kent

HEADLINE BOOK PUBLISHING
A division of Hodder Headline
338 Euston Road
London NW1 3BH

www.reviewbooks.co.uk
www.hodderheadline.com

Illustrations on pages 101 (FAO 1924), 119, 122 (both FAO 1914) and 157 (FAO 1925)
by Ley Kenyon © RAF Museum;
page 226 © John Frost Newspapers

To all who fight for freedom
and against oppression

My guide and I came on that hidden road
to make our way back into the bright world;
and with no care for any rest, we climbed –
he first, I following – until I saw,
through a round opening, some of those things
of beauty heaven bears. It was from there
that we emerged, to see – once more - the stars.

– Dante, *Inferno*, Canto 34 (translated by Allen Mandelbaum)

Per ardua ad astra

Motto of the Royal Air Force

Contents

Contents

Acknowledgements

This book is in part the result of extensive research into the history of the Great Escape by United Productions for a television documentary. Some of the material used here is based on interviews conducted by United with participants in the escape or their relatives, for few remain of those who survived Hitler's wrath then. For this book I have to acknowledge the help of Les Brodrick, Alex Cassie, Russell Cochran (Dennis Cochran's younger brother), Beryl Fitch (Dennis Cochran's sister), Jimmy James, Colin Kirby-Green (Tom Kirby-Green's son), and Jack Lyon. I have also drawn on testimony and material from Marie Brochin (née Marchant), who is 'Jack' Grisman's widow, and from Joan Ellwood (née Cook), who was Brian Evans' fiancée; as well as further contributions from Tony Bethell, Sydney Dowse, Malcolm Freeguard, Graham Hall, Henry Lamond, Jens Muller, Ken Rees, Frank Tams and Reg Van Toen. For their expertise, thanks are also due to M. R. D. Foot, the historian of MI9, and the espionage authority Nigel West, as well as the staffs of the Library and Archives at the Imperial War Museum; the staffs of the London Library and the Public Record Office, and the staff of the Bundesarchiv Militärarchiv, Freiburg i. Br. At United Productions I have to thank Steven Clarke, the documentary's producer and director, Louise Osborne, its assistant producer, and Liz Stevens, its production manager; and at Headline Book Publishing, Heather Holden-Brown, head of non-fiction, and Lorraine Jerram, the editor of this book. Finally I should like to thank Marji Campi for her patience and support during the time I took researching and writing; Kenneth Cope; Matthew Parker for marshalling additional material; and Stephen White for additional information on espionage.

Glossary

A short glossary of abbreviations, acronyms, contemporary slang and German terms may be useful:

Dulag-Luft: *Durchgangslager Luftwaffe* (German Air Force Transit Camp)

Gestapo: *Geheime Staatspolizei* (State Secret Police)

'ghost': prisoner who fakes an escape, but hides within the camp, in order to make a genuine escape later

'goon': POW slang for a German soldier, and specifically a German guard

'goonskin': POW slang for a German uniform (usually mocked-up by the tailor's shop within the escape organisation)

'kriegie': POW slang for a prisoner-of-war, from the German word for a POW, *Kriegsgefangene*

Kripo: *Kriminalpolizei* (plain-clothes police, akin to the CID in Britain; then closely affiliated to the Gestapo)

Oflag: *Offizierlager* (prison camp for officers)

Orpo: *Ordnungspolizei* (regular uniformed police)

'penguin': POW slang for a prisoner whose job was to redistribute soil or sand dug up during the excavation of a tunnel. The earth was concealed in sewn-up long johns hidden down the prisoners' trouser legs, and dispersed by untying the bottoms when the coast was clear. The weight of the earth or sand made the prisoner waddle, hence the name

'purge': POW slang for the movement of a group of prisoners from one camp to another, or in and out of a camp

RAAF: Royal Australian Air Force

RAF: Royal Air Force

RCAF: Royal Canadian Air Force

RNZAF: Royal New Zealand Air Force

RSHA: *Reichssicherheitshauptamt* (State Security Head Office) - a huge organisation of seven departments and some 180 sub-departments including the Kripo and the Gestapo, with its Berlin headquarters at Prinz-Albrecht-Straße 8

SAAF: South African Air Force

SBO: Senior British Officer (the chief prisoner officer in a prison camp predominantly containing British and Allied troops)

Stalag-Luft: *Stammlager-Luftwaffe* (German Air Force Permanent Prison Camp)

USAAF: United States Army Air Forces

Vorlager: sub-compound of a prison camp compound containing, in the case of the North Compound of Stalag-Luft III, the guardhouse, the cooler, the hospital and the coal store.

Author's Note

Every effort has been made to verify facts but memories of events which took place sixty years ago can be treacherous. Some sources state that Roger Bushell flew Spitfires, others say that he flew Hurricanes, for example; one source gives it that his right eye was deformed; another that it was his left. It is very hard to tell from photographs which is correct.

All incontrovertible errors, however, must be laid at my door.

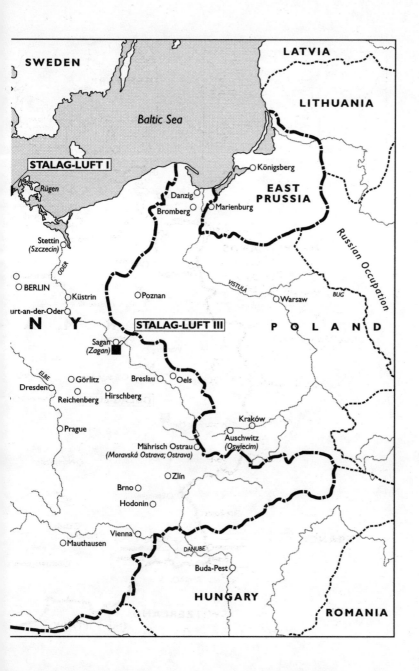

Foreword

WHY DID PEOPLE TRY TO ESCAPE ONCE TAKEN prisoner? Was it not rather a relief to be removed from the fighting, to sit out the conflict in relative safety? These are not simple questions, and answers depend on a variety of elements. In any war, the conditions of confinement are a factor governing any decision to get away. During the Second World War, the Japanese generally treated their prisoners-of-war with great cruelty, and means of escape were minimal. Camps in the east were surrounded by inhospitable jungle, and in any case the distance between them and any Allied lines, let alone home itself, meant that escape could rarely be taken into serious consideration; quite apart from the punishments meted out to those recaptured.

In Europe the distances between prison camps and a neutral country were not so great, and Germany was at least a nominal signatory of the Geneva Convention, which guaranteed certain basic rights for prisoners-of-war (under the Weimar Republic, Germany had been the first nation to sign it, in 1929). However, the distances were still long enough, and to reach safety hundreds of kilometres of enemy-occupied territory had to be crossed. Spies and police informers were everywhere, and whereas it was far easier for an Englishman or a Caucasian American, for example, to pass unnoticed while on the run in Europe than elsewhere, he could not pretend to be dumb; even if his forged papers were as near-perfect as could be, the jig would be up the moment he was obliged to open his mouth, unless he had faultless French, Italian or German, or one of the languages of Eastern Europe. Then as now, the English-speaking nations were not famous for their command of foreign tongues, though the study of them in prison camps was a practical way of alleviating the boredom and filling time profitably.

Prison camps were sited carefully – especially those for elite or troublesome captives – in remote places and in a terrain which would add to the difficulties of escape: sandy soil or a high water table would make tunnelling harder, for example. In the beginning, however, escape 'over the wire' or through the gates, disguised as a German soldier or a worker, was easier than it was later on, as guards became more experienced.

Some captured soldiers, sailors and airmen no doubt elected not even to try to escape: they may have been too badly wounded, they may have lacked the resources to get anywhere, or they may simply have been grateful to be out of the war. However, for most, on whatever side, there was a sense of duty that they should at least try to get back into the fight. This was recognised by the Geneva Convention, which decreed that no punishment more harsh than a couple of weeks' solitary in the punishment block, or 'cooler', as both Germans and Allies called it, should be meted out to recaptured prisoners. Most escapers fully expected to enjoy no more than a few days' liberty at most before being returned to their camps. And for every man who escaped, up to ten who did not belonged to the escape organisation within the camp which was responsible for getting him out: the tailors who could make civilian suits out of military jackets and greatcoats; the engineers, surveyors and miners who could design and build tunnels; the artists and printers and graphic designers who could forge documents; the look-outs (or 'stooges', as they were known) and the messengers and the diversion-creators; the German-speakers whose job it was to befriend and bribe or blackmail German guards into cooperation; the intelligence-gatherers; the entertainers who kept up morale and also provided cover for secret escape activity (among those RAF prisoners at Stalag-Luft III who went on to successful theatrical careers were Peter Butterworth, most famous in later years for his roles in the well-known *Carry On* comedy film series; John Casson, the son of Lewis Casson and Sybil Thorndike, and Rupert Davies, the creator of the role of Maigret for British television); and finally the administrators who held the whole thing together.

The sense of duty may have decreased among Axis prisoners-of-war as the tide turned after Stalingrad in November 1942, and conditions in Germany and central Europe worsened; but for Allied prisoners by the same token it increased. It would have been particularly keenly felt by elite troops – pilots and aircrew, submariners, paratroopers and commandos. But something else has to be taken into account, which is the youth of most of the men concerned in the story which follows: few were older than thirty-three, most were in their early twenties. They had been highly (and expensively) trained for a particular job, and instead of doing it they were condemned to sit around, bored to death, badly fed and sex-starved, knowing that the action, their chance to participate in it, their chances of promotion and glory and their very lives, were all passing by. Some of the men who figure in this story had been captured very early in the war, and had hardly seen any action, which was an additional frustration.

No-one knew how long the war would last, except that after the euphoric hope of a short conflict died within the first few months, everyone knew that it would be a long one.

The frustrated energy of youth, the boredom enforced on energetic minds, and the inactivity forced on energetic bodies, focused the attention of the best prisoners on ways of getting out. This, in turn, provided a means of deflecting those energies from conflicts within the prisoner populations, which were inevitable among so much stress and stagnation. Coupled to the idea of escape was the thought that in trying to get away, even if one only succeeded in eluding recapture for a few days, the escaper was diverting a few German resources from fighting to tracking the escaper down. To escape was to contribute to the war effort, and all elite prisoners on either side knew that their captors would be specially keen not to let them get away. This was particularly true of Allied aircrews as the war entered its final phase and Germany began to suffer the shock of concentrated air-raids by day and night deeper and deeper into its territory, spreading increasing destruction and demoralisation.

Allied air force prisoners were guarded in camps run by the Luftwaffe. There was some sense in this: at least captors and captives would understand the same profession. Plenty of Germans had lost friends and family in Allied raids by the middle of the war, and would be unlikely to look kindly on captured bomber crew especially. An escaping airman would run an additional risk once on the loose: that of falling into the hands of a vengeful civilian population. But it was not until late in the war that Hitler threw out all regard for the Geneva Convention, in the case of the Great Escape from Stalag-Luft III.

Although as the war progressed German guards became more experienced at detecting escape plans and thwarting escape attempts, prisoners by the same token became more adept at the planning and execution of escapes. German guards were, with few exceptions, not plucked from the ranks of the fittest and most able conscripts, and as shortages in

Germany grew, and quasi-friendships developed between guards and prisoners in the camps, it was not unusual, especially as the outcome of the war became more and more inevitable, that guards would clandestinely help escape efforts in exchange for some real coffee or chocolate from a Red Cross parcel. Acorn coffee can be a great persuader that one's country's military fortunes are on a downward turn.

Unfortunately, as a totalitarian power collapses, those most fanatically attached to it, and its leaders, become increasingly desperate, and increasingly savage in their desperation. The Jews of Hungary were deported to, and slaughtered in, the concentration camps after D-Day, and a new concentration camp was opened as late as spring 1945. At the time of the Great Escape from Stalag-Luft III, in March 1944, it was no longer a question of if Germany would be defeated, but when. That year saw Hitler unleash his greatest savagery against the Jews, actually redeploying rolling stock and other *matériel* away from the war effort to ensure his programme of destruction. That year, too, he would cease to recognise that escapers from a prison camp should be protected from serious reprisal by the Geneva Convention. He paid scant regard to international opinion and he still had plenty of men, notably in the Gestapo and the SS-Death's-Head Brigades, in charge of the running of the concentration camps, ready to do his bidding. Nor did he or his henchmen care that their acts of reprisal and mass slaughter would be carried out, not as if they had some ideological, moral or ethical imprimatur, however warped, but as criminal deeds, to be covered up – not executions or even assassinations, but simple murders. At the time with which we are concerned, the cynical device of killing someone and then officially describing the death as 'shot while trying to escape' was becoming so current that when the famous Stauffenberg Plot against Hitler failed in July 1944, and the German Army chiefs in Paris who were involved in it were obliged to set the SS officers whom they had imprisoned free, the SS refused to leave their prison, convinced that as soon as they made a move, they would be 'shot while trying to escape'.

To all Prisoners of War!

The escape from prison camps is no longer a sport!

Germany has always kept to the Hague Convention and only punished recaptured prisoners of war with minor disciplinary punishment.

Germany will still maintain these principles of international law.

But England has besides fighting at the front in an honest manner instituted an illegal warfare in non combat zones in the form of gangster commandos, terror bandits and sabotage troops even up to the frontiers of Germany.

They say in a captured secret and confidential English military pamphlet,

THE HANDBOOK
OF MODERN IRREGULAR
WARFARE:

". . . the days when we could practise the rules of sportsmanship are over. For the time being, every soldier must be a potential gangster and must be prepared to adopt their methods whenever necessary."

"The sphere of operations should always include the enemy's own country, any occupied territory, and in certain circumstances, such neutral countries as he is using as a source of supply."

England has with these instructions opened up a non military form of gangster war!

Germany is determined to safeguard her homeland, and especially her war industry and provisional centres for the fighting fronts. Therefore it has become necessary to create strictly forbidden zones, called death zones, in which all unauthorised trespassers will be immediately shot on sight.

Escaping prisoners of war, entering such death zones, will certainly lose their lives. They are therefore in constant danger of being mistaken for enemy agents or sabotage groups.

Urgent warning is given against making future escapes!

In plain English: Stay in the camp where you will be safe! Breaking out of it is now a damned dangerous act.

The chances of preserving your life are almost nil!

All police and military guards have been given the most strict orders to shoot on sight all suspected persons.

Escaping from prison camps has ceased to be a sport!

Chapter One

ONE MAN STOOD OUT AMONG THE GROUP OF NEW Royal Air Force prisoners-of-war who arrived, in the autumn of 1942, at Stalag-Luft III, the vast, recently built prison camp complex just outside the nondescript town of Sagan deep in the eastern hinterland of Greater Germany. Just thirty-two years old, Squadron Leader Roger Joyce Bushell had already been a prisoner for over two years, though he hadn't taken captivity lying down, and was the veteran of several escape attempts.

He was lucky to be alive now: he'd been recaptured with a friend while hiding out in a flat in Prague in the wake of the assassination in late May of thirty-eight-year-old *Obergruppenführer* Reinhard Heydrich. Heydrich, the son of an eminent musician, had established himself as head of the Reich Security Service, Deputy Reich Protector of Bohemia and Moravia, administrator of the concentration camps, and a specialist in Nazi terror techniques. Heydrich's brutal putting-down of the Czech resistance led to a decision by Czechoslovakians in exile in London to strike back. On 27 May 1942 three young men were parachuted into the outer suburbs of Prague. Two days later they lay in wait for Heydrich's car and ambushed it, throwing a bomb which fatally wounded the SS general. In retaliation the Germans

executed 860 people in Prague and another 395 at Brno.
The entire village of Lidice, whose population was accused
of aiding the assassins, was razed to the ground. Its menfolk
and older boys, 172 in number, were killed, as were most of
the women. Others were transported to concentration camps,
where they died. Most of the children of the village suffered
a similar fate, though some of the youngest were taken to
foster homes where they were indoctrinated in Nazi ideology.

Bushell and his fellow-escaper, a Czech officer with the
RAF called Jack Zafouk, were delivered into German hands
when their hosts were betrayed by the apartment block's
porter, one of many Czechs who turned in their fellow-
countrymen and resistance operators to save their own necks
as the Germans arrested people by the thousand in the wake
of Heydrich's assassination. Both men were subjected to
lengthy interrogation by the Gestapo. Zafouk ended up in
Colditz, the fortress-prison reserved for the most hardened
escapers, and believed to be completely escape-proof. How
Bushell, himself a seasoned escaper, avoided a similar fate, is
uncertain. Paul Brickhill, the original chronicler of Stalag-
Luft III and the Great Escape, and himself a prisoner there,
suggests that Bushell could well have been shot had it not
been for the intervention of Stalag-Luft III's chief officer in
charge of censorship (censoring letters home and so forth),
a man called von Masse. Von Masse, a regular air force officer
and no Nazi, knew and liked Bushell; he had heard that the
Gestapo were holding Bushell and trying to pin a charge of
sabotage on him. As von Masse's brother was a *Generaloberst*
(Colonel-General) in the regular army, von Masse asked him
to intervene on Bushell's behalf. But when Bushell arrived
at the camp, von Masse warned him that nothing would save
him if he tried to get away again. Bushell, an active and
highly intelligent man, brushed this off. The next time he
escaped, and he had every intention of doing so, he would

succeed in getting back to Allied lines or a neutral country, from which he could make his way home.

Though Bushell never discussed his experiences at the hands of the Gestapo very much, it's likely that von Masse wasn't his only German friend. There had been several in the skiing fraternity to which Bushell had belonged in the pre-war years.

Roger Bushell was born in South Africa in August 1910, the son of an English mining engineer who had emigrated there. He went to school first in Johannesburg and, later, Wellington in England, where his housemaster noted how quickly he became a ringleader. In 1929 he went up to Cambridge to read law. Once there, he established himself as a vigorous all-rounder. He shone in his academic work, but he was also a tireless party-goer, and a good enough skier to represent the university. Later on, he became a member of the famous Kandahar Club at Mürren, named after Lord Roberts of Kandahar, who had donated a skiing trophy. The club was founded by the downhiller Arnold Lunn. Bushell even had a black run at St Moritz named after him, to honour the fact of his having achieved the fastest time ever down it. His attitude to skiing mirrored his attitude to life: he approached it with a fearlessness that bordered on reckless-ness; his success lay in his ability to calculate the degree of risk and take that to the limit. He was the fastest British downhiller of the early 1930s, though injuries after a bad fall during an international downhill event in Canada left him with a slight disfigurement: as he fell one of his ski-tips caught the corner of his right eye. Luckily it did not blind him, but the gash, after it had been sewn up, pulled the corner of the eye down in a slight, but sinister, even intimidating, droop. It was something he could turn to his advantage when he wanted to.

His love of speed drew him to flying, and in 1932 he

joined 601 Squadron of the Royal Auxiliary Air Force, which attracted the sons of the great and the good, and carried the not entirely enviable nickname of The Millionaires' Squadron. They lived and played hard, gaining a reputation for indefatigable partying; in those days, Bushell was making his way in society.

As his social life developed (though there was no serious romantic attachment) so did his career. He was called to the Bar in 1934 and quickly established a reputation as an acute defence lawyer who thought on his feet, and whose acid tongue could reduce opponents and prosecution witnesses to jelly. Within him the kind of amoral cynicism necessary for such work was tempered by a young man's high-handed moral sense. On one occasion shortly before the outbreak of the Second World War in 1939, he defended a well-known London gangleader on a murder charge, and got him off. The villain – a prototype Kray – wanted to shake hands with his lawyer in gratitude afterwards. Loftily, Bushell declined to do so: 'I don't shake hands with murderers,' he said, and added, with an adolescent vaingloriousness which was a mark, some-times positive, sometimes negative, of his character: 'I only do what I'm paid to do.' The villain was unfazed and simply told Bushell that if he ever ran into trouble in London all he had to do was whistle. Bushell remained aloof. He was equally singleminded as a prosecutor, so much so that his success rate at courts-martial of RAF personnel on charges of dangerous flying caused High Command to block more cases being passed his way – he was having a deleterious effect on Public Relations. Later, however, it was said that his skill as a lawyer helped him stay one step ahead of his Gestapo interrogators.

His was the kind of *Boy's Own* character which has been superseded by other role models today. He was influenced by the heroes and escapers of the First World War, and by nineteenth-century British imperial enterprise; but he also belonged to the fast, quasi-nihilistic generation of privileged children that grew up in the economically bitter and politically insecure years that bridged the two world wars. His character contained precisely the correct mixture of arrogance, intelligence, patriotism and daring to form him for action. Deprived of that ability through being taken prisoner early in the 1939–1945 war, it is no wonder that he turned all his intellectual, organisational and physical energies to the question of escape.

Bushell had reached the respectable rank of Flight Lieutenant by the time Britain declared war at the beginning of September 1939. Soon afterwards, in mid-October, he was promoted and given the job of setting up a squadron (number 92) of twin-engined Blenheim night-fighter-bombers at Tangmere, just east of Littlehampton and near the West Sussex coast. As a historian of the Great Escape, Jonathan Vance, puts it, 'When he arrived at the station . . . he discovered that he had no equipment, no other officers, and only a skeleton ground crew.' He was nevertheless given a hearty welcome by a fellow squadron based at Tangmere and got royally drunk with them.

Ninety-two Squadron quickly became properly operational, but in the early years of the war the organisation of military forces was very much in flux. At the outset, German fighters were superior to most of those of the British or the French, and the Allies were fighting as yet without the support of America. By spring 1940, as the phony war came to an end, and real hostilities began, Bushell's squadron had changed its configuration to light Hurricane attack fighters (some sources give Spitfires), ready to beat off the threatening waves of bomber raids from Germany as Hitler launched Operation *Seelöwe*. As early as May 1940, Bushell's squadron was twice involved in action covering the evacuation of the British

Expeditionary Force as it lay prone to attacks from *Stuka* dive bombers (Junkers Ju 87 *Sturzkampfflugzeug*) on the beach at Dunkirk, waiting to be ferried back to England by the courageous fleet of small civilian boats which set out voluntarily to rescue the soldiers involved in the doomed and precipitate attempted bridgehead on the occupied mainland. Meanwhile, in the poorly pressurised cockpits of the *Stukas*, pilots and bomb aimers were bursting apart as their aeroplanes plunged too fast towards the earth. Nevertheless, at that early stage of the war, German air-power was greatly superior to that of the British in numbers and in experienced pilots.

As for Bushell, his first sortie was, if not a success, at least without incident. On his second, he became involved in a dogfight with a vastly superior intercepting force of Messerschmitt Me-110 twin-engined fighters. He managed to shoot one down, no mean achievement from a Hurricane against superior aircraft, but the end of the combat was inevitable and Bushell crash-landed near Boulogne. He'd managed to contain the fire in his aircraft and walked away from it unscathed, but he was quickly taken prisoner by a German motorcycle patrol. With the war only nine months old, it seemed to him an ignominious and unacceptable end to what he had planned as a dazzling military career.

Bushell was a big man (for his day) with plenty of charisma, a dominating personality, and cold, penetrating blue eyes that could quell a man with a look. His organisational skills were, however, his best asset, and with them he would convert the escape efforts at the new camp into a coordinated single-minded operation. He was helped in this by being reunited with several other veteran escapers, brought to Stalag-Luft III as it was supposed to be a camp from which it was next to impossible to escape.

At the beginning of the war, though, the system of prison

camps set up by the Germans was in its infancy. No-one expected a long conflict, and during the phony war the influx of POWs was small. Castles and fortresses were taken over and roughly converted for holding captive enemy troops, and small purpose-built camps were laid out. Some camps were designated especially for officers. However, with the invasion and fall of France, the Germans, initially successful beyond their expectations, found themselves with many thousands of prisoners from each of the services to look after, which meant finding food and lodging for them – a logistical problem for which they were not entirely prepared.

The organisation with responsibility for POWs, a branch of the *Oberkommando der Wehrmacht*, or Army High Command, quickly found itself up to its neck in difficulties. The complexity of the task it faced was not eased by the fact that the camps for army, navy and air force prisoners were each run by the related German services. Liaison between them was often confused; and resources varied greatly from camp to camp; and conditions, in terms of food and clothing, deteriorated as the war progressed and the German military swallowed up an ever greater share of the nation's supplies. The expected oil and wheat from a conquered Russia never materialised, since Russia was not conquered, and goods, money and valuables confiscated from the Jews, which brought in a rich treasure in the early years, soon came to an end. By the time that the German-Soviet Pact of Non-Aggression, concluded between Hitler and Stalin on 23 August 1939, collapsed in the summer of 1941, Germany was already in trouble. This was compounded by the Japanese attack on Pearl Harbour at the end of the year; and the fate of the Nazis was sealed after Stalingrad fell in 1942.

POW affairs were not the sole preserve of Army High Command. The Reich Security Service also had a hand in them, since they had the responsibility for recapturing escapers.

One of the objectives of escapers was simply to escape, to tie up German resources and manpower, a task in which they were helped by a rising crime rate within Greater Germany, as its fortunes crumbled, and by an increasing number of deserters, criminals and fugitive foreign forced-labourers. Two arms of the Reich Security Service, the Gestapo and the Kripo — the secret police and the conventional plain-clothes department — responded to these challenges with energy and with ever greater severity, particularly on the part of the Gestapo, who, as politically committed Nazis (at least in theory), faced the risk of dire punishment from post-war Allied and Democratic German courts if the Third Reich collapsed.

The rank and file Gestapo were, however, not trained investigators: they relied on stool pigeons for their information, and on the fear of punishment for non-conformity that preys on all but the bravest civilians in a police state. The Czech family that sheltered Bushell and Zafouk were all slaughtered, as an example to their fellow citizens, for the most part unwilling denizens of Greater Germany, the empire Hitler had managed to carve out, with scarcely a whisper from other powers, from Austria and the Czech Sudetenland. Only the invasion of Poland, which he was sure he'd get away with too, led to the outbreak of war. But any criticism of the Allied politicians of the time must be tempered by the realisation that it was only twenty years since the bloodbath of the First World War, the Great War, the War to End All Wars, had come to an end. It hardly seemed possible that history should be repeating itself so soon.

The museum at the former Nazi prison at Plötzensee in Berlin contains chilling evidence from law reports of what life was like for the ordinary German, too, under the *Nationalsozialistische Deutsche Arbeiterpartei* (the NSDAP, or, National Socialist German Workers' Party, from which the abbreviation 'Nazi' comes). The reports also convey something of the cold-bloodedness of the regime, an image the Nazis were keen to promulgate, with their constant rhetoric of being 'iron-hard' and 'steel-cold'. In the original (the following translations are by the author), these reports are self-consciously cold and factual, and peppered with outraged exclamation marks, which are a feature of Nazi documents.

They also indicate what escapers were up against, particularly those (the majority) who went on the run in what passed for civilian clothes, thus risking charges of espionage:

> Emmi Zehden, executed at 1pm on 9 June 1944, aged forty-four. A member of the Jehovah's Witnesses. She helped three young men avoid their call-up. Her punishment was death by the guillotine. Sentence took seven seconds to carry out.

Like everyone sentenced by the Nazi courts of crimes against the state, the cost of her own trial and execution was drawn from her estate or from her surviving relatives. The Jehovah's Witnesses were courageous resisters to the Nazi regime, and many thousands of them perished in the concentration camps.

> Karl Robert Kreiden from Düsseldorf. A musician. While lodging in Berlin during a concert tour he tried to persuade his landlady, one Frau Ott-Monecke, to join the Resistance. He described Hitler as a brute, and told Frau Ott-Monecke, a convinced National Socialist, that she had better change her ideas. She informed on him and he was tried on 3 September 1943, executed on 7 September, aged twenty-seven.
>
> Otto Bauer, a fifty-six-year-old businessman, unguardedly said on a train in June 1942 that Germans had only

two alternatives: to kill Hitler or be killed by him. He
was overheard by a married couple who reported him.
He was beheaded on Thursday 16 September 1943 for
fomenting discontent and unrest.

Erich Deibel. On 29 April 1940 he drew the symbol
of the SPD [the *Sozialdemokratischepartei Deutschlands* –
or German Social Democratic Party: a far more left-
wing grouping than the present British Liberal
Democrats] – three arrows – on the wall of a lavatory
in his factory, adding the words: 'Hail Freedom!' On 22
July the following year he chalked up: 'Workers! Help
Russia! Strike! Up With the Communist Party of
Germany!' and drew the Red Star and the Hammer and
Sickle. He also allegedly listened to broadcasts from the
BBC [the British Broadcasting Corporation, in those
days an important disseminator of news overseas].
Accused of sabotage and treason, he was executed on
15 August 1942.

As for the methods of the Gestapo, already touched on, one
small example of their work is encapsulated in the story of
a couple of agents who raided a Berlin intellectual's flat on
a tip-off provided by an informer. They found books on
archaeology, and, recognising only the 'arch' part of the word,
arrested her for being an anarchist. (If that may be found
incredible, one should not forget that in 2000 in Britain a
paediatrician was hounded from her home by a mob which
suspected her of being a paedophile.)

In Germany during the Second World War, there were
those who embraced Nazism ideologically – the social reform
programme of the Party, though funded by capital looted
from Jewish Germans, was in itself a model of its kind –
though most who were not fanatics grew disaffected as Hitler's
folie de grandeur became less deniable. There was a very small

number with the foresight and the insight to become members of the Resistance to Nazism from the outset. The majority, as in any society, went along with the status quo, grumbled a bit (but not much), and tried to get on with their lives – ever more wretched under the Nazi yoke. The most popular way of letting off steam against the regime was the joke – and in the very early days, the Minister of Propaganda, Josef Goebbels, even sanctioned certain cabarets critical of National Socialism. By the mid-1930s, however, after only two years of the regime, that came to an end, and some of Germany's most famous comedians died in the concentration camps. An example of the kind of joke for which they lost their lives was given to the present author by Christabel Bielenberg, an Englishwoman married before the war to a German lawyer who became a hero of the Resistance:

> The story goes that at Hitler's birth three good fairies came to give him their good wishes, and the first wished for him that every German should be honest, the second that every German should be intelligent, and the third that every German should be a good National Socialist. An uplifting thought. But then came the bad fairy, and she stipulated that every German could only possess two of those attributes. She left the *Führer* then with intelligent Nazis who were not honest, honest Nazis who had no brains, and intelligent, honest Germans who were not Nazis. A funny little story, perhaps, but one not too far from the truth: for it seemed to me that those three categories of Germans did indeed live and work together side by side, unable, because of the nature of the regime, to maintain more than the most superficial contact with one another.

The joke provides more than an indication of the German side of the story with which we are concerned.

When an escaper was caught, he was to be held by the civil police authorities until he could be returned to the prison camp from which he'd got away. As we've seen, under the terms of the Geneva Convention he could then expect a couple of weeks' solitary in the *Kittchen* – the 'cooler', or punishment block, for his pains. From a military point of view, whatever the nation, escape was regarded as a legitimate activity, and also a respected one; though naturally the captors did all they could to inhibit it.

Quite apart from the numbers of French POWs, 1940 brought a large influx of British prisoners. The Battle of Britain had been a great success, but it had by no means won the war. British fighters and bombers would gradually gain the ascendancy, technically, and in range, numbers and development as the German economy faltered; but for the moment the RAF was sustaining big losses. Bomber Command, which later in the war, under its leader Arthur 'Bomber' Harris, would inflict heavy casualties in raids on targets such as Dresden and Leipzig (as reprisals against German attacks on London and Coventry), suffered major losses during the Battle of France, and across the board the RAF lost, either to death or to imprisonment, hundreds upon hundreds of aircrew in the early months of the war, once it had been engaged in earnest.

But of those who had escaped death, and became the ignominious victims (as they saw themselves) of an enforced incarceration – which, at least at the beginning, meant spacious quarters but little to do, frustration and boredom – many energetic figures stood out. Some accepted the fact that for them 'the war was over'; they would sit it out, hopeful of a quick return home if the war didn't last too long. Others couldn't cope with being cooped up, and of standing by while the fate of democracy was at issue. Some just wanted to get the hell out of a boring and tedious situation. The desire to escape was stimulated by a variety of emotions – sexual frustration, the feeling that life was passing by, a desire to rejoin the battle, homesickness and simple cabin fever. During the First World War, the Germans in some camps ensured that their prisoners had plenty of alcohol to drink. This simple disincentive to rebellion was not understood by the Nazis; they couldn't afford it, nor could they allow it: their *Führer* was a teetotaller and a vegetarian who understood little of the normal urges of the human psyche – particularly the stressed human psyche.

Among the first to be captured, days after the war had broken out, were two members of an Armstrong Whitworth Whitley twin-engined bomber squadron en route for a propaganda leaflet-dropping mission over northern Germany. Pilot Officer Alfred 'Tommy' Thompson, a Canadian volunteer, was flying his aircraft accompanied by Squadron Leader Philip Murray, a fluent German speaker. Their mission accomplished, engine failure brought their plane down on enemy soil.

In those very early days, Germany had absolute confidence that it would win the battle of the skies. After a desultory interrogation the two were taken by rail for the seven-hour journey to Berlin, where they were escorted to a bizarre alfresco meeting near a railway siding with the First World War fighter ace and now *Reichsmarschall der Luftwaffe*, Hermann Göring. Göring in those early days of the war, assured of ultimate victory, could afford to show a degree of camaraderie to fellow flyers.

The RAF and the *Luftwaffe* were the new military legions. They were the freshmen, the fighters who had to prove themselves. It's hard to believe now that only sixty-odd years ago, aerial combat was a very new form of war. It had had its beginnings during the First World War, but then, however deadly, it was glossed with a veneer of chivalry. Enemy combatants would wave at one another during a dogfight. The Second World War was to usher in a harsher form of fighting in the skies. No mercy would exist any more, and no chivalry. War in the air quickly assumed the brutal mantle of war on land and on sea.

Göring exchanged a few friendly words with Murray, who saluted the already booze-bulky and cocaine-fuelled head of the German Air Force, and nodded in the direction of the junior officer. After that, the two prisoners were shipped off to Itzehoe, a newly established camp near Hamburg. There, they had few companions – a handful of Frenchmen, 600 Poles, and, soon afterwards, a New Zealander. But in terms of what was to come, they lived in luxury: each had a room of his own, and they were well fed. They even had access to fruit and soft drinks. The only problem was that there was nothing whatsoever to do.

Bored as they became, Thompson, Murray, and the New Zealander were soon shipped off to a new camp, the medieval fortress of Spangenberg, an officers' camp not far from Kassel. Here they were confronted with a diet composed of black potato-bread, salty bacon, and – a foretaste of what was to become a feature of the POW's diet, and another factor in driving some to escape – cheese derived from fish waste, saccharine-sweetened jam whose ultimate source was a chemical by-product of coal, turnip stew with wisps of what may once have been meat, and 'coffee' – a lukewarm drink derived from acorns. As the war progressed, the guards hardly did better; but in the early days such food was barely acceptable, let alone digestible. Its nutritional value was extremely low, and prisoners quickly lost weight and energy.

The accommodation was poor, too. There was a huge dormitory on the ground floor, with iron bunks furnished with damp palliasses set round the whitewashed walls. In the centre of the room stood a couple of refectory tables. The POWs spent most of the day in the long room, for as winter set in it became too cold, towards freezing, to venture into the grim little courtyard that was their only chance of open air. Miserable and homesick, the young men played cards in a desultory way; but there were few serious squabbles: most of the prisoners were centred on themselves, coming to terms with God-knows-how-long a stretch of confinement: months? years? Escape from Spangenberg was out of the question, and few POWs were yet considering that possibility. Home seemed one hell of a long way away, and to have been caught so soon was very dispiriting.

Frank Tams, who ended up in Stalag-Luft III, was on his twentieth operational sortie flying a twin-engined Beaufort when he was shot down:

'From tea and cakes, eggs and bacon and dates with girl-friends one minute, to being shot down, caught, put behind barbed wire a few hours later. The sheer speed of this was traumatic in itself and the fact that the transition was never contemplated automatically meant that one was a reluctant and awkward captive. Bloody minded, in fact!'

The compensation was the growing company, though it was a backhanded way of making friends, seeing so many compatriots and allies taken out of the conflict. Language could be a problem, since many of the other inmates were French, but in mid-October 1939 a new consignment of prisoners included a British officer, Wing Commander Harry Day, an old man of forty-one, nicknamed 'Wings', after the air force anniversarial 'Wings' Day'. He would be a driving force, years later, in the Great Escape.

Tall and balding, Day had already seen service with the Royal Marine Light Infantry in the First World War, and he'd been commissioned a lieutenant at the age of eighteen in 1916. After the war, he remained in the service and transferred to the recently established RAF in the 1920s. From then on his military career took off, and by the time the Second World War started, he'd reached the rank of Squadron Leader. He was offered a staff job, which meant a desk, and refused it in favour of a command (which also involved promotion, after a few strings had been pulled) of Blenheim bombers.

Day was another early POW. He was shot down by a flight of Messerschmitt 109s during a daylight reconnaissance sortie in a Blenheim over Kaiserslautern in south-west Germany in October 1939. Soon afterwards, he was taken to Spangenberg, where at once he ran into one old friend, Flight Lieutenant Mike Casey, a fellow RAF officer, who introduced him to Murray and Thompson. All of them would end up in Stalag-Luft III.

They didn't remain together until that time. It was early German policy to break up groups every so often in order to destabilise any nascent organisations or networks within the prisoner populations. Like Itzehohe, Spangenberg was a dull place, with no real facilities, and the 'kriegies' – as prisoners-of-war called themselves, borrowing the German word for them: *Kriegsgefangene* – spent a good deal of their time kicking their heels. In prison camp society, captured officers were waited on by captive other-rankers, who served as orderlies. Mike Casey's air-gunner, who'd been shot down with him, fulfilled this role in the present event. Day held the highest rank, and became SBO – Senior British Officer, a post whose duties included liaising with the German camp commandant and other prison staff on matters regarding prisoner welfare, but who also acted as a consultant and arbiter regarding escape plans and attempts. This latter duty, however, did not gain currency until a little later in the war.

It came as a relief when a group of them – six Frenchmen and six Britons – were transferred to another camp at the end of the year. They were sent to Dulag-Luft, the Luftwaffe Transit Camp about fifteen kilometres north-west of the centre of Frankfurt-am-Main. Initially the prisoners there were housed in a large building which had formerly been part of a farm, but by April 1940 the purpose-built camp nearby, which had been under construction for several months, was ready for occupation. It was a relatively civilised place, with three barrack blocks: one contained the recreation room and the washrooms, as well as a number of twin- and single-bedded rooms for senior officers; a second was designed to accommodate a further sixty-five prisoners; and a third held the messrooms, the kitchen and the storerooms.

It was at Dulag-Luft, despite its shifting population, that the first moves towards organising escape attempts were made.

Chapter Two

ARRY DAY SHARED MANY OF ROGER BUSHELL'S charismatic qualities of leadership, which were supported by the fact that he was twice the age of many of his fellow prisoners – an older brother, if not a father figure. He was lean, with greying hair and a lived-in face, which made him look older than he was; he also possessed great energy and vitality. His character was volatile, and he could swing from a mood of high bonhomie to one of frosty aloofness; but his age and experience endowed him with great authority.

The prisoners had not been informed formally that they were now in a transit camp, but they quickly found out. The primary function of the place was to act as a reception centre for new prisoners, to interrogate them and to acclimatise them to prison life before sending them on to a permanent holding camp for all ranks, or to an officers' camp. However, to assist them in the processing of what quickly became a flood of confused, frightened, unruly and belligerent young men, the German staff of the camp found it necessary to select from the older senior British prisoners a permanent staff (who as their name suggests were to remain in the Dulag). The Camp Commandant, Theodor Rumpel, who had some knowledge of how British society worked in those days, tried to make his selection as far as possible from among men of good family. The Germans had always rather respected the idea of British gentlemanly behaviour, and Rumpel hoped that the officers he chose would set a good example to the other ranks. But having appointed Day as the prisoner SBO, Rumpel allowed him (subject to approval) to pick his own staff.

He was quick to choose men who would not only appear to fulfil the role Rumpel had in mind, but who were also adventurous and intelligent spirits capable of continuing to contribute to the war effort by all means possible within the confines of captivity, and by working towards a variety of schemes for escape.

Frank Tams became one of the hundreds involved in the escape from Stalag-Luft III:

'"For you the war is over," so often repeated by our captors, was just not accepted. The captor has guns, bullets, spies, dogs, barbed wire and countless refinements of mental oppression which make life as a POW a special sort of hell. The captive has only his wit, inventiveness, his brains, endurance and mental attitude as well as pure cussedness, never admitting defeat or letting the enemy think he is defeated and more important than anything, unlimited time to plot and scheme.'

As his Number Two he chose the Royal Naval Lieutenant Commander James Buckley, a career Fleet Air Arm pilot who'd served on the aircraft carrier HMS *Glorious* before the war and who'd been shot down while leading his flight on a strafing mission of German gun emplacements at Calais at the end of May 1940. Taken prisoner immediately, he'd already managed to get away briefly on the long march across France. Buckley brought in a fellow officer, John Casson, son of the actors Sybil Thorndike and Lewis Casson, who'd himself been shot down six weeks earlier than Buckley near Trondheim in Norway, during the famous attack on the German battle-ship *Scharnhorst* (named after the noted Prussian general of the Napoleonic wars). Each man shared with Day a frustra-tion at having failed to strike any blows against the enemy before being taken out of the action, and this sense fuelled their interest in escape.

Newly arrived prisoners were first subjected to an inter-rogation by German intelligence staff, though the word 'inter-rogation' should not be construed in this context as having anything of the third degree about it, unless a captive was suspected of lying. Usually the sessions were mere formali-ties, after which the prisoners were handed over to the British permanent staff and inducted into the camp. They were assigned a bed in one of the small dormitories (many rooms had no more than four occupants), given a toilet kit and a Red Cross parcel – that staple and saviour of prisoners-of-war, which the Germans seldom tampered with before handing it on – and whatever clothes they might need, before sitting down to a square meal. German policy while they could maintain it, was to give POWs a relatively comfort-able life, in the hope that it would soften them up and act as a disincentive to escape or rebellion. In this they were not wrong in many cases. Big repasts were arranged regularly for the men, and Rumpel entertained the officers to dinner in his own quarters from time to time. There were other motives for this apparent kindness: there was the propaganda value of making the captives think that their enemy was not so bad after all; and there was always the chance that if a prisoner were sufficiently won over, he might let drop some vital infor-mation about what he knew, say, of British military strength or general morale. For the first eighteen months to two years of the war, while Germany enjoyed great success in its campaigns, this policy would continue. The Reichsbank at least appeared to be bursting with money (only later would it appear how irresponsibly Hitler was leaching the economy away), and German soldiers' uniforms were still being made of cloth, and not (as came later) wood fibre.

The British officers who formed the permanent staff naturally let the Germans believe that their tactic was working; but in the meantime Day had made Buckley responsible for setting up an escape committee. By now the permanent staff had gained a new recruit, a squadron leader who'd recently arrived in the Dulag and who had all the qualities Buckley was looking for in an escaper and potential rebel. His name was Roger Bushell.

Buckley quickly made Bushell his deputy. They were well aware of the difficulties facing any real escape activity from Dulag-Luft itself: the members of the permanent staff were all too well known to the Germans for them to try to get disguised either as a civilian worker or as a German guard, and because the compound was small, any attempt to try to get out 'over the wire' would almost certainly be doomed to failure. At the same time, the period which any other prisoners apart from the permanent staff had to spend in the Dulag was uncertain. An escape attempt could take weeks of planning, and there was no point in engaging in such activity if the potential escaper might be moved on without notice at any time.

It seemed to them that at least they could provide some experience in the art of escaping, which could be carried on by prisoners to the permanent camps. But the art of escaping was in its infancy – it could even be said to be non-existent. Against that, the Germans themselves had not yet fully honed their security skills: prisoners at the Dulag were allowed to attend church services, and to go on supervised walks in the surrounding countryside and woods. A certain mutual humanity and even fraternity existed, which never wholly disappeared between prisoners and German guards of the regular forces, even in the Luftwaffe, a relatively new service, and regarded by the Nazis as their most reliable.

The Navy had tarnished its reputation by siding with the Communists in 1918 and 1919, and the Army was full of old-school senior officers (many of whom would be replaced) who disapproved of Hitler (an ill-educated lower-middle-class Austrian) and his upstart minions. The Luftwaffe could be staffed with younger officers steeped in Nazi ideology even if they belonged to the regular military and not to the SS battalions. The older services had many elements which, while remaining loyal to Germany, had reservations about Nazism, and as for having the country run by an Austrian, many senior staff (who were mostly from Northern Germany) believed that Hitler had simply bludgeoned his way into power past the elderly Hindenburg, who had always disapproved of him. And hadn't Bismarck himself made the famous joke: 'A Bavarian, gentlemen, is a cross between an Austrian and a human being'? Resistance to Hitler in the army had existed since the moment he took power in 1933. One of the reasons the Führer had for hastening the start of the war (at least a year before his advisers had told him Germany would be ready) was to consolidate his grasp on power. Having underestimated his determination, the military and political opposition was caught on the hop, and then it was too late, as fighting for the Nazis and fighting for the Fatherland became confused, and Hitler replaced older officers with younger ones who had been influenced by his political brainwashing since their adolescence.

Luckily for escapers, the staffs of prison camps were older men, or men who were either physically or mentally not tough enough for front-line duty – men who had served in the First World War, and those who were perhaps C3 rather than A1 in military terms. Punishments for close fraternisation included, as time passed, posting to the Eastern Front – a punishment which also awaited concentration camp staff who dragged their feet – and that was an effective death sentence. Nevertheless, as the war reached its desperate latter years, guards, by then suffering from conscious or unconscious fatalism, were prepared to commit what amounted to acts of treason in exchange for a few grammes of coffee or a chocolate bar out of a Red Cross parcel.

In the Dulag, the escape committee of the permanent staff decided to try digging a tunnel out. This was also something new, though it had the obvious attraction, at least in theory, of being something that was sustainable. As more prisoners-of-war joined their ranks, escape committees would in time acquire the expertise of trained civil engineers, miners, surveyors and architects, graphic artists and painters who would make good forgers, radio engineers, linguists, the occasional career con-man and many others who could apply their knowledge to the art of escaping; but these were still early days. None of the men who started the first tunnel at the Dulag really had much idea of what they were doing, except that a tunnel could be carried on by members of the permanent staff, and any transients who wanted to get some practical experience. It was a kind of school for escapers, with the teachers being their own students.

They did have some knowledge of surveying between them, and they decided to dig a tunnel out towards a foot-bridge over a dry stream-bed a short distance beyond the wire. The hope was to break out in the ditch and under its cover get plenty of people out before the Germans noticed. This plan was evidently one of Bushell's – that one tunnel should serve its maximum purpose was an idea that stayed with him. As long as it was well planned, carefully made and properly concealed, why not use it for a mass break-out? It was a simple question of investment. Bushell began work on the tunnel with Casey and others, having decided, if they were successful, to make their way roughly south-west towards the Swiss border at Schaffhausen, which meant crossing almost half of Germany, clearly a mad scheme, but in accord with the daring of a black-runner whose motto in skiing was effectively: 'keep them together, and keep them pointed downhill'.

The tunnel was a failure. The Dulag stood on a high water table (though it's not clear whether the Germans had planned this intentionally or not: later they would choose their camp sites with much care, taking into account the geological and geographical lie of the land). Dressed in scratchy long underwear to spare their uniforms any telltale signs of dirt and mud, the tunnellers, still fairly fit on a good diet and trying to maintain some kind of exercise regime, found that the dry stream-bed wasn't that dry after all. Their tunnel flooded, and they found themselves struggling against oozy mud. They were lucky that the earth above them held, and that there were no fatalities. One or two of the diggers had attacks of claustrophobia from working in the narrow tunnel in near darkness alleviated only occasionally by unreliable makeshift lamps fuelled with ersatz margarine (which burnt with the help of a bootlace wick). After a few weeks of digging with their hands, shifting the muddy dirt into metal basins and hauling it back to the shallow shaft, they had to give up only two metres short of their goal. Unperturbed, they started another dig, but the Germans found it and became a little more alert. Then the winter set in, and the escaping season was over. The Germans from the outset sited their camps far from friendly borders. Even a successful escaper from a camp would then have faced hundreds of kilometres, with poor clothes and little food, to cover on foot in icy conditions. It just wasn't possible.

Nevertheless, they had gained some experience. They'd learned that tunnelling was a long-term project which needed the proper technical backup, but that it could work: the Germans, after all, had been all but oblivious to what they were doing, regarding the tunnel they'd found as a fair crack of the whip, and Rumpel's cordial dinner parties went on uninterruptedly.

In the meantime the permanent staff had absorbed into their company a new man who was to prove a great asset in the lonely, isolated war would-be escapers from POW camps were to wage in the years to come, against captivity and against the drain on their own spirits and the damage to their own psyches that imprisonment brought with it. It was important to the younger prisoners, and Bushell was already at thirty a senior citizen, to have a handful of 'older brothers' or father-figures, who were nevertheless still men of action, to stabilise and encourage them. Harry Day was now joined in that category by an American well qualified to fill that role.

John Bigelow Dodge, known to his companions as 'The Artful Dodger', was one hell of a guy. One of the oldest of the escapers, he was 46 in 1940, and by the time he arrived at the Dulag, he was trailing greater clouds of glory than his relatively modest army rank of major warranted. But he was too much of a loose cannon to be a conventional career soldier, and his background was colourful.

Dodge's mother was Mrs Charles Stuart Dodge, the daughter of John Bigelow, a writer and diplomat who'd edited the *New York Evening Post* from 1850 to 1861, when he went as consul to France. Four years later, Bigelow spent a year as Abraham Lincoln's US Minister to France, and later became Secretary of State for New York. He published a biography of Benjamin Franklin in 1874. His son, Dodge's uncle Poultney, was a journalist and traveller who, ironically, was also a great friend of Kaiser Wilhelm II.

Dodge's quite grand family was related by marriage to Winston Churchill, a fact which would not go unnoticed by the Germans later on. After completing his education in the USA and at McGill University in Canada, he sailed to England in 1914 as a volunteer and joined the Royal Navy, with whom he fought at Antwerp and Gallipoli before transferring to the Army in 1916, where he saw service in France. At the end of the war he was a twenty-four-year-old colonel in the Royal Sussex Regiment, decorated with the Distinguished Service Cross, the Distinguished Service Order, and the Military Cross, with two mentions in dispatches.

He'd become a British citizen in 1915, reacting against his germanophile uncle and identifying with his more august relative and half-fellow-American, Churchill. After the war, he took on an investigation into the problems posed by it to commerce (he always remained an unregenerate capitalist), and travelled the world, visiting Australia, New Zealand and Japan, China and Mongolia, and travelling 1700 miles on horseback into Siberia – his mission provided the excuse for his love of adventure. Not content with that, he turned his attention to Burma and Thailand, Afghanistan, and Iran, as well as Mesopotamia, before being arrested in Batumi (then Batum) on the eastern coast of the Black Sea in Georgia, where Soviet secret police had found drawings of agricultural implements among his belongings. He was only under lock and key for a few weeks, but then, and this was still only 1921, he tried to establish a trading station in the town. This met with predictable failure, and he returned to England, where his boundless energy propelled him into politics. He worked for the then London County Council in Mile End, east London, from 1925 to 1931, and also joined the Stock

Exchange, though his attempts to get elected as a Conservative MP in working-class Mile End failed twice. But his career never faltered. He married, fathered two sons, became the director of a New York bank, and would have continued with his political ambitions had he not been interrupted by the war.

Although of an age at which he might have avoided another fight, Dodge pulled strings through Churchill and got himself a commission almost immediately. Serving with the Middlesex Regiment as part of the British Expeditionary Force near Dunkirk in the early summer of 1940, he was cut off in the fighting. Nothing daunted, when he noticed a small craft a couple of miles offshore, he took off his boots and set out to swim for it, but before he reached it the Germans noticed it themselves and turned their guns on it, upon which it fled, and Dodge was forced to return to the shore – not a mean feat of swimming for a man in his mid-forties. There he was picked up by a German patrol. He escaped almost immediately, jumping off a steamer that was taking a consignment of prisoners up the River Scheldt and swimming towards the sea; but he was quickly recaptured. Fate decreed that the local police, not recognising his uniform, turned him over to the Luftwaffe, and he was duly sent to Dulag-Luft, where Commandant Rumpel thought he'd be an ideal man for the permanent staff, and discreetly had his POW papers register him as a member of the RAF. But Rumpel had introduced a serpent into the bosom of the German Air Force POW system and Dodge got on well with Bushell and Day, who had similarly adventurous spirits.

As 1940 drew to a close, the stream of POWs increased, for the war was going in Germany's favour and, with Europe taken over except for the island of Great Britain (Eire, after the treatment it had received from Britain before achieving independence, was understandably neutral), and with the USA still dithering about getting involved, there seemed little to stop Nazi domination of Europe from the Atlantic seaboard to the western frontier of the USSR (then still their ally).

Among the many hundreds of RAF and Allied aircrew who fell into the hands of the Germans during the latter months of 1940 were three more who were participants, in one way and another, in the Great Escape. They were the Pilot Officers Paul Royle, an Australian, Dick Churchill and B. A. 'Jimmy' James. Royle had been shot down in a Blenheim, James in a Wellington and Churchill in a Hampden. They were all to become key figures in the escape organisation of Stalag-Luft III, but they were to cut their teeth as POWs in a new facility the Germans had set up in the face of a hugely increasing prisoner population, a camp designated Stalag-Luft I.

Stalag-Luft I was as deadly a posting for the German staff as the Allied inmates, except that the Germans had the quadruple reliefs of being on their home turf, access to alcohol, sex, and a kind of freedom. It was built near the bleak little town of Barth, on the equally bleak Baltic coast, about seventy kilometres north-east of Rostock. The camp itself was a dire place, though its design conformed with most of its fellows and successors: a bare compound in which barrack-blocks were regularly distributed, surrounded by a high barbed-wire fence guarded at regular intervals by watch-towers, with a ditch and a low wire inside the main fence to demarcate the limits of where POWs could walk. An immediately adjacent compound held one additional block containing the guardhouse, the cooler, and the hospital; two more small sections of the camp held NCOs and officers. The location was windswept, comfortless and bare – the very last kind of place to discourage prisoners from thoughts of escape.

★　★　★

It wasn't far into 1940, therefore, before the POWs at Barth organised their own escape committee, led by a career Royal Navy officer, a Fleet Air Arm Lieutenant-Commander called Peter Fanshawe. He'd joined the service fifteen years earlier, aged thirteen, and had been serving as John Casson's navigator when their aircraft was shot down in 1940 over Norway during the famous attack on the German battleship *Scharnhorst* (named after the noted Prussian general of the Napoleonic wars). Fanshawe was a rather stiffnecked career officer, whose English reserve meant he could appear aloof – you couldn't call him by his first name. As a result he later earned the nickname (used behind his back) of Hornblower, after the two-dimensional naval hero in the novels of the late C. S. Forester. One of the surviving members of the Great Escape, Les Brodrick, remembers that 'I put my foot in it one day when I heard the others talking about Hornblower, and I said that I was reading about someone called Hornblower.' The nickname was appropriate. According to Brodrick, Fanshawe was 'very snooty, a permanent Naval type and very Dartmouth'. Nevertheless Fanshawe was an able organiser. Quickly he led his team towards the decision that a tunnel would be the best means of escape.

In those early days the Germans had not yet learned that the prisoner barracks should be raised above ground so that tunnelling directly through the floor would be impossible to undertake undetected, so it was a relatively easy matter to cut a 'trap' (a concealed entrance, like a trapdoor) in the floor of a room in one of the blocks. Getting rid of the displaced soil wasn't hard either, since the Germans had built the blocks to civilian standards architecturally, and there was enough ventilation room under the floor to conceal it. The would-be escapers dug a shallow shaft of about a metre and a half before beginning to go laterally towards the wire. Such a shallow tunnel indicates the naïveté of the escapers of those early days – and the naïveté of their guards, whose security arrangements were no more than basic. And despite the absolute horrors perpetrated in both the world wars of the twentieth century, martial cynicism still yielded, in pockets of military association, to a sense of honour. That would outlive 1945.

The escapers estimated that they'd have to dig for about 120 metres before being able to break out into the safety of the woods beyond the wire. There was no problem with security at Stalag-Luft I, because the Germans mounted very few guards, and therefore very few prisoner lookouts, or stooges, as they were called – a slang corruption of 'studious' – were required.

With these advantages, the tunnel reached almost to the wire before it was discovered by the Germans. The result was that the barracks had their skirts removed – in other words, their wooden supports were exposed, so that any future tunnel would have to burrow through the concrete foundations of the washrooms (which for drainage purposes had to run from the floor of the barrack to the ground below), or those of the chimneys and stoves. In addition, new specialised guards were introduced. The Germans had recognised the fact that tunnelling was a means of escaping, and recruited miners and pot-holers to check out the possibilities. They wore drab overalls, and carried long, strong, thin steel probes to check the ground. Later they would sink sound-detectors into the ground, which proved very successful at picking up the noises of men working in what were then relatively shallow tunnels – the shafts sunk were often no more than a metre and a half deep. Two new words entered POW slang: if the tunnellers were rabbits, the special guards were ferrets. One of them at the camp at Barth, who was quite popular with the prisoners, and whose fate would be bound up with theirs for the next few years, was called Karl Pfelz, known affectionately as Charlie.

The early tunnels were very foolhardy undertakings, and would-be escapers could easily have been buried alive. As the Germans became better at security, however, so the prisoners developed more sophisticated ways of outwitting them. Two more tunnels were started at Barth, though neither came to anything; and a handful of POWs managed to walk out of the camp disguised as workmen. They were recaptured, but they remembered the lessons they'd learned.

Increased RAF raids on mainland Europe and the resultant losses as German fighters and anti-aircraft defences took their toll, meant that there was an increase in the number of prisoners arriving at Dulag-Luft, the Luftwaffe transit camp. The escape committee there took on a number of new recruits, among them Flight Lieutenant Brian Evans, a Welshman in his early twenties, who brought with him a useful skill: he was a trained surveyor. He'd been captured early in December 1940 when his plane's engines had failed over Paris. His stay at the Dulag was, however, short, since he was transferred to Barth in mid-February, before the escaping season could really get under way again with the coming of the spring and warmer weather. This didn't stop Evans and three fellow prisoners jumping off the train en route to Stalag-Luft I, though Evans injured one of his legs and all four men were quickly recaptured. One of his fellow escapers on that occasion was another flight lieutenant, a career airman who'd been in the RAF almost since its inception – for seventeen years. This older man was Henry Marshall, known as 'Johnny', who, like Evans, would play a pivotal role in the Great Escape. For the moment, however, they were carted off to Barth, where they would meet fellow escapers, as the network of contacts spread and further experience was gained. The keenest escapers were the prisoners who'd been held longest, but the exercise of planning and whenever possible carrying out escapes had the additional function of staving off the boredom which was a prisoner's worst enemy. Not only that, but if men's minds were focused on a common task there was less chance of dissent between them, and dissent was a major problem where a large number of men who hadn't chosen each other's company were cooped up in a confined space for years with nothing to do.

Back at the Dulag-Luft transit camp, during spring 1941 the escape committee reopened the tunnel they'd been forced to abandon the previous year because of flooding. They found that it was salvageable, and they were able to solve the water problem by digging drainage channels. The Dulag was built on good, solid ground, so that there was no need to shore the tunnel up, and work progressed so well that it had been cleared, repaired and completed by May. Work was further facilitated by the fact that the barrack blocks at Dulag-Luft, unlike those at Barth, still had walls which went right down to the ground.

The escapers decided to break out on the first moonless night in June, which happened to fall on the first weekend of that month. Roger Bushell was to have been one of them, but as he planned to travel alone, and needed to catch a train from Frankfurt to the Swiss frontier, he decided to go it alone on a weekday – the train service at weekends and especially on Sundays was slower and less frequent.

Bushell spoke German fluently but with a Swiss accent – a by-product of his skiing days. His plan was to hole up in a shed at the edge of the exercise-field, which lay next to the camp compound. He would not be missed until roll-call the following day, and he would slip away the previous evening, so he'd have a good start. The only problem was that the shed had an occupant – an elderly and very smelly goat. The goat was harmless, but its presence sparked a fairly predictable gag: Buckley pretended to be concerned, on

Bushell's behalf, about the smell. One of the other prisoners picked up the cue by reassuring him: 'Oh, I'm sure the goat won't mind that.' While his fellow prisoners diverted the guards' attention by staging a mock bull-fight with the goat, Bushell slipped into the shed unobserved.

Armed with rudimentary false papers (the system of forging German documents would become very sophisticated in time) and dressed in what could pass for civilian clothing, and with some German money raised over time by the escape committee by stealing from guards or occasionally selling them delicacies from their Red Cross parcels, Bushell made a successful getaway. He caught his train and reached the small town of Stühlingen on the Swiss border late the following afternoon. At that point a small pocket of Switzerland projects into Germany; once over the border it would be a relatively simple matter to cover the sixty-odd kilometres to Zürich. Bushell opted to make the crossing in daylight, posing as a German ski-instructor on leave from the army, planning the winter season's cross-country routes. He decided to act drunk, hoping that his story – however tenuous it was – and his bonhomie would get him across the border into Switzerland unchallenged. But despite his excellent German he was stopped by a border guard, who took him to the police station to check his papers. At that point, with the mountains of Switzerland so close he could almost reach out and touch them, Bushell had to admit defeat and give himself up.

Meanwhile the major escape party was preparing to use the tunnel. Those not taking part gave a wild party to distract the guards. Those who were, including some of the senior members of the permanent staff, dressed themselves in RAF tunics or greatcoats recut to look more or less like civilian clothes, and opened the trap of the tunnel, which was located under a bed in Day's room. The tunnel worked perfectly, but bad luck, and vigilance on the part of the Germans ensured that all of them were recaptured, most within twenty-four hours. Dodge was caught as he crossed a guarded bridge; Buckley made it as far as Minden, well to the north, where he fell foul of a railway official. Day himself managed to stay out for two whole days, but was captured by a forest ranger on the third. Mike Casey stayed out longest, but he and his fellow escaper were asked for their papers in a village near Darmstadt. They had none – in fact they'd done very well to get so far without papers, since in wartime Germany everybody was stopped and asked for them frequently by officials of the state – so their bid for freedom came to an end.

The tunnel escapers were returned to Dulag-Luft, whence they were transferred to Barth. Commandant Rumpel, who lost his job as a consequence of the escape – close to twenty prisoners had used the tunnel to get away – nevertheless ensured that a case of champagne accompanied the recaptured airmen on the train to Stalag-Luft I.

On his recapture Bushell found himself transferred to a terrible camp far to the north, near Lübeck. It wasn't specifically for RAF personnel, although there were fifty RAF officers there, along with a number of British army officers who'd been taken prisoner in Crete. The camp was cold and dirty and the food was poor. To make matters worse, an RAF bomber had recently flattened the German officers' mess, so the British airmen were given a particularly hard time. Notwithstanding, Bushell organised another tunnel there, but it was nowhere near completion before – to their relief – the entire population of the camp was relocated to an *Offizierlager*, or Oflag – a camp for officers – a few kilometres north-west of Kassel, near Warburg.

The journey from Lübeck to Warburg, covering some 300 kilometres, was to be made by train. The prisoners were herded into goods waggons, thirty men to each, with three guards over them. It was dark and noisy in the waggons, and no sooner had they set off than Bushell started to organise an escape attempt which had been mooted in the camp the minute the prisoners knew they were going to be transferred by train.

The opportunity seemed too good to miss, and one of Bushell's comrades, a man called Filmer who had jumped off the Barth-bound train with Evans and Marshall, had come prepared with a table knife, filched from the camp kitchen and notched to give it a rough serrated edge. Also with Bushell in the waggon was the Czech airman, Jack Zafouk.

The guards positioned themselves near the door, and to cover the escape work they were doing, a group of prisoners gathered round a game of cards on the opposite side of the waggon. The watchers and the card-players concealed Bushell and his comrade, who sawed away at the floorboards of the waggon with their knife. It was slow and hard work, but finally, after several hours, their fingers cut and bleeding, they had managed to make a big enough hole to squeeze through. Getting out wouldn't be easy: they had to wait until the train slowed, then drop onto the track below the waggon, then roll off the railway line between the wheels of the waggon. This was a very dangerous manoeuvre and they were lucky that no-one was injured. Filmer went first, followed by Zafouk and Bushell, then another pair. All of them got away from the train, and though all were recaptured, one couple got as far as Stettin (now Szczecin in modern Poland), where they hoped to stow away on a ship. This was the escape attempt that took Bushell and Zafouk as far as Prague, where they were picked up after several frustrated attempts by the Czech Resistance to smuggle them out through Hungary and Yugoslavia, and thence to Turkey.

Despite increased German security at Barth, no fewer than

forty-eight tunnels were dug there. Tunnelling itself was easy: the ground was firm and no shoring was needed. Not all the tunnels were completed, and most were discovered, but the experience was valuable and the knowledge that one was at least making an effort to get away was of great psychological value. Morale was given a fillip at the end of June 1941 when a prisoner called Harry Burton managed to worm his way under the wire and made his way to Sweden – the first member of the RAF to complete a successful escape. The other area in which significant progress was being made, and this was perhaps the most important aspect of development at Barth, was in the organisation of escaping. Gradually, many of the men who had gone through Spangenberg and Dulag-Luft were coming together again at Barth and fusing into a formidable team. Day and Buckley were its leading lights, with Buckley as commander of what they called the X-Organisation. Buckley was known as Big X.

Tunnelling was not the only means of escape used. One man was able to concoct a passable set of dark grey overalls, and walked out of the camp disguised as a 'ferret'. Another managed to get hold of a black suit, made himself a top hat out of cardboard and coloured it black, smeared his face with soot and walked out of the camp looking like a traditional German chimney-sweep. On another occasion a Swiss delegation visited the camp. Switzerland, as a neutral state, had taken on the office of Protecting Power; that is to say that it looked after the interests of the belligerents during the suspension of diplomatic relations between them. One of the Protecting Power's rights is the inspection of prisoner-of-war camps to see that the nationals of the country it represents are being treated properly. During the Second World War, Switzerland was the Protecting Power in Germany and Italy for Great Britain and the USA; for the USA in Japan; for Germany, Italy and Japan in the USA, and so on. While the

Swiss were in one part of the camp, a group of prisoners in makeshift civilian suits walked out through the gates, trying to look grave, diplomatic and unassailable. One distinguished POW, Douglas Bader, the fighter ace who'd lost his legs in a flying accident in the early 1930s, managed to sneak out of Stalag VIIIB (Lamsdorf) with a group of prisoners designated to work at a nearby airfield, where he hoped to steal a plane and head for home in it. Unfortunately a guard recognised him. Bader was sent to Colditz.

On 20 August 1941 a tunnel from the west block of the camp was ready to 'break' – that is to say, it had been completed barring the last foot or so of earth that separated its exit hole from the surface, which obviously wouldn't be dug out until the last minute because otherwise it would have betrayed the tunnel's existence to the German ferrets who patrolled the area immediately outside the camp's perimeter. Thirty people were involved, including Jimmy James. Tunnels represented a great investment of time and labour, and as they could only be used once, it made sense to maximise the number of people who used them. The first five to go through found that the narrow bore of the tunnel made it hard to get their escape kit, which included a blanket, through. They also made so much noise that the guards were quickly alerted, and only three prisoners got away. One was quickly caught, but the other two made it as far as Rostock, a major port on the German Baltic coast about sixty kilometres south-west of Barth, but there their attempts to get away to Sweden on a ship were thwarted at the last minute.

Despite this setback, James was soon working on another tunnel, whose trap led from beneath a rubbish incinerator near the wire. The advantage of the location was that a tunnel would only need to be seven or eight metres long. James and the comrade who worked with him, John Shore, needed to work from inside the incinerator, and to disguise their activities enlisted the aid of a bunch of fellow prisoners who instituted a daily game of football. These included others who would later be involved in the Great Escape: Dick Churchill, Paul Royle, Squadron Leader Lawrence Reavell-Carter, a former Olympic athlete, and Flight Lieutenant James Long, whose nickname 'Cookie' derived from his uncontested skill at distilling moonshine liquor. The tunnel took only four days to complete, but those four days were spread over three weeks as it wasn't always possible to gain access to the incinerator, and with so many escape attempts going on, the Germans were very much on the alert. At last, in October, the escapers were ready to make a break for it, waiting for an air-raid to provide them with suitable cover. When it came, the half-dozen men involved in the attempt, including James and Shore, were to make their way one by one to the incinerator during the confusion. The men had been holding themselves ready for days, but four of the escapers didn't even make it to the trap. James was recaptured but Shore, the first to go, managed to make his way to Sassnitz on the island of Rügen. From there he boarded a ferry to Sweden, and became the second successful RAF escaper of the war.

Winter was now setting in, and although that meant the end of the escaping season, it did not signal any slowdown in tunnelling activity, though burrowing through the much harder cold ground was considerably more difficult. The winter also brought a fresh intake of prisoners, who included fellow crew-members Lester Bull and William 'Jack' Grisman, whose Wellington bomber had been shot down over France early in November, both of whom quickly became involved in tunnel work. They were soon joined, in another transport of prisoners, by Flight Lieutenant Roy Langlois, from the Channel Islands, and the dashing and eccentric Tom Kirby-Green, a squadron leader of twenty-three, who'd been born in Nyasaland (modern Malawi), where his father had been governor.

Kirby-Green joined the RAF in 1936, having first tried to join the fight against Franco in Spain. When war broke out he was attached to Bomber Command. He flew an astonishing twenty-seven raids in the first half of 1940 (most bomber crews were lucky if they got past five), before being relocated as a training officer with a free Czech squadron. Thereafter he flew Wellingtons, and it was on his thirty-seventh raid that he was shot down, in October 1941. He was considered such a catch that his capture was announced by Lord Haw Haw (William Joyce) in the German propaganda radio transmitted to Britain. Kirby-Green was hardly a typical RAF officer. He loved Cuban music, and was passionate about Latin America. He played the maracas and the drums. He loved to cook. He was a passable artist and counted Matisse and Gauguin among his favourite painters. His son Colin, a young boy at the time of his capture, remembers him as a romantic – 'quite Byronic in a way'. Kirby-Green and Langlois were both participants in the Great Escape. Langlois made it home after the war. Kirby-Green did not. Later on, Langlois would marry Kirby-Green's widow, Maria. Colin Kirby-Green remembers that Langlois 'was smashing to me, and that helped a lot. In fact there was a time when I asked him – when I was at boarding school and he was still in the air force – if I could take his name. It seemed odd to me to have a different surname from my mother and stepfather, and you know how it is in schools, any kind of difference is a burr under the blanket . . . and he very gently said to me, yes, I could if I really wanted to, but wouldn't it be nicer for Tom if I didn't?' Colin kept his father's surname, but remembers Langlois' suggestion with deep gratitude: 'He was hugely supportive in that way.'

Tom Kirby-Green had an eight-year-old son, Colin:

'When I heard that he was a prisoner I was also told that he would now be safe. It wouldn't be nice for him and it could be for a long time, but most people viewed having their families as prisoners as the next safest thing to them coming back.

'So I was given to understand that he was safe in the meantime and I always thought that I would see him again, as did my mother. Nobody knew what would happen. I just knew that I missed him and that he was this wonderful kind of distant hero there all the time. That was pretty sustaining for me in prep school when I didn't want to be there.'

Information about the war filtered into the camp. Now that the former allies, the USSR and Germany, had turned against each other, some of the pressure had been lifted from Britain; but Germany was still experiencing great success, and if the news that the USA had entered the war in December 1941 brought some relief, the numbers of RAF POWs continued to increase, bringing with them news of an increased air offensive, but also stories of successful German defence, and many deaths. The tide of the war had not yet turned by any means, and those with loved ones, perhaps especially those with young wives, were going through a very anxious time. The prisoners did what they could to keep their spirits up, experimenting with different ways of making alcohol (one based on dried fruit from Red Cross parcels and yeast bought from a guard turned out to be particularly successful), and putting on a show whose content is suggested by its title: *Alice and her Candle.*

As more POWs arrived, the camp began to feel distinctly

overcrowded. Despite the fact that it was still winter, a number of escape attempts were made early in 1942. One of them was made by the indefatigable Jimmy James. By this time the prisoner population was, within the X-Organisation, becoming proficient at setting up escapes and providing backup and resources to anyone who came to it with a viable plan. 'Departments' began to be organised which exploited the civilian-life skills of those POWs belonging to them: though still in a relatively primitive state, there were departments for forging documents and mapmaking, for example, and tailor's shops for creating, by adapting whatever clothing was available, civilian clothes ranging from passably smart suits to workers' garb, and even German uniforms. The German guards were known to the POWs as 'goons' – the name of the stupid, sub-human beings who occasionally featured in the early Popeye cartoons. Hence their uniforms were called 'goonskins'. Jimmy James acquired one of these, and during a blackout simply ran towards the main gate shouting *Los!* (Let's go!), in the hope that he could just simply run through it in the confusion. But as he approached, power was restored. There was no way his uniform would stand scrutiny when bathed in floodlights, so he turned on his heel and returned to his block fast – goonskins were too precious to be given up – it could be used again when another opportunity presented itself.

If escaping sometimes seemed like a game, one incident occurred that winter to remind the prisoners that it was not. A sergeant pilot in the non-commissioned officers' compound, John Shaw, who had flown Brian Evans' plane, was cutting through the wire one night with a fellow escaper when a guard surprised him. He surrendered immediately, but for reasons which are unclear the guard shot him. He was the first RAF crewman to die while attempting to escape.

As February arrived, the occasional rumour began to

circulate about a huge new camp the Germans were constructing somewhere far to the south, in Silesia. RAF prisoners were concentrated in Barth and at the Dulag, but others were dotted about all over the place. The very first American flyers to be captured were beginning to arrive, and there were already members of the Australian, Canadian, New Zealand and South African air forces in the camps. It seemed that the Germans were planning to centralise all air force prisoners in one large holding area in an inaccessible location from which escape would be very difficult, and even if achieved, so far from any friendly or neutral country that virtually no-one would avoid recapture. Aircrews, like commandos, paratroopers and submariners, were regarded as crack troops, expensive to train in terms of cost and time, and capable of doing more damage per man than ordinary soldiers. They were therefore regarded as requiring the strictest security, and, as the war progressed and bombing raids on Germany became increasingly successful and destructive, they were regarded with only the thinnest sympathy by the majority of their guards, despite the professional association of belonging to complementary air forces.

The rumours proved true, and in the second half of March the first contingent of officers left Barth to take up residence at their new home, Stalag-Luft III.

Chapter Three

THE NEW CAMP WAS SITUATED A COUPLE OF KILOMETRES south of the town of Sagan (modern Zagan), then in Germany, now in Poland, in the midst of a vast and dreary pine forest through which the Bober River runs. Sagan lies midway between Berlin and Breslau (modern Wroclaw). It is about 625 kilometres as the crow flies from the Swiss frontier, about 275 kilometres from the nearest point on the Baltic coast, and 175 kilometres from Berlin. The countryside is flat and featureless, consisting of pine forest or bleak, open farmland. In winter temperatures can drop to well below -15 degrees Celsius.

To begin with, the Germans had cut a large clearing in the forest near the river and laid out two compounds, one for officers and one for enlisted men. There were six barrack blocks in each compound, and all were built on stilts, apart from the concrete foundations below the washrooms and the stoves. Trapdoors in the floors and ceilings allowed ferrets to make easy inspections to ensure that no illicit escape materials were being concealed. Not only were the blocks set well back from the perimeter wires, so that any tunnel would have to be very long indeed to reach a safe exit point beyond them, but the double fences themselves were daunting: three

Jimmy James:

'First of all the huts were built on very soft sand, which the Germans didn't think we would be able to make tunnels in. Secondly the huts were a very long way from the wire and the camp itself was a very long way away from neutral territory. In addition to this there were three guard boxes on each side of the camp with a good field of fire everywhere. Also there were scismographs to detect tunnelling. For these reasons the Germans did consider Stalag-Luft III escape-proof. But no camp is really escape-proof. Some are more difficult to get out of than others but I don't think there has ever been a camp that's been escape-proof.'

metres high, with thickly coiled barbed wire laid in the two-metre gap between them. The top of the fences had an inward-sloping crown which made them impossible to scale, but no prisoner was supposed ever to get close enough even to attempt such a means of escape. About ten metres inside the inner fence another, single strand of barbed wire ran all the way round each compound. This 'warning wire' was only forty-five centimetres high, but any prisoner who stepped across it was immediately open to being shot at from the machine gun posts on top of the watch-towers, or 'goon-boxes', which were placed along the outer perimeter fence at intervals of about one hundred metres, and equipped with powerful, wide-beam searchlights. The final security measure lay in the nature of the ground on which the camp was built. Under a thin crust of grey soil there was wet, yellow sand. If a tunnel were attempted, it would have to be a miracle of engineering and would require solid wooden shoring along its whole length; but even if that were possible, there would still be the problem of getting rid of the sand displaced by it. There could be no question of mingling much of it with the grey topsoil – it would soon show up; and there was no way of dispersing it either below the blocks or in their roofs, open as they were to inspection at any time by the guards.

But there were chinks in the German security arrangements, and in time the prisoners would find them out.

A basic error was to put all the most troublesome escapers together, though it may be that the Germans had enough faith in the physical obstacles they had put in place to reassure themselves that the spirit of even the most cussed escaper would be dampened. From the German point of view, it made good administrative sense to have everyone under one roof, as it were, and under the same eagle eye. But fellowship among the prisoners helped morale. There had been a couple of escape attempts even on the first transport, including one by Cookie Long, and another by an officer who'd had himself shut up in a packing case which should have contained supplies. The officer had managed to get away, but was recaptured after a couple of days and shipped off to Colditz.

Allied aircrew knew they were wreaking terrible destruction on the German population. For some, it was a relief once shot down to reach military custody. Alex Cassie:

'We were briefed that the Germans observed the Geneva Convention and, in fact, most of us captured bore that out. I knew what was going to happen once I got to Dulag-Luft. It was before you got to the interception camp that was the dangerous period. If you encountered the public before you were in military hands you could be attacked by anyone. Once you got into the military's hands – the Wehrmacht, the Luftwaffe, or the Navy – you believed they observed the Geneva Convention. Certainly my experience was that they observed it in a sensible way. I was handed over by a fishing crew to the Navy. Although not luxury, of course, my treatment was perfectly good. The young German officer who escorted me on the train to Dulag-Luft near Frankfurt-am-Main was a perfect gentleman. He was interesting and we got on very well together. My only worry was to remind myself that I shouldn't talk too freely in case of what I might inadvertently reveal. I had to remind myself from time to time that he was my enemy. But he was very nice, and kept me well supplied with cigarettes and things.'

Despite the support of a feeling of fellowship, arrival at the bleak camp, so far from anywhere, was a grim experience. At Barth, the simple fact that the sea, with its hope of escape to Sweden, was so close, acted as a source of comfort. Trying to get to sleep at night was one of the worst times, as Alex Cassie still remembers: 'There was a sense of being forgotten, and that there was a whole war going on between me and home.' Cassie was very much involved in the Great Escape, and he was one of the lucky ones. It was all too easy, without anything to occupy one's mind, to drift into a state of hopelessness, and although a theatre company was quickly formed at Stalag-Luft III, and sporting events were organised with the help of equipment sent by the Red Cross and the YMCA, it was hard for a POW to shake off the malaise engendered by the fact that he wasn't doing anything useful, that he was listless owing to poor nutrition, and that he was horribly sex-starved.

Although the distribution of food was fair, and the ever more basic rations were occasionally eked out by a Red Cross parcel, concern over food could become an obsession. Bill Armitage, a former POW at Stalag-Luft III, remembers taking forty-seven minutes to choose a slice of bread. The Red Cross parcels, with their cans of soup and corned beef, made up for the camp diet of grey bread, margarine, acorn coffee, thin soup and horrible concoctions such as chemical jam and fish cheese. Red Cross parcels also contained tins of powdered milk, known as Klim. The empty cans ought to have been removed by the camp authorities, but Commandant von Lindeiner didn't always run things by the book, and the POWs were able to hoard them for later use in escape activities. Everything was saved, because everything could be converted, with a little ingenuity, to another use. Old tin cans, as it turned out, could yield any manner of tools and utensils, from wire-cutters to knives, bowls and spoons.

Jack Lyon:

'We all did things in the prisoner-of-war camp that we might not have done otherwise. As with men living together anywhere, it doesn't always bring out the best in them. We all tended to live our own little lives and follow our own interests. I was trying to study at that time and carried out my limited escape committee duties. Above all, the proximity of ten men forced to live together, eating together, causes you to develop your own interests, as far as possible, to live your own inner lives shall we say.'

Day-to-day life, however, was grim, and fights often sprang up as tensions mounted and petty grievances became festering sores. Senior officers and NCOs tried to maintain military discipline and a sense of order, but the best way of channelling energy and forgetting one's woes – or at least pushing them into a corner – was to get involved with the escape organisation. There was a sense of purpose and a sense of belonging which could quite literally be a life-saver. It is hardly surprising therefore that so many tunnels – over one hundred at Stalag-Luft I alone – were started throughout the camp system.

The central core of serious escapers among the officers were soon reunited at the new camp: Harry Day and two fellow officers had hardly been in the place twenty-four hours before they made what both must have known was no more than a symbolic gesture: they roughly adapted their RAF uniforms to look like Luftwaffe uniforms (as at Barth, the guards were all Luftwaffe personnel), which luckily were more or less the same colour, and boldly marched towards the gates. The guards there were unimpressed, and the two officers were sent off to the *Kittchen* for a couple of weeks' solitary confinement. The *Kittchen*, or cooler, was used so often that the Germans soon dropped their word for it and adopted the English expression. The Commandant of the camp, Friedrich von Lindeiner-Wildau, a highly decorated First World War cavalry officer and now a Luftwaffe colonel in his sixties, was a regular soldier untainted by Nazism; but he knew what he would face if he was at all negligent in his duty, just as he knew the damage his charges could do to his country if any of them ever got back to their own lines. But the cooler was the standard punishment, and that was all that was meted out. It was unpleasant enough: two weeks alone in a dank, narrow cell on basic rations was enough to crack some already fraught spirits, though that was not Colonel von Lindeiner's purpose. He recognised that the POWs still saw themselves as at war; it was their duty to try to get away; and he respected that.

The biggest thorns in his side started to rebuild their infrastructure as soon as they arrived. Jimmy Buckley and Harry Day set up a new X-Organisation, and they were joined by Mike Casey, John Dodge, Peter Fanshawe, Jimmy James,

Cookie Long and Johnny Marshall, among other by-now veteran escapers with a good deal of tunnelling experience between them. New recruits came in not only from Barth, but from Spangenberg and the Oflag near Warburg, as well as other, more recently captured POWs, who would bring a new injection of special skills to the X-Organisation. The organisation itself became a much more sophisticated outfit as a result.

Among the new sections was 'Dean and Dawson', named after the famous London travel agency. It was run by a man who would later become one of Alex Cassie's room-mates, Flight Lieutenant 'Tim' Walenn, one of the key members of the escape organisation. 'Dean and Dawson' was the forgery department.

Walenn was twenty-six when he arrived in Stalag-Luft III. The son of a London graphic artist who'd served with the Royal Flying Corps during the First World War, he'd followed in his father's footsteps at first, before switching from design to banking, in the hope that he'd earn enough money in that field to fund his love of flying. This was such a successful ploy that he ended up founding a flying club for the bank, which subsidised it. The club was inaugurated in 1937 and, perhaps with an eye on the gathering clouds in Europe, the bank allowed Walenn six months' leave to train as an instructor. Thereafter he spent his weekends teaching his fellow club members to fly.

He joined the RAF Volunteer Reserve late in 1937, while continuing with the teaching of the club, but in March 1939 he left civilian life altogether and joined 97 Squadron. He grew an extravagant reddish-brown RAF moustache. He was such a good instructor that the air force kept him working as one until they finally heeded his repeated requests to go into active service in August 1941; but scarcely a month later his plane crash-landed near Rotterdam, and he fell into enemy hands.

Walenn's gentle, humorous and easy-going personality hid a steely character. Cassie remembers that he was secretive about his past, liking to make it appear rather more glamorous than it actually was. But there was hidden tragedy there, too: a girlfriend had been killed in a car accident. This event he only mentioned once or twice, and never elaborated on. During the long years of imprisonment, he never gave in to cigarettes, which for most of his comrades helped stave off the constant feeling of hunger common to all prisoners-of-war; he also strove to keep fit, knowing that it would be to his advantage when he eventually escaped – something he never doubted that he'd do.

He hadn't forgotten his other skills – those of a graphic artist – and he now deployed them as his contribution, from his restricted position, to the war effort. He possessed all the infinite patience needed to reproduce or invent typewritten documents by hand, and the ability to inspire others to follow suit. Given the Nazi administration's mania for paperwork, and given that convincing documents were essential for any successful escaper, the input of 'Dean and Dawson' to the X-Organisation was crucial.

The tunnelling section had to adapt its skills to the new terrain, but Fanshawe and Marshall were joined by a Scotsman called Robert Ker-Ramsay and a Canadian called Wally Floody – both had mining experience and inventive brains. They started a number of shallow experimental tunnels, which either caved in of their own accord, leaving embarrassing grooves in the floor of the compound, or were discovered by the Germans, sometimes by chance. When a heavy horsedrawn waggon caused a tunnel to collapse when it drove over it, the Germans took note, and afterwards frequently used the same means deliberately to expose a tunnel if they suspected one existed. The biggest give-away was the yellow sand that was so difficult to conceal. The early tunnels were too shallow, and unshored-up. It quickly became apparent that deep shafts would have to be sunk, and some means found of keeping the unstable earth at bay, if a tunnel was to be successful. That meant a much larger investment of time than hitherto, and the thought of working in a confined, dark space many metres below the surface was not one that had massive appeal.

In the meantime, German resources were beginning to feel stretched for the first time. Long lines of communication had to be maintained for the Russian campaign, though continued German successes meant that a large number of Russian POWs (though seldom treated with any regard for the Geneva Convention) had to be accommodated. At the same time, defence of Allied bombing attacks on the Ruhr and other industrial areas to the west meant that an increased number of British, Colonial and American flyers were ending up as POWs. The camp was filling up, and the Germans guarding it found that they had their work cut out for them.

Lindeiner's team was not first rate, but among his officers and the ferrets at least he was ably served. Hans Pieber was one of the camp administrative officers, and had close contact with the prisoners. Pieber was a former schoolteacher who had joined the Nazi Party early on; in fact he was one of 1500 men entitled to wear Hitler's *Blutorden*, or Blood Order, the highest honorary decoration of the Party, as one of those who'd taken part in the abortive 'Beer Hall Putsch' of 1923 in Munich. Pieber, like Hitler, was an Austrian; but he had refused to wear his decoration since the German takeover of Austria in 1938, and he had not risen in the Party hierarchy. He was a pleasant enough man, more interested in watching his own back than anything else, and oddly popular with the prisoners. As the war progressed and its outcome became all the more obvious to all but the most blinkered follower of the Führer, Pieber cultivated the POWs increasingly. A more shadowy figure was the security officer, a man by the name of Major Broili.

The ferrets were often to be seen in the compound. Their chief was Sergeant Hermann Glemnitz, known as Dimwits, though he was far from that. He was the best and most perspicacious of the ferrets, and as he'd worked with a mining firm in Yorkshire before the war, he not only had a knowledge of the mechanics of tunnelling, but also of the English character. He was not without humour, but completely conscientious in his work, despite which he had the respect, if not the unreserved affection, of the prisoners. His second-in-command was equally conscientious, but lacking in any other redeeming feature. Corporal Karl Griese, whose nickname, Rubberneck, reflected the unusually long column of flesh that ran between his shoulders and his chin, had few friends either among the Germans or the prisoners. He was inflexible in his dedication to his work, which he was extremely good at; to make matters worse, he actively disliked the prisoners. Perhaps an Allied air-raid had affected his family.

Among the rank and file ferrets were Karl Pfelz – whom some of the prisoners had encountered at the camp at Barth and called 'Charlie' – usually active in the East Compound of the camp, and two others only remembered by their nicknames: a young one called Keen-Type, and another, older one whose toothbrush moustache inevitably got him the name of Adolf. As for the rank and file guards, it seems curious that a camp designed to be all but escape-proof and containing such valuable prisoners should have been so ill served. Perhaps the Prison-Camp Service of the High Command felt that the camp's installations and situation provided sufficient security; certainly as the war progressed the need to have the best, and even the second-best, soldiers employed elsewhere, was understandable. The guards at Stalag-Luft III were a real Achilles' heel, and a weakness the POWs would not be slow to exploit.

In the meantime, although various attempts were made to get out of the camp by simply leaving in disguise, the best option, despite all the drawbacks, remained tunnelling. Jimmy James and a comrade, Charles Bonington (father of mountaineer Chris), pretended to leave the camp as part of a group to be vaccinated for typhus (a disease with thrived in the crowded and unhygienic conditions of prison camps), but spirited themselves into a coal store near the wire. They had originally set out to try to cut their way out, but when the hoped-for wirecutters had not been forthcoming, they opted for tunnelling, planning to drive a shallow shaft down inside the store and then burrow the seven or eight metres that would take them beyond the compound. It was a desperate scheme, but could have succeeded had not a guard entered the store to shelter from the rain and caught them there.

Far more successful was a scheme thought out by Bill Goldfinch. When he put it to the escape committee, they thought it almost suicidally daring at first, but as Goldfinch knew what he was talking about, they gave him the go-ahead.

The first thing Goldfinch and his two comrades in the venture, New Zealander Henry 'Piglet' Lamond and Jack Best, needed was a safe place near the fence from which to dig. Such a location was next to impossible to find, but there was an ablutions hut about five metres from the wire, which looked as if it would provide the ideal cover. Goldfinch arranged to block its drains, and after a short time effluent was seeping up through the soil. Goldfinch then approached Pieber through Day and Buckley and volunteered to dig a sump to clear it. Pieber, short-staffed, agreed, and even laid on shovels and spades, which, however, had been carefully counted.

Once they'd dug a trench about one and a half metres deep, Goldfinch and his team, watched over by a group of stooges, started a lateral tunnel from it towards the wire. He chose his spot carefully because he did not want to alert the sound-detector microphones already sunk into the ground. Every day they dug a little further, and every day when they finished and cleaned up for evening roll-call, they sealed the mouth of their hole with mud. There was still enough water in the drainage trench to justify their continuing work there, but they would have to be quick.

By 21 June they'd managed to dig a tunnel about fifteen metres long. After roll-call, they made their way back to the sump with a prisoner whose job it would be to cover their tracks. As soon as they were sure that they were unobserved, the three escapers lowered themselves into the pit, entered the tunnel, and closed it behind them, while their fellow prisoner made sure that the water in the ditch covered their tracks. The tunnel was very shallow, only just over a metre below the surface, so that they could push thin sticks up to the surface to get oxygen; but it was pitch dark, and only just wide enough to accommodate them. That evening Goldfinch dug a further eight metres, while the two men behind him shovelled the sand back to their rear, filling in the tunnel as they moved forward. Then they stopped for the night in case the dog patrol detected them. The next day, working in unimaginable conditions, they made another twenty-five metres, trying to prod open air holes as infrequently as possible, for they knew steam from the heat of their bodies would rise through them and possibly betray them. But they went undetected, and, lying up again until the camp was quiet, they dug the last few metres to where they calculated they could surface. It was very much rule of thumb, and few would have been capable of burying themselves alive for forty-eight hours or so even if escape at the end of it had been certain, but they managed it.

For the first day they lay up, filthy, stinking and exhausted. Travelling by night, since they only had their RAF uniforms, they eventually managed to reach the River Oder, where they stole a rowing boat and made their way downstream, hoping to reach the Baltic. But the boat's owner reported it missing, and they were picked up by the police the following night. Lamond was returned to Stalag-Luft III and the cooler. Goldfinch and Best were sent to Colditz.

There followed a flurry of activity on both sides. The Germans dug an eight-foot trench between the warning wire and the fence, and doubled the number of seismographic microphones. The prisoners responded by making two attempts to emulate the Goldfinch party's effort by blitz-tunnelling their way out from the new German trench. Neither attempt succeeded, but the Germans quickly filled their anti-tunnelling trench again. Nevertheless, Goldfinch's method wasn't tried by anyone else at Sagan: the chances of being buried alive were high enough at the best of times, and one didn't have to have more than mild claustrophobia to view the 'mole' method of tunnelling unenthusiastically.

Like everyone in the camp, Henry Lamond suffered from the lack of privacy and space:

'You got to know a few people you lived with but I developed this capacity to completely ignore them. You had to do that otherwise your life would have been a misery. The arguments that went on and the shouts and screams – you were locked in the hut in the winter from about half past four and you weren't allowed out until nine or ten in the morning. It was terrible, it really was. And it was cold, every room had a fire, but it was cold and misery all together.

'You could be entirely on your own, you could wipe out the noise, the shouts and screams and be in your own little sphere and you wouldn't even know what was going on . . . you got very good at that sort of thing.'

But escapes continued. Under the distraction of a boxing match set up to draw the attention of the guards on the nearest watch-tower, an Irish airman and an American from one of the RAF 'Eagle' squadrons walked in makeshift civilian clothes towards a place on the perimeter where they reckoned there was a blind spot, and cut their way through both sets of barbed wire fence as well as the coiled barbed wire in between. It took them ten minutes, the operation went faultlessly, and they walked off into the woods. They got as far as the town of Frankfurt-an-der-Oder before they were picked up, as their forged papers were not quite in order. When they were returned to the camp, von Lindeiner gave them a bottle of whisky in recognition of their sheer audacity. If they'd been caught in the attempt, they would certainly have been shot.

Les Brodrick:

    'There was one fantastic Czech, and when we had a sports day he did the triple jump and he won it with something over 40 feet, and he only had one leg! Amazing! He was so strong that he didn't do the normal hop, step and a jump – he just did three hops and he won the event.'

Jack Lyon:

    'There was an impromptu game of rugby and the ground was as hard as rock but it didn't interfere with the exuberance of the game. It was led by a very hefty chap by the name of Ken Toft, and Glemnitz watched this game with a certain amount of interest. They said to him, "Look, this is rugby, what we call rugby. What about getting up a team with the camp staff?" He said, "Yes, if you let us keep our guns."'

The tunnelling continued in a modified form. Because of the

increased number of sunken microphones, it was clear that the tunnels would have to run much deeper. The experts decided on a new approach: they dug two shallow dummy tunnels, and from them dropped further shafts to a depth of ten metres, disguising the mouths of the second shafts in the hope that if the Germans discovered the dummies, they would not think that they hid the main tunnel, which could be re-excavated when the heat was off. Unfortunately, and more by luck than judgment, the Germans discovered the whole set-up, but not before a new member had joined the tunnelling teams. He was a Rhodesian called John Travis, who kept himself sane in the camp by turning himself out every day as immaculately as possible. He was a genius at improvising digging tools, though he also made baking dishes from old tins and shaving brushes from bits of wood and frayed string. One of his early innovations was the fat-burning lamp – consisting of a tin containing boiled-down margarine, with a pyjama-cord wick. These considerably alleviated the problem of working without light down in the tunnels, but they required air to work. After experimenting with an old accordion, a rudimentary air-pump was developed made of a kit-bag fitted with wooden hoops and circles of shoe leather as valve-flaps. These innovations would be of prime importance.

Travis joined in the tunnelling for a time, but he suffered badly from claustrophobia since he'd once been trapped 1200 metres down a gold mine by a fall of rock. Digging at Stalag-Luft III was particularly dangerous because of the friable nature of the sand. Diggers always worked in twos so that if there was a fall, one could pull the other out. In the end Buckley decided not to risk losing his technical skills and took him off digging. The guards were beginning to accept small bribes from Red Cross parcels – a piece of soap, a few grammes of coffee or cocoa, for example – in exchange for tools. Even a bit of broken file had its use, and a broken kitchen knife could be transformed by filing into a useful chisel. Travis could convert a bit of old stovepipe into a useful hand-shovel. A workshop was soon established under his supervision. At the same time, a food section, which would experiment in developing high energy food concentrates, was set up under David Lubbock, a nutritionist in civilian life, and Tommy Guest organised a tailors' shop for converting uniforms into civilian suits and German uniforms. There was soon a mapmaking section, and to make the overall operation more streamlined, the X-Organisation designated three overall categories of escape: Over (across the wire), Under (tunnels) and Through (walking out through the gates in disguise or hidden in a group of civilian workers).

About the time of Goldfinch's escape attempt, Roger Bushell arrived at Stalag-Luft III, frustrated and filled with a profound dislike of the Germans. He had managed to smuggle in with him a real civilian suit in grey cloth, which he'd been given by his Czech host in Prague and managed to hang on to throughout his imprisonment by the Gestapo, who were more interested in information than personal effects. It was almost a talisman for him, something he would wear when he escaped, and something which 'ensured' that he would do so. He joined the escape committee immediately, but before he could help them develop their operation further, the Germans struck.

For some time it had been clear to them that, in order to put a stop to the vigorous escaping activity that was going on, they would have to break up the group responsible for it. Since the ringleaders were not difficult to identify, von Lindeiner decided to have them transferred to an army camp for officers, Oflag XXIB. They left in November 1942, the same month that the critical battle of Stalingrad, which had been raging since September, turned at last in favour of the Russians. Among others packed off were Jimmy Buckley,

Dick Churchill, Harry Day, Peter Fanshawe and Jimmy James, as well as the indefatigable John Dodge, who leapt from the train that was transporting them, only to be picked up immediately, as it was broad daylight. 'No harm in trying,' was his only comment.

The Oflag was located at Schubin, near Bromberg, on the site of a girls' school, in pleasant countryside. The twelve brick barracks which housed the prisoners were less pleasant: they were cavernous empty spaces, and any privacy was only achieved by rigging your clothes up around you like curtains. On the other hand, by comparison with Sagan, Schubin was like an open prison. The escape committee was immediately reformed, gathering strength from a separate group of airmen transferred from Warburg. A 'mole' tunnel was started, but had to be abandoned when a bad fall buried one tunneller so completely that his friends had to dig him out from above. The tunnel was four feet below the surface and they were only just in time.

Security remained lax, however, and a more substantial tunnel was planned, its trap skilfully concealed inside the prisoners' latrine, a place even the keenest ferret would hesitate to inspect. It prefigured later tunnels: a deep shaft ended in a chamber large enough to function as a small workshop. There, bedboards taken from the bunks were cut to size with makeshift saws and used as props in the tunnel bore, greatly reducing the risk of falls.

A second tunnel was started by another group, fully shored, and even fitted with electric light tapped from the camp's supply – this tunnel would provide the inspiration for later work back at Stalag-Luft III, but it was discovered before it could be used.

The earth became harder to cut through as winter approached, but on the other hand there was no problem in getting rid of the soil displaced by the digging: it was taken in metal containers up to the communal latrine and dumped through the holes cut in the wooden boards perched above the massive ditch into the effluvia below, which was regularly cleared away by a Polish workman with a 'honey waggon'. Work continued almost unabated through the winter, though naturally it slowed, and during the bleak and dark winter months two young airmen met their deaths: one, unable to stand the confinement any more, rushed the wire in daylight and was shot dead. Two months later, another fell to his death from the top of the camp's main building. The other prisoners shuddered and sympathised – they knew very well the feelings that had driven the young men to their deaths. But the escapers carried on with their work.

In February 1943, rumours began to reach the prisoners that they were to be taken back to Sagan. If they were transferred before the tunnel was completed, all their effort would have been for nothing. They continued to work frantically, and at the end of the first week in March they were ready to go.

The tunnel was a triumph of Anglo-American planning, for several USAAF airmen had been involved this time and the engineer in charge was an American. As the thirty-three escapers lay in the tunnel waiting for the head man to break out into the open, they all prayed that the calculations hadn't erred. They'd been perfect: the tunnel came out in the bottom of a drainage ditch, allowing the escapers to crawl along it to the shelter of the woods unseen by the guards. The only problem was getting out of the narrow hole. Harry Day was last out – except for an opportunistic South African who followed on the spur of the moment and made the thirty-fourth man – and he could scarcely extricate himself, so much soil had fallen back into the opening.

It wasn't until morning roll-call that the Germans realised what had happened, and even then they were not immediately sure, for some of the remaining prisoners drew themselves up in ranks of four, only a little spaced out, rather than in the ranks of five usually demanded and expected by the Germans. When they realised what had happened, they went berserk – this was one of the first really major escapes of the war, and apart from anything else, they were terrified of the consequences to themselves. Five thousand police, Hitler Youth and Home Guard were mobilised for the search, and within a fortnight, most of the escapers had been retrieved. Those who had set out on foot were the first to be recaptured. Harry Day and his partner were seen hiding in a barn by a member of the Hitler Youth, who raised the local Home Guard to flush them out. The train travellers lasted somewhat longer, but all of them, too, eventually returned to Schubin.

Only two men got away – in a sense. Jimmy Buckley, for so long a vital driving force behind the escape attempts, teamed up with a young Danish airman serving with the RAF. They managed to get to Denmark and reached the Sjaelland coast, where they acquired a small boat in which to make the eight-kilometre crossing over the Sound to Sweden. There the story ends. The Dane's drowned body was found weeks later, washed up near Copenhagen. Buckley's body was never found. It was assumed that their little craft was hit by a large vessel either in the darkness, or in fog.

Chapter Four

ROGER BUSHELL'S ARRIVAL AT STALAG–LUFT III HAD been preceded by his reputation. A fellow prisoner who was to join him on the Great Escape, Tony Bethell, remembers him as 'an extraordinary man. I remember the day he arrived. The effect was electric. He wasn't the senior RAF officer in the camp but we knew right away he was in charge.'

When Day, Buckley and the others were taken away to Schubin, it was natural that Bushell should take over escape activities, and he was immediately assigned the duties of Big X following Buckley's departure.

Because Bushell had liked the Germans, and had had many friends in the skiing fraternity, when he joined the war against Hitler, it was from a desire to protect the values he believed in against a foe that was not only threatening democracy everywhere, but also, he felt, stifling the country in which it bred. But following his return from the hands of the Gestapo, though he was never specific about his experiences with them, something in him changed. His family noticed a hardened and personal resolve in his letters home from the camp. It was clear that even if the Gestapo had not tortured him, he had been made aware of their brutal methods in a way which both horrified him and aroused his hatred. There was also the problem all prisoners with any spirit faced, and which was well expressed by Jimmy James, the arch-escaper: 'It was the boredom and frustration that were worst, because when you are in a small compound surrounded by barbed wire, you can't help feeling depressed. As Churchill said, the hours crawl past like paralysed centipedes. Armed guards watch your every move. But above all you feel your loss of freedom. The actual conditions weren't so bad, but you felt that life was passing you by, and you felt that you were no use to the war effort, that your friends were out there, seeing the action, getting promoted, and so on.'

Roger Bushell's arrival at Stalag-Luft III had a huge impact. Alex Cassie:

'Everybody knew about Bushell, he was a familiar name, one of the legendaries where escaping was concerned. He'd been out several times, he had stayed out and he hadn't appeared back again. I remember a distinct note of elation when people said that Roger Bushell was coming back; he was a much respected figure. Almost within weeks he had been put in charge of escaping. One felt then that the whole thing was in safe hands and things would be organised properly. Before it was so badly organised you had to find your own resources – find somebody who would make civilian clothes for you, organise documentation and so on. There were cases of a tunnel meeting another one. There was a case of one hut almost collapsing as too many tunnels were passing under one spot.'

Reg Van Toen (aka 'Van'), who was shot down over Holland in 1942:

'[Bushell] was as hard as nails. When he came into the camp, the SBO made him Big X and no-one did anything without his say so. He would decide who made an escape. He was totally ruthless. He knew full well that if he escaped again [and was caught] he would be shot.'

There were plenty of experienced escapers left at Stalag-Luft III for Bushell to draw on, and in one sense it was a blessing in disguise that the older leaders of the X-Organisation had been removed, because Roger had a free hand to reform and restructure what had still been quite a loose system. Ker-Ramsay was head of tunnelling operations, together with Wally Floody; and an officer called Norman Canton coordinated escape attempts 'over the wire'. A recently arrived American airman, 'Junior' Clark, was put in charge of security, ensuring that all escape activities were kept secret from the German staff, and from any stool pigeons planted among the prisoners. The theory was the classic one – that the smaller the number of people was who knew about an escape attempt, the better. Clark's designation was 'Big S'. His job would be of vital importance for the big enterprise already forming in Bushell's mind.

In the tailoring department, Tommy Guest was joined by Ralph Abraham, and most of their staff were recruited from the Czech and Polish RAF airmen in the camp. Their task was eased by the occasional stroke of good luck. Once, Lawrence Reavell-Carter found the German clothing store unlocked and unattended, and managed to remove four suits and three raincoats, from which patterns could be made using old newspapers, for the cutters to duplicate. Tim Walenn's forgery department needed real documents to serve as models to copy. These were occasionally stolen, more often 'borrowed', in exchange for a small bribe, from camp staff.

One of the key positions in the escape chain of command was held by a Czech Flight Lieutenant in the RAF, Arnost

'Wally' Valenta. Valenta, a quiet man who most unusually neither smoked nor drank (if and when the occasion arose), spoke fluent Russian and German, and was in charge of intelligence gathering, and of the other German-speaking POWs whose job it was to befriend and suborn the increasingly demoralised German guards. Selection of these guards, who would become willing or coerced aides to the escape effort, was a delicate matter, but it was one which Valenta was well qualified to direct. He had to keep a low profile, however, for if the Germans had known more about his background and the other work he was doing for the war effort, even within the camp, he would certainly have been taken out and executed. Very few of his fellow prisoners, even within the X-Organisation, were aware of the dual role he was fulfilling.

Jack Lyon:

'None of the escapes were successful in the early summer of 1942. I really passed through the worst period of my life. That was when we had the terrible outbreak of dysentery because the latrines became a breeding ground for flies. I also contracted a skin disease which was allied, I think, to athlete's foot but it actually appeared on my hands. I had great difficulty in shaking it off. I really was at a low ebb.

'The war news was very bad at the time and in 1942 we were just about being thrown out of Africa. It looked as though we might lose. The Far East was at a very low ebb. It was really the only time in my four years that I felt it might be a good idea to end it all over the wire.'

He was born in 1912 in Svebehov, a town in a partly German area of northern Moravia. Because of the tensions between local Czechs and Germans, Valenta grew up a Czech patriot, and as the Nazi Party began to rise within the tottering Weimar Republic at the beginning of the 1930s, he applied to enter an Infantry Reserve officers' training school as a cadet. He started there in 1933, the same year that Hitler came to power, and the following year transferred to the Military Academy at Hranice, near Olomouc. He passed out in 1936 and joined the 39th Infantry Regiment, based at Bratislava, the capital of Slovakia, where he successfully applied to study military history at Comenius University. He excelled in the subject, and while studying for his degree gave lectures for the benefit of his fellow junior officers. The gathering storm, however, prevented him from taking his final exams.

The Czechoslovak Republic was a young one, formed after the collapse of the Austro-Hungarian Empire at the end of the First World War. The two nations which formed it – the Czechs and the Slovaks – contained large minority groups of Germans and Hungarians respectively. Hitler was not slow to exploit the discontent among a proportion of these minorities, who saw themselves as second-class citizens and wished to belong to their countries of origin. Soon the fledgling democracy was in danger of being pulled in two, thanks to the vocal representations of the pro-Nazi Slovak leader, a renegade priest called Hlinka. Britain and France turned a deaf ear to the pleas of the country's elected representatives, thinking that Czechoslovak independence was a small price to pay for peace, and Hitler proclaimed the independence of Slovakia on 14 March 1939, and the following day occupied Bohemia and Moravia. They met with such hostility, however, that they had to maintain an army of occupation a quarter of a million strong. After war had been declared, vicious atrocities were carried out against the Czech civilian population.

In the run-up to the events of March 1939, Valenta's military duties included peace-keeping missions in western Bohemia, and the evacuation of Slovaks from the Hungariandominated areas in the south-east. But when he was ordered, along with the rest of the army in the region, to swear an oath of allegiance to the newly formed Nazi puppet state of Slovakia, he and four fellow officers refused. They crossed the Tatra mountains to the north, which divided their crumbling state from Poland, and entered that country on 15 March – the day of the Nazi invasion.

The Poles welcomed them and, needing information on the state of affairs in Czechoslovakia, with which the frontiers had now been sealed, gave them a crash-course in intelligence work. The five Czechs slipped back into their homeland as spies early in April and remained until the end of August, when they successfully returned to Poland, and enlisted in the Czech Legion at Cracow.

Following the German invasion of Poland at the beginning of September, Valenta and the Legion made for the north-east of the country, but soon found themselves caught between German and Soviet forces. They turned back towards Lvov, hoping to head south to Romania, then still a safe haven, but the Legion was overtaken by the Red Army in mid-September and disarmed. They were taken to Jarmolince and interned, spending Christmas in a semi-ruined monastery.

In the spring, things took a turn for the better. The Soviets decided that those members of the Legion with valid passports should be allowed to leave the USSR, and in mid-March 1940 Valenta was among the first group of Czechs transported to Odessa on the Black Sea, where they boarded a steamer bound for Istanbul. The free Czech consulate in the city organised the next stage of their journey, on a French cargo ship, which took them to Beirut, then controlled by France. There, they were enlisted into the French Army and a further voyage took them to Marseilles. Valenta himself transferred to the military administration of the free Czech National Committee in Paris. In mid-June he applied for transfer to the air force, and

IWM HU 21013

HENRY LAMOND

IWM HU 1609

Top: Stalag-Luft III, Sagan. The barrack blocks were set well back from the perimeter fences to deter escape attempts.

Above: An aerial view of the camp.

Left: Commandant Friedrich von Lindeiner-Wildau.

JONATHAN VANCE

ELIZABETH CARTER

Above: Roger Bushell (third left) with the Cambridge University ski team in 1932. He was the fastest British downhiller of the early thirties.

Left: Bushell – 'Big X' – was already a veteran escaper by the time he arrived at Stalag-Luft III in autumn 1942.

Opposite top: Tim Walenn (front right) was a flying instructor before going into active service. But it was his skill as a graphic artist that proved most useful to the X-Organisation.

Opposite left: Czech-born Arnost 'Wally' Valenta, who spoke fluent German and Russian, was head of intelligence-gathering.

Opposite right: George Harsh pictured in around 1970. One of the many Americans to arrive in the camp, this tough southerner became deputy head of security.

JOY TROUGHTON

JONATHAN VANCE

JONATHAN VANCE

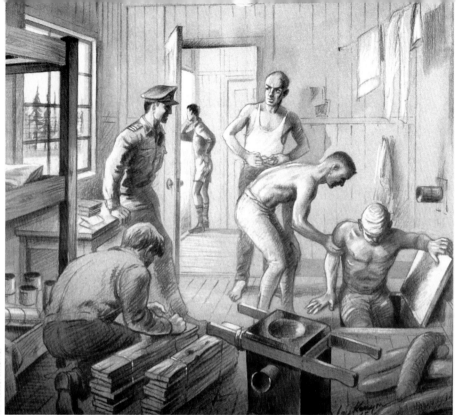

Above: One of Ley Kenyon's drawings depicting prisoners at work on a tunnel.

Left and below: The construction of the tunnels at Stalag-Luft III was a tremendous feat of ingenuity and engineering: Harry's entrance and a wooden trolley built for removing sand.

Half Way.
Transfer of sand from
Trolley to Trolley
at a Half way House.

These Ley Kenyon sketches give an idea of how the prisoners worked in the
cramped conditions below ground.

Clean up after
Collapse.

IWM HU 21218

IWM HU 21220

Above: The device used for pumping air into the tunnels.

Left: A German guard demonstrates the 'trouser-bag', the ingenious method by which prisoners dispersed sand from the tunnels around the compound.

Opposite top: Tools and other instruments, like this compass and wirecutters, were hidden inside books in the library.

Opposite middle: The forgery department was one of the most active. It was crucial for the prisoners to have authentic-looking papers to make good their escape.

Opposite below: A collection of the escapers' materials, including fake German money. The attention to detail and resourcefulness of the escape team were remarkable.

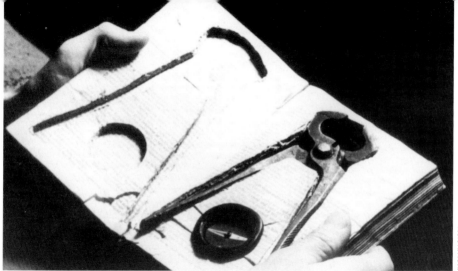

The handwritten POW card reads:

Kriegsgefangenenlager — Prisoner of War Camp: **Stalag Luft 3** — Datum / Date: **2-11-42**

Name / Surname: **Cochran** — Vorname / Christian Name: **Dennis Herbert**

Dienstgrad u. Truppenteil / Rank and Unit: **Pilot Officer R.A.F.**

Geburtsdatum / Date of birth: **13.8.1921** — Geburtsort / Native-place: **London**

Letzter Wohnort / Last dwelling: **Dulag Luft**

Adresse meiner Angehörigen / Home Address: **144, Essex Road, Leyton. E.10. London.**

Unverwundet — ~~leicht verwundet~~ — in deutsche Kriegsgefangenschaft geraten —
Unwounded — ~~slightly wounded~~ — prisoner of war in Germany —

befinde mich wohl.
I am well.

(Nichtzutreffendes ist zu streichen)
(Passages non opposite to the point to be cancelled)

Signature: *Dennis. H. Cochran. P/O.*

Above: Flying Officer Dennis Cochran, seen here in a pre-war photo, was captured late in 1942, as detailed on the card filled in by him and sent to his family from Stalag-Luft III.

Right: The capture of Tom Kirby-Green, in October 1941, was considered such a coup that it was announced by Lord Haw Haw.

was accepted. By the end of the month he was in England, and by the end of July he was posted to 311 (Czech) Squadron as a Wellington bomber radio operator, commissioned into the RAF Volunteer Reserve. He flew five sorties between December 1940, and February 1941. On the last, lost over northern France and running out of fuel, his pilot was forced to crash-land, and the crew were immediately picked up by a German patrol.

Valenta ended up in Stalag-Luft I, at Barth. Some of his history trickled out there, and partly on account of his intelligence experience in Nazi-occupied Czechoslovakia, he was discouraged from escaping at that time. He kept a low profile, studied classical Chinese from books in the camp library, taught Jimmy James Russian, and alleviated the boredom of his fellow POWs by giving the occasional lecture on military history: he was an expert on von Clausewitz. Ultimately transferred to Sagan, his linguistic and organisational abilities, and not least his amiability – he was well-liked by his fellow POWs and well regarded by the Germans – made him the ideal man to manage the escape department he was allocated.

The intelligence and contact network was crucial to the success of the X-Organisation. Without it, none of the other sections could have functioned with anything like the success Roger Bushell envisioned for them. Most of the tools and some of the instruments needed for escaping could be made by the prisoners, using stolen materials or adapting what was available in the camp. Among the most obvious things which could not were a camera and film, vital for the photographs to go on fake identity papers. Other useful tools and aids included wire-cutters, knives, German military insignia and uniform badges, real civilian clothes, German money and authentic German documents (for the purpose of copying). A typewriter was almost too much to hope for, and the noise it made might have attracted attention. Not all guards, and certainly not many officers or ferrets, were corruptible.

Several guards, once enticed, were, however, very willing to smuggle in whatever was required (within reason) in exchange for chocolate, coffee, cigarettes or soap from the Red Cross parcels, the more so as the war situation in Germany worsened and supplies of these things became difficult or impossible to obtain beyond ersatz substitutes. Morale was falling, too, among the Germans, and once a guard was hooked, he had little choice but to do what was asked of him; exposure would lead to court martial for treason.

Les Brodrick:
    'We could receive parcels via the Red Cross. It was quite an event if you received a parcel. My parcels always seemed to turn out to be tobacco. I smoked a pipe at the time and actually pipe tobacco was at a premium. There were hundreds of cigarettes available, which you could swap or buy at the store. This was run by a Dutch squadron leader, who worked out this plan of credits — say a tin of Spam would be worth so many points, twenty cigarettes would be so many points. All had their values, so if you got something in your parcel you didn't like, you could go to "Foodacco", as he called this store, and just hand it in and then you would be credited with so many points and you could buy something else in the store. He took his rake off of one percentage or two percentage or something of that order and it ran very well.'

The first line taken with a guard, in a process known as 'taming', was usually to gain his confidence and even friendship. In this the German-speaking POWs working with Valenta specialised. The process might start by inviting him out of the cold into the block for a cup of coffee and a cigarette or a chunk of chocolate. There'd be conversation, which would lead to family and home, which the guard probably missed as much as the POW, and the course of the war. Naturally POWs were not supposed to know anything about this, but 'tamed' goons could be persuaded to smuggle in valves and other parts from which a radio receiver could be constructed by prisoners with the right expertise. On one occasion a young and naive guard was actually inveigled into signing a receipt for some chocolate he'd received in exchange for a pair of pliers. With this proof of his collusion in his possession, the 'kriegie' controlling him had him in the palm of his hands. One or two Germans were all but voluntarily biddable. One of the prisoners, Sydney Dowse, didn't even need a knowledge of German to suborn Corporal Hesse, one of the interpreters. The two men struck up what in normal circumstances would have been a genuine friendship, and Hesse provided suits, hats, food coupons, money, and – just as important – information.

Information – intelligence – formed the backbone to the other, secret side of Valenta's activity in the camps, and though he was one of the most significant players, he was not alone. A number of POWs were, almost from the first, acting as field agents, reporting back to a highly secret information-gathering offshoot of MI6, called MI9, formed in the early days of the war.

MI9 was created in December 1939, when it was headed by Colonel Norman Crockatt. He was succeeded by Colonel J. M. 'Jimmy' Langley, who'd lost a leg at Dunkirk. In the early days MI9 had its headquarters at The Metropole Hotel on Northumberland Avenue, London. Its initial brief was to organise an escape-line to get valuable airmen who'd been shot down home before the Germans could capture them. In this they were aided by local Resistance cells, sometimes working with MI9 agents who'd been parachuted into occupied territories, principally France. Along with MI6, it built up a network of secret agents, saboteurs, radio operators, couriers and escape organisers, all operating behind enemy lines. Along with MI6 it was at the heart of Britain's clandestine war effort.

However, MI9 was also part of the intelligence-gathering network, and, as increasing numbers of aircrew ended up as POWs, the opportunity arose to create a spy network behind enemy lines. This became all the more important after the fall of France in 1940, which had meant the loss of MI6's entire network of spies deployed in mainland Europe.

The best sources of information, especially in the early years of the war when Germany still had supremacy, now lay with captured German servicemen, who could be interrogated, and with Resistance cells. Neither were always cooperative or reliable, however, and an extra source, against which existing data could be cross-checked, could, it was argued, be tapped from Allied POWs now captive in German camps. Any information would be of value, especially if a 'goon' dropped his guard enough to let his POW contact know what was going on in Germany. Even general knowledge of the enemy's national mood was important. The question was, how to communicate with the kriegies.

The initial answer came from a totally unplanned source – an informal and personal arrangement which already existed between a young British bomber pilot, Graham Hall, and his wife, Vera. 'My first sortie was on the second day of the war,' Hall remembered, 'and, of course, Vera worried about what would happen if I were shot down. Would she ever hear from me again?' Letters were permitted between POWs and their families, but they were heavily censored. What if the Halls wanted to exchange anything of a personal nature?

Between them, they hatched a plan. Before the war, when-ever either of them had written to a relative or a friend, the other would read the letter before it was sent. Hall never remembered to put enough punctuation into his letters, and his wife used to chide him about it. 'One day Vera said, "Give me your pen, I'll put the full stops and commas in myself." Without any thought, I replied, "If I am ever a prisoner-of-war, and I use punctuation in a letter, underline the next word. It will be a coded message." It was as simple as that.'

Some time later, Hall was shot down, and taken to Stalag-Luft I. Writing to his wife, he tried out the code he'd suggested, hoping that she'd remember it – it had only been an offhand comment that he'd made. But Vera hadn't forgotten, and when she saw an unusual amount of punctuation in the letter she received, she duly underlined the word that followed the full-stop, semi-colon or comma, and from an otherwise innocuous letter which the German censor had passed with scarcely a stroke of the black pencil, a message to her which was not for the censor's eyes emerged.

Vera had the initiative to take their code to a friend in Army Intelligence, and soon Hall found himself receiving coded messages from her requesting specific information on behalf of MI9. According to Hall's recollection: 'My wife was wined and dined by the Intelligence Services. She kept MI9 supplied with my letters to her, and hers to me. They inserted coded messages into her replies and returned them to her to write in her own hand. MI9 was desperate to expand this spying network as quickly as possible, so a number of bomber crews were gathered together for a top-secret briefing. They were told that by the law of averages some of them would become POWs, and if they did they should try to make contact with me. They were taught a simple code to pass on.

'Within three months a flyer did turn up at my camp, and a second turned up two days later. From that moment on we were in touch with MI9 for the whole war. I worked with a score of other prisoners at Stalag-Luft I. Each would send one sentence of a given message in their letter, and I would link their letters in the order they were to be read, in mine. The first use of the code was to make a monthly report of how, when and where our aircraft had been shot down. We also sent details of any troop movements we were able to observe. And as the others and I were moved from camp to camp, we created further teams of letter-writers, spreading the net to cover most of Germany.'

This so-called 'dotty' code was just the start. MI9 quickly developed a codebook and a code system. Aircrews were given extra briefings about what to do if taken prisoner. As the means of communication became more sophisticated, British Intelligence became able to send specific questions to specific POW contacts in specific locations within Germany. In this way, facts were gleaned about troop movements, bomb damage, potential targets for bombing raids, political developments within Germany and German morale. They were even able to get information about the German advanced aeronautic and secret weapons programmes. It is reputed that in the course of its wartime life MI9 briefed and equipped hundreds of thousands of British servicemen, especially aircrew. And in time, out of MI9 grew Special Operations Executive. Also spawned by MI9 was IS9, a kind of Intelligence School for anyone behind enemy lines who might want to get involved in escape and evasion (known as E&E), both of which were taught at IS9, along with information gathering and relay techniques.

At Stalag-Luft III, Roger Bushell himself ran, with Valenta, not only an escape operation but an intelligence-gathering unit whose work included the de-briefing of all new prisoners regarding what they'd seen before, during and since capture, and the location and circumstances of their aircraft's being shot down. The information was then relayed back to MI9, usually via letters to prisoners' families. At home, the

ANTON GILL

families delivered their encoded letters to MI9 at their secret
base, Wilton Park, at Beaconsfield in Buckinghamshire, on
the north-west perimeter of London.

Wilton Park was a place that thrived on this kind of cloak-
and-dagger arrangement. It was populated by brilliant
oddballs and obsessive technicians with preternaturally inventive minds, so when one officer was officially described as
'somewhat eccentric', it was recognised that the man in question was quite extraordinary. This man was Clayton Hutton,
known as 'Clutty'. He was to play a unique role in the lives
of British prisoners-of-war. The prototype for James Bond's
'Q', he specialised in inventing ingenious gadgets to be smuggled into POW camps. The historian of MI9, M. R. D. Foot,
has explained that 'Clutty invented the most amazing variety
of gizmos. He had Waddington's Games in on it: they placed
real German money inside Monopoly sets, and hid other
objects in the boards. He invented a system of disguising
clothes as blankets: when they were washed, the dye came
out, revealing the pattern that the cloth should be cut along.
He once had over two million miniature compasses distributed, disguised as collar studs.'

The question of how these items were smuggled in to the
POWs has been deliberately obscured since 1945. There are
reports of many documents having been destroyed after the
war; others in the Public Records Office remain classified
for the foreseeable future. The reason for all this is that British
Intelligence was prepared to contravene the Geneva
Convention, and compromise the integrity of the Red Cross.
As Foot has pointed out, 'The official version is that no-one
ever tampered with the Red Cross food and medicine parcels
destined for the POWs; but in fact the Red Cross was the
mechanism for delivering all kinds of parcels to the camps.
MI9 simply invented fake welfare organisations and had the
Red Cross take them in past the guards in good faith.'

They were taking a huge risk, and the stakes were enormously high. The Swiss Red Cross was the only guarantor of prisoners' welfare and good treatment; and the Geneva Convention was the framework that gave protection from the excesses of the SS and the Gestapo. In the Nazi regime, engaged as it was in the genocide of the Jews, there were plenty of senior figures who regarded the Geneva Convention with contempt, and themselves flouted it when they could get away with it. But the discovery that Britain was abusing the system could have been catastrophic.

The parcels were packed by a small team at MI9. Each packer placed his or her own secret 'signature' on the parcels. The POWs at the receiving end were alerted to what to look out for. Former prisoner Tony Bethell remembered that 'you needed to be quick to avoid the guards spotting what was going on, but the system worked well.' As well as useful equipment, some of the 'secret' parcels contained bribes for use in suborning guards – additional packets of good quality coffee, and Wills and Players cigarettes.

The smuggling was so successful that most camps, even without the help of 'tamed' goons, managed to assemble radio receivers. That opened up a whole new range of secret communication. MI9 approached the 'Radio Padre', whose job was to broadcast uplifting sermons. When he prefaced his talk with the words 'Good evening, Forces,' Jimmy James remembers, 'I had to start taking shorthand. It was his signal that his sermon included a coded message.'

Intelligence gathering became so entwined with the POW network that some key figures were ordered by MI9 not to escape: they were more valuable where they were. One of these men, who knew they were all running huge risks, for discovery would have been fatal, was the original inventor of the 'dotty' code, Graham Hall, who expanded the network across the thirteen camps in which he was successively held during the war.

In Stalag-Luft III, the intelligence gathering work went on around the camp with only a handful of the POWs having any idea of the grand schemes hatched at Wilton Park, or even of the existence of an organisation like MI9. Bushell's developing scheme for a mass escape on the grand scale, which he would set in motion in the spring of 1943, created the need for a serious amount of intelligence gathering in its own right. This was a good cover – for there was always a high security risk – for data destined to be sent home. Acquiring information about train timetables, for example, could be done hand-in-hand with gaining knowledge of bomb damage.

A huge number of men – over six hundred – would be involved in planning and organising the Great Escape, though only a fraction of them would actually make the break. Most of them simply went about their work on behalf of the escape plan as their way of 'doing their bit'. A select few only were aware of the espionage element. One was not even a serviceman. 'Flight Lieutenant' Harold Cunlan was in fact a civilian scientist involved in the development of the RAF's top-secret radar. Shot down over France, fortunately he was mistaken for a serving RAF officer, and ended up at Stalag-Luft III. The camp was close to a military airfield, and some of the POWs regularly observed German aircraft movements. Using the information these observations yielded, Cunlan was able to send back to MI9 enough information to enable the RAF's radar team to track the development of the Luftwaffe's own night-fighter radar system.

But apart from the specialised few, escape remained the chief priority, and gradually, under Bushell's iron direction, a cohesive and highly organised escape machinery was built up, impressive in its ability to draw together so many different men, of different skills, nationalities and outlook, all working towards a common aim. The influx of Americans in particular had been a breath of fresh air. As soon as they got used to being POWs, they would run the Germans ragged. The Germans weren't used to such loud, fast-talking, confident and well-fed people, and they were confused and agitated by them. The confusion permitted the Americans to rob them of anything that might be useful, and they joined in the escape movement with a will.

Among them was a tough southerner called George Harsh. He was the son of a wealthy family, but he had a chequered past. As a teenager during the days of Prohibition, he and three equally rich college friends got together for a night to drink moonshine whiskey. They decided in their cups that they were capable of anything, even committing the perfect crime, but unlike most teenagers they stayed with the idea after they had sobered up, and launched themselves on a series of carefully planned holdups. They robbed a number of grocery shops quite successfully, threatening the owners with a revolver they'd acquired, and managed to stay one step ahead of the police. One night, however, things went wrong. A storekeeper refused to knuckle under and produced his own gun and opened fire wildly. In the panic Harsh, who had the gang's pistol during that heist, fired back, and a few moments later both the storekeeper and his assistant lay dead. Soon afterwards, Harsh and one of his companions were arrested and charged with the murders. They could scarcely claim self-defence, especially in the state of Georgia in those days. It took the jury less than half an hour to find them guilty, but owing to their families' wealth and influence, the death sentence was commuted – in exchange for pleas of guilty – to a long stretch on a chain gang.

Harsh spent the next twelve years in jail, living under the toughest conditions, and during that time stabbed another man to death in a fight over a bar of soap. As time passed, however, he found himself transferred from the chain gang to a regular prison, where he became a 'trusty' and worked as an orderly in the prison hospital. There, he saved the life of a fellow convict by successfully performing an emergency appendectomy on him, and through that earned his parole. Once out of prison, he and his family decided that it would be best if he made himself scarce. He signed up with the Royal Canadian Air Force and quickly earned a commission. The only person in Stalag-Luft III who knew about his background was Canadian Wally Floody. Floody also knew that despite his wild past, Harsh was a young man of great endurance, with a hardened prisoner's knowledge of how to buck the system. Harsh became deputy head of security under fellow American 'Junior' Clark, with particular responsibility for tunnelling activity.

For the moment, however, beyond continuing individual escape attempts, little could be done on a grand scale. Not only was 1942 drawing towards winter, which in central Europe can be very cold indeed, but the inmates of the compound could see that the Germans were preparing something.

The existing two compounds at Stalag-Luft III were overflowing, and beyond the wire the POWs could see that a large number of Russian POWs, thin and miserable, had been drafted in to cut a large clearing in the forest immediately to one side. As they finished digging up the tree-stumps and levelling the ground, the early new year saw a small army of civilian forced-labourers arrive to erect the familiar barbed wire fences and begin the work of putting up the familiar drab, wooden barrack blocks. Though the winter had been milder than the previous year, it wasn't the best season for building work: the snow fell heavily and regularly, and the wind was icy; but slowly and inexorably a new compound rose in the middle of the grim forest; and it was vast.

Bushell talked to Captain Hans Pieber, one of the duty officers of the camp, about the new compound, and Pieber told him that officers would be transferred there in the New

Year – probably in March. Bushell tucked this valuable information away, and bided his time. The ground was hard and
covered with snow. The Polish airmen had formed a choir,
and gave a beautiful performance at Midnight Mass on
Christmas Eve. Thanks to the Red Cross, there was enough
dried fruit to make plum pudding and plenty of hooch. It
was so cold that the prisoners had been able to create an
ice-rink. The Red Cross had supplied enough skates for each
prisoner to have thirty minutes' skating each per day. There
were ice-hockey matches; and the steel blades of the skates
would prove useful later.

Frank Tams:
   'The Polish contingent, who occupied one of the huts in
the centre of the camp, used raisins and sugar from parcels to
produce wine. Having tasted this I decided it was too sickly
and decided to distil this product. The Germans issued jam in
large metal containers of about two gallons. I obtained one of
these from the German cookhouse, made the lid a tight fit and
soldered an outlet tube to the top of this container. This metal
tube was fed into a trombone, which was positioned in a
wooden trough filled with water. An extension soldered to the
trombone outlet allowed the "hooch" to drip into our bottles.
   'I progressed through the night making periodic tasting
checks; unfortunately the metallic taste of the trombone came
through very strongly and it was not until after two or three
bottles that I got rid of this flavour. I decided to distil this
batch again and was so pleased with the result that in all future
distillations I used this double-distillation process. It was of
course sacrilege to use food in this way but three good snorts
of this reduced the duration of the war by one day at least.'

During the winter, the collecting and collating of information continued. The German-speakers, like Polish Flight Lieutenant Jerzy Mondschein, read all the German newspapers that came into the camp from cover to cover. Every detail that could be of any possible use was noted, from the names of officials and their appointments to the opening of factories or changes in transport systems. Various individuals had responsibility for various areas in Europe, which they had personal knowledge of from before the war. Bushell looked after Germany, for example; a Lithuanian airman, Romas Marcinkus, covered the Baltic coast and the Netherlands. Mondschein himself, though a career airman before the war, had acquired other skills before joining the Polish Air Force; he was a good tailor and, from experience in the building trade, was an expert in casting concrete. Marcinkus spoke fluent English, French, German, Polish and Russian, and worked as a foreign language adviser in Walenn's forgery workshop.

No detail was too small not to merit consideration. A New Zealander, Arnold Christensen, whose father had emigrated from Denmark before Christensen was born, kept a packet of biscuits relatives had sent him from Denmark. He planned to take them with him if and when he escaped, as proof of sorts for any suspicious official that he was genuinely the Danish workman he intended to pretend to be while on the run. Another airman, Bob van der Stok, who'd flown with the Dutch Air Force before his country was conquered and had later managed to get away to England to join the RAF, was shot down in July 1942 and sent to Sagan. He brought with him valuable knowledge, because before fleeing to England he'd lived in Holland under the German occupation. Many prisoners knew something of occupied Europe from various attempts to escape through it; others knew parts of Europe, including Germany, well, but from before the war.

Van der Stok's experience of life under the occupation was very valuable: he knew something about how German officials operated; what kind of people were likely to arouse their suspicion; what kind of questions they might ask; and what kind of documents they'd demand to see. Even points of etiquette and general behaviour had to be learned: no-one in occupied Europe would offer his seat on a crowded train or bus to a woman, yet in those days that was a common politeness in England. Never fall asleep on a bus or train, in case you talk in your sleep; above all, never get tripped up by answering in English when a suspicious policeman suddenly says, 'Good luck!' in your native tongue.

In the camp, each new inmate was treated with only guarded friendliness until the X-Organisation, through veiled questioning and independent enquiries around the camp had satisfied itself that the newcomer was not a German stool pigeon. In such a vast and often shifting international community of prisoners-of-war as then existed in Germany it was very likely that nearly everyone's path had crossed before with someone somewhere. Then the line of questioning changed – but anyone working for the Germans would still have had to answer eager questions about anything from favourite football teams and film stars to the latest on the gorgeous *Daily Mirror* comic-strip heroine, Jane, who was constantly losing her clothes and who was a darling of the forces. Once accepted, the newcomer would find Stalag-Luft III, by the autumn of 1942 and the winter of 1942/1943, a not unpleasant place. There was a good library, with books supplied courtesy of the Red Cross, a thriving amateur dramatic society which had access to texts of all but the very latest Broadway and West End plays and shows, and decent sports facilities. There were lectures on almost any subject under the sun, and if you wanted to, you could learn any European language you chose. German and French were favourites, closely followed by Czech and Polish. Organisation of enforced leisure time was a hedge against boredom and the social decay that it could lead to, despite the fact that with few exceptions the prisoners still observed military discipline. Rank was still acknowledged. Only in the X-Organisation was the chain of command independent of it; but within X, discipline was tighter than anywhere else.

The activities provided useful cover for escape work, too. If you had any linguistic, artistic or engineering skills, you could develop them; and if you hadn't, you could learn them – once you had been properly vetted – within the X-Organisation. But involved or not, every prisoner knew better than to question any activity that seemed odd or out of place. As Bushell impressed on newcomers, 'If you see me walking around with a treetrunk sticking out of my arse, don't ask any questions, because it'll be for a damned good reason.'

The information gathered by the X-Organisation was relayed to MI9 and also served in the escape effort. Escapers who were able to speak a foreign language and had the necessary documents were often able to use the railway system to make their getaway, and these needed only rudimentary maps and a knowledge of the timetables that affected their travel. But for those who were travelling on foot, the so-called 'hardarsers', detailed maps were needed, sufficient to show not only the location of small villages, but every other possible detail of the topography of the regions through which the escaper would be passing – rivers and their bridges, streams, woods, mountain ranges and their passes. A map section was therefore organised under the direction of Flight Lieutenant Des Plunkett. Maps could occasionally be obtained from 'tame' guards, but Plunkett and his team also had to rely on descriptions of areas from fellow prisoners who'd known them well before the war. Distances and scales had to be worked out painstakingly, and paper was not always easy to supply. Fortunately Plunkett was a skilled draughtsman who had had some experience of aerial reconnaissance before the war. His team's biggest problem was how to mass-produce maps – there simply wasn't the time or the manpower to hand-draw each of them. A method of printing them had to be found. Plunkett addressed himself to the problem.

The closing months of 1942 saw a handful of escape attempts 'over the wire'. None was successful. The last was made by Sydney Dowse and a Polish officer called Stanislav 'Danny' Krol. They were caught before they'd even cut their way through. Bushell kept a low profile. He knew that the answer lay in something far more than a number of isolated attempts. Individuals could be tracked down and picked up with relative ease, and therefore caused little distraction to the German war effort. As he looked across at the new compound that was being built, Bushell knew that the best chances for a major break-out lay there. In any case it was pointless to undertake anything big where they were, if they were going to be transferred so soon.

He called a meeting of his heads of department and told them that they could best use the time between now and the move to the new compound in planning. He also described his own scheme to them. It was to construct not one, but three major tunnels from various points in the new compound, and to dig them simultaneously. The advantage of this would be that if the Germans discovered one, or even two, it was unlikely that they'd discover all three – so that a major escape through one at least was a near-certainty. There was a certain amount of protest at the amount of time such a project would take, and at the manpower it would need. Bushell replied that the point of the scheme was that it would absorb virtually all escape resources. Individual attempts would still be permitted, judged as always on their merits, and indeed they should be encouraged, for the Germans would inevitably grow suspicious if suddenly all escape activity appeared to end. But there would be no other tunnels. Apart from anything else, the amount of sand displaced would amount to hundreds of tons, and that alone would be hard enough to disperse without the goons noticing. As for the time-frame, Bushell said, there would be no tight schedule. If the Germans ever grew suspicious, operations would be suspended until the heat was off. Such a massive undertaking would in any case be a long job. But it was turning into a long war, even though the news of its progress trickling in from new arrivals, and gathered from listening carefully to BBC broadcasts, especially the sermons, was beginning to sound – very cautiously – encouraging. Apparently the German Sixth Army was now badly pinned down by the Russians near Stalingrad, deep inside Russia.

There was one other major objection: how could such an operation possibly be planned, when no-one knew the layout of the new compound? That, replied Bushell, was one of the beauties of the scheme. X-Organisation would volunteer to help with the construction of the compound: prisoner workers' parties could get a good idea of the layout, plumbing, electrical system and so forth as the place was being built. If they were able to make maps and plans of where the infrastructure was before wires and pipes were buried or covered with planking and plaster, it would be of enormous value later.

'How many men do you hope to get out?' someone asked.

'I want tunnels big enough to get two hundred out in one night in one break. We might get lucky and be able to use more than one tunnel, and even one tunnel more than once. Either way, it'll leave the Germans with something to remember us by.'

All of the heads of department were aghast at the scale of the plan, but all of them equally were intrigued and stimulated by the challenge it presented, and they had a few months at least, before winter had passed and the new compound was completed, to prepare themselves. The work that confronted them was enormous: in the two hours that the meeting took, they had roughly thrashed out a scheme that involved three tunnels sunk ten metres down (to avoid detection by seismic microphones), and God-knew-as-yet how long they would have to be. The tunnels would be far wider and higher than hitherto, they'd have to be lit, there would have to be a way of ventilating them and of transporting sand quickly and efficiently perhaps as far as one or even two hundred metres from the workface to the shaft-head, and then getting rid of it. There would have to be underground workshops. Shovels, saws, chisels and knives would have to be made. Wood would have to be obtained to shore up the tunnels, because there was no way that the sandy soil of Sagan would support itself. And even allowing that they achieved all that, there would then have to be mass-production of civilian clothing, documents and maps. There would have to be a large supply of German money, compasses would have to be made or obtained for those setting off on foot through the featureless forest, and then people would have to be found who could make or organise all these things. They would also need tight security, and a mass of information. MI9 would help all it could from outside, but for an undertaking of the size Bushell was looking at they would largely have to rely on their own resources. How many people had he envisaged getting out? At least two hundred?!

Bushell took the plan to the Senior British Officer, Group Captain Herbert Massey, a First World War veteran who'd volunteered for service in the Second. Massey walked with a limp, the result of severe wounds to the same leg in both wars. There would be no escape for him, but he had to know what was going on. Massey warned him about the personal risks he was taking – he was a veteran escaper who'd already been in trouble with the Gestapo in the wake of the Heydrich assassination, and if the Germans found out about his secret service connection they'd shoot him for sure. Bushell assured him that this time he'd get clean away. Massey, who may privately still have thought that if Bushell were caught again he'd be lucky if all the Germans did was send him to Colditz, nevertheless approved the plan, though he warned Bushell to stay in the background as far as possible. Massey also agreed to talk to Kommandant von Lindeiner about organising prisoner work parties for the new compound.

Bushell had several more individual meetings with his department heads over the next days, walking with them round and round the perimeter of the compound, within the warning wire. This was no unusual activity for prisoners. As Paul Brickhill wrote: 'You could walk there for hours till you were numb and didn't worry about home or the war or even the more important things like sex or liquor.' But you could also talk in the safe knowledge that you wouldn't be overheard by a lurking ferret.

During these walks, Bushell appalled his lieutenants with his demands. From Tim Walenn, he wanted two hundred sets of forged travel documents, including passports and railway tickets. From Tommy Guest, he wanted two hundred full sets of clothes, of different types, from suits to workers' overalls, even German uniforms. Guest's problem was not only how to lay his hands on the material and the patterns, let alone the civilian buttons, the thread, the needles, and everything else he would need, but even if he could complete the impossible task, where would he hide the stuff until it was needed? Bushell sympathetically told him they'd cross that one when they came to it. Rhodesian Johnny Travis was required to think out the means of supply for the tunnels, from shovels to pipelines for the air that would have to ventilate them. Des Plunkett needed to find a way of reproducing maps quickly. But no-one really demurred: their regard for Bushell and their trust in his judgment was too great for that.

In the meantime, the Germans welcomed the help they were getting from the Allied POWs in the new compound, and the enthusiasm with which they approached the job didn't strike them as odd. Clearly the kriegies wanted their new quarters to be as comfortable as possible, and to be ready as soon as possible, too. Certainly they worked more efficiently than the forced-labourers (though that was hardly surprising), and they took a lively interest in everything that was going on, from the number of bunks there would be and how many bedboards each bunk would need, to where the stores would be located. One or two of the German surveyors and builders supervising the work were surprised and pleased to find among the POWs German-speaking colleagues who asked intelligent questions about the work, and even suggested, deferentially of course, minor improvements.

Of course, the prisoners made none of this obvious. Still less obvious were the mental notes they made, as they schlepped sacks of cement and planks for the walls of the blocks from place to place, of the distances they were pacing out, all to be carefully recorded when they got back – the distances between the blocks, the proportions of the blocks, and the distances from the blocks to the wire. One prisoner managed to purloin a blueprint of the new compound's underground drainage system – very important for any tunneller to know about. And if the drains were wide enough to accommodate a man – and a thin POW didn't need much room – they might even find themselves with a ready-made tunnel.

Towards the end of March 1943, as the new, so-called North Compound neared completion, the recaptured men of the big Schubin escape, including Day, Dodge, and Jimmy James, were returned to Sagan, and were quickly reabsorbed into the newly structured escaping fraternity. Then, on 27 March 1943, the transfer of prisoners to the new camp began.

Chapter Five

THE NORTH COMPOUND WAS DESIGNED TO BE EVEN harder to escape from than the old one, but was built hurriedly as the old lags were moved there to make room for the large numbers of new prisoners who were coming in from every Allied air force, as the air war against Germany was stepped up. On the face of it, it was the same as the old, East Compound; and both these compounds were reserved for officers. The former inmates of the old compound were joined by about fifty prisoners from the Oflag at Warburg, and the population of the North Compound grew initially to around nine hundred. Two-thirds of that number would be engaged, in one way and another, in escape activities. It was an organisation on an almost industrial scale, and its efficiency and security were a tribute to its leaders, as well as a reflection on the naïveté of the camp's officials, though perhaps they placed too much confidence in the security measures they had taken for the new compound. Most of the German staff of the old compound followed their charges to the new one, which provided the prisoners with a further advantage: few new relationships needed to be struck up. It worked to the prisoners' advantage, too, that the Germans worked to a predictable routine. If they raided a block, they'd leave it alone until after they'd raided all the other blocks, often in order. As Bushell once observed drily, 'There's madness in their method.'

The new compound was about three hundred metres square, with two perimeter fences, each about three metres high and separated by a gap of nearly two metres. The warning wire again ran ten metres inside the inner fence. The fences themselves were strung with twenty strands of barbed wire, and the gap between them was filled with coils of more barbed wire, so thickly that, as Paul Brickhill remembered, 'you could hardly see through it'. The watch-towers were placed along the outside of the outer perimeter fence at intervals of about 150 metres. At night, guards patrolled the perimeter fences, and a dog-handler made his rounds within the compound, in the company of a German Shepherd trained to kill if necessary. Beyond the fences, the monotonous ranks of dreary greyish pine trees blocked any other view.

The main enclosure comprised fifteen blocks arranged in three rows of five and aligned lengthways on a north-south axis. The northernmost row of blocks were numbered, from west to east, 101, 103, 104, 105 and 106. The main gate of the camp, which led to the *Vorlager*, was more or less opposite the north end of Block 104. At the eastern end of the *Vorlager* was the guardroom, then came the hospital block, the cooler, and the coal store. South of the first row of prisoners' blocks, counting now from west to east, ran blocks 107, 108, 109, 110 and 112. The library was located in the western side of Block 110, and between 110 and 109 was the fire pool – a small square reservoir holding water for use in case of fire.

The building that housed the compound kitchens was situated between blocks 110 and 112, and its limited function included boiling water for potatoes and soup. The rations issued by the camp authorities were sparse and became sparser:

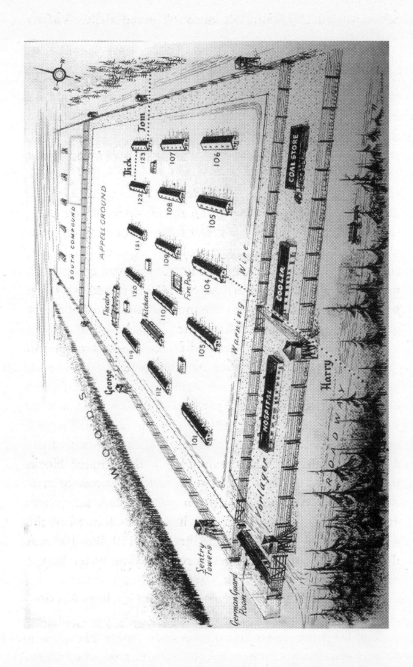

breakfast now consisted of a thin slice of bread, with margarine and ersatz jam, and two more plain slices of bread came with lunch and dinner, which might consist of potatoes, occasionally green vegetables or other root vegetables like turnips, and barley, and once every few weeks a small amount of minced meat, usually horse. The Red Cross parcels provided a welcome addition to this fare in the form of corned beef, Spam, and chocolate, as well as coffee, cheese and real jam.

The third and last line of blocks, counting again from east to west, were 119, 120, 121, 122 and 123. Beyond them lay the wide open space of the *Appellplatz*, or parade ground, where roll-call was taken, and in whose north-eastern corner the theatre building would be built.

Each wooden block was divided into eighteen rooms, most of which were designed to house four men, though a few accommodated only two. To begin with, there was more room in the North Compound than there were prisoners, though conditions were nevertheless relatively cramped. In each block additionally there was a minute kitchen with a coal-burning stove, a washroom with a concrete floor, and a privy. The living-rooms were (again relatively) comfortable. They contained an unplumbed sink which could be filled with water from jugs for washing, lockers, stools, a table, and a small stove in one corner on a tiled base which was used for heating and boiling water for tea or coffee, as well as cooking what little extra food there was. The bunk beds consisted of four corner posts with planks screwed across the sides and ends, the bedboards, arranged laterally, measured about seventy centimetres by fifteen – a perfect size for shoring tunnels. On them a palliasse was laid – a mattress-shaped paper bag filled with wood shaving. Each prisoner was issued with an army blanket.

The furniture was movable so inmates could arrange it to their mutual convenience and taste. Later, when the still-growing influx of POWs meant that the population of the compound increased, the number in each room increased to six and even eight, and some of the lockers were moved into the block's central corridor to make more space. Prisoners were allowed to keep the Red Cross packing cases (which the individual parcels came in), and these robust wooden boxes were dismantled and reconstructed as extra furniture – anything from bookshelves to armchairs. The Germans allowed the POWs to have large-scale maps of Europe. These were fixed to a wall in most rooms, and the progress of the war, based on reports culled from a variety of sources, was marked on them by means of pins, with lengths of string stretched between them to represent the front lines.

The compound itself was still far from finished. There were trees remaining, which gave some relief to its overall drabness, but some were in the process of being cut down, and the area was dotted with stumps. After the move had been completed, it took a week or so for the inmates to settle down and accustom themselves to their new quarters, but Bushell's first act was to send an experienced tunneller down through one of the manhole covers (noted on the stolen drainage plan) to see if the system of pipes underground could be of any help to the escapers. No-one was entirely surprised, given the general care and attention the Germans had lavished on the compound to make it escape-proof, when the POW came back up after only a minute or two, looking grubby and disappointed. The pipes were only about fifteen centimetres in diameter. 'You couldn't pull a greasy piglet through them,' he said.

It was frustrating, and it meant a lot more work; but Bushell accepted the news philosophically.

As things stood, so far from being demoralised, the inmates of the new compound were soon in the grip of a kind of escape fever. The Germans weren't completely organised yet, there was a lot of coming and going as the compound neared final completion, and opportunities to get away were plentiful – so much so that X-Organisation wasn't able to authorise every attempt that was being made.

Jack Lyon knew that in the normal course of events, it was safer being a POW than a serving airman:

'I thought I was unlucky but it turned out to be exactly the reverse. I jumped out of a burning aeroplane and thought, "What a pity! Here are the others going home and eating eggs and bacon in a few hours' time." But looking back, considering the casualties and that the average life of a bomber crew was five operations, I was lucky wasn't I? It puts it in perspective.'

One of the most popular methods was to make use of the lorries that came and went, laden with the branches and debris from the trees within the compound that were still being chopped down by Russian POWs, grey with hunger. As the lorries drove past the blocks, POWs concealed on the roofs would drop down onto them and bury themselves under the pine boughs. So many people used this means of attempting escape that it wasn't unusual for a lorry to be carrying more than one would-be escaper out of the camp. It wasn't without its dangers, however: the branches of the trees could deliver nasty scratches, and even more unpleasant was the way the guards took to probing the lorryloads with pitchforks. Very few who tried escaping in this way even made it outside the camp, but the attempts meant that the German guards had their hands constantly full. Besides the 'tree' escapes, the more conventional techniques, such as trying to get out under cover of a work party, of which there were many coming and going, also continued.

Two men who had managed to get away were the Canadian Kingsley Brown and RAF Flight Lieutenant Gordon Brettell. Both spoke fluent German, and had prepared themselves for a serious attempt, sanctioned by the X-Organisation. They were provided with passports, maps, money and even the addresses of safe houses at Mulhouse and Strasbourg, each lying roughly six hundred kilometres south-west of Sagan. Disguised as Bulgarian steelworkers travelling from one factory to another, their plan was to make the initial part of their journey on foot, before catching a westbound train.

They burrowed out under the wire of the old compound on the night of 27 March 1943, taking advantage of the upheaval occasioned by the first transfers to the new North Compound. After walking that night and all of the next day, they caught a train to Cottbus, where they changed for another bound for Leipzig. On the second train they found themselves sharing a compartment with five ordinary German infantrymen and a sixth soldier who wore the uniform of the Afrika Korps. The last, considering himself a cut above his fellow soldiers, began to brag of the exploits of the Korps in North Africa, ignoring a poster which bore the German equivalent of the British wartime slogan, 'Careless talk costs lives'. Brown and Brettell listened carefully, determined to remember as much as they could, though Brettell, who liked to sail close to the wind, was tempted to remind the boastful soldier of the poster and tell him that, 'for all he knew, we might be disguised British officers'.

They continued their journey successfully as far as Chemnitz, where they were turned over to the police by a suspicious booking clerk. The police passed them on to the local Gestapo, but after a routine interrogation to determine whether the two might be spies or not, the secret policemen became more friendly. It turned out that their interrogators had both escaped as regular soldiers during the First World War, and they were quite sympathetic. One of them even wished Brettell and Brown 'better luck next time' as he sent them back to Sagan.

Bushell and his executive officers had recently been joined by Peter Fanshawe, alias 'Hornblower', now returned from Schubin. Fanshawe was put in charge of the group whose duty it would be to disperse the huge quantities of sand which the tunnellers would excavate as they worked. As early as 11 April, sites had been chosen for the three tunnels, which had acquired the codenames of 'Tom', 'Dick' and 'Harry'. From now on these were the only names by which the tunnels could be referred to, under the strict security code established by Bushell.

Tom was to lead west from Block 123. There had been much discussion before choosing as its starting point a block next to the wire, since such a block would naturally attract more attention from the Germans than another, further away. On the other hand, the advantage of Tom was that it would not have to be very long; and as Block 123 was the farthest from the guardhouse, the security system of stooges would have plenty of time to warn diggers to get out and close up and disguise the trap down into the tunnel before any roaming ferret or other guard arrived.

Dick was planned to run in the same direction, but from 123's neighbour, Block 122, parallel to Tom but just to the south of it. The thinking here was that Block 122, being relatively far from the perimeter fence, would not be highly suspected as the source for a tunnel. Additionally, if Tom were discovered, it was unlikely that the Germans would think of looking for another tunnel right next door.

The third tunnel, Harry, was sited on the other side of the camp, in Block 104, and would run north, under the *Vorlager*. Its close proximity to the main gate raised serious security questions, but precisely because of that proximity, and because it would have to run a long way before getting beyond the *Vorlager* and into the trees, it was argued that the Germans would be unlikely to suspect its situation.

It was now necessary to recruit a 'Little X' and a 'Little S' in each block. Little S had the job of organising security around his block, and recruiting stooges who would keep a round-the-clock watch on guards and ferrets; Little X took responsibility for recruiting prisoners with various specialised skills to the escape effort, and introducing them to the heads of department and their deputies, as well as vetting individual escape proposals before passing them up the line. Bushell and Massey, the Senior British Officer, met the escape represen-tatives of each block once a week and kept them abreast of progress. At the same time, all prisoners new to the compound were assembled in groups as they arrived (later on these assem-blies would take place in the compound's own theatre) and given a general talk on escape activity by Massey, who referred them, if they were interested, to report to their block's 'X'.

The next job was to have a detailed scale map of the entire compound drawn up, on which all the sightlines from the watch-towers could be calculated, and from them, areas which lay in the guards' blind spots. These areas were not, of course, safe from the ferrets, who were apt to turn up anywhere at any time, but they did represent places of relative safety. To monitor the ferrets, the compound was divided into two areas – S and D, separated by an imaginary line roughly bisecting the camp on a north-south axis running through the fire pool, leaving the camp's main gate just to its west. The S – or safe – zone was on the east of this line, and the D – danger – zone on the west. The standing order was that the moment a ferret crossed from S to D, all work on the tunnels would be shut down. If three ferrets or more entered the compound at any point together, all work would similarly cease. Colonel

'Junior' Clark and his security team also set up the position of so-called Duty Pilot. Whoever was on watch in this position sat near the main gate and recorded all traffic and all pedestrians entering and leaving the compound. The duty pilot would sit in a homemade armchair, smoking and reading, apparently idling his time away – though the Germans came to realise that he was there to monitor movements. But he didn't apparently do anything. The trick lay in a complicated system of signalling. By him might lie a couple of objects, for example an old crate with a lid and a bucket. Different combinations of these objects would convey different messages to watching stooges, who in turn had a relay system between them for getting the message across the compound fast. If the box had its lid on, that might mean that ferrets were approaching D-zone; if the bucket were the right way up on top of the box, that might indicate an all-clear; and so on. Stooges had to concentrate very hard, because on them the whole system of security rested. Also, however casually a man might appear to be lounging around, if he was seen by a German to be doing it for too long in the same place, it would arouse suspicion. Therefore shifts were short and the number of prisoners working as stooges was high.

At the outset of the planning of the Great Escape, the experts Bushell and his team needed were surveyors and mathematicians. As a trained surveyor, Brian Evans was one of the first to be recruited. His work and that of his colleagues was hampered by the lack of real theodolites to use, but makeshift ones were constructed in the workshops run by Travis. These, however, only allowed for rough calculations to be made, with a degree of error that could mean a miscalculation of up to six or seven metres in a tunnel's length, which might mean the difference between coming up in the safety of the trees, or several metres short of them. To compensate for this, several teams were put onto the calculations for each tunnel, and the results of their surveys collated, in the hope that this would yield as accurate a measurement as possible.

Materials for the tunnels were 'organised' in a variety of ways – but a prison camp like Stalag-Luft III was a large, disorderly, untidy, dirty and overcrowded place. Guards were disinclined or simply unable to check up on everything. Travis, the head of the engineering department, had need of a heavy hammer and could not obtain one. Then one day, the honey waggon – the great, horse-drawn tanker used to pump out the latrines – trundled into the compound and came to a stop. The old peasant who drove the thing got down, attached his pumps, and started them. Meanwhile, a couple of prisoners started a mock fight to divert the driver's attention while a third crept up to one of the wheels and drew out the massive pin that attached the hub of the wheel to the axle. The fight came to an end, and when the honey waggon was full, the driver climbed aboard and whipped up the heavy horses for the journey to the sewage dump. Turning the corner by Block 101 the wheel came off, the tank crashed to the ground, and effluvia spilled and spread in all directions. Travis accepted the makeshift hammer happily, remarking that it would do perfectly, but observing, as he held a near-spotless handkerchief to his nose, that he wondered if it had been worth the cost of its acquisition.

The camp theatre was being constructed at that time by the prisoners themselves, and they had been lent tools by the Germans to do the job; but these tools had been lent in good faith, under the parole system, and it was a point of honour, which no-one ever broke, not to purloin them. The theatre, for which the Germans had built a double-block, was otherwise constructed entirely by the prisoners. It had a raked floor, and three hundred proper tip-up seats, all made from Red Cross crates. When it was up and running, the theatre had a regular company which put on shows which ran for three nights, once a fortnight. They managed to get the scripts of the latest shows through the Red Cross, and the theatre company, though not all its members were interested in escaping, provided a huge input of morale-boosting for all the POWs, and the theatre initially was excluded from any association with escape activity: no risk of its being closed down was to be taken. The Germans attended performances and, on the whole, enjoyed them; though much of what they saw and heard (perhaps mercifully) passed them by. And of course it was in their interest to make sure that their charges were amused. As far as possible, a man who is not bored and does not feel frustrated does not think of escape. But most of the prisoners did feel unfulfilled and frustrated, and entertainment and distraction, no matter how good, are not substitutes for good food and good sex, especially if you are young.

Les Brodrick:
    'Not everybody was involved in escape activities, quite a
lot spent their time studying and others took to acting. They
put on various plays, usually about one a fortnight. They had
some luscious girls actually, they tarted them up and dressed
them up. No, they weren't really very luscious, I must admit,
but the lot of them were known forever thereafter by the
names of the parts they'd taken. We were all keen on seeing
the shows and I think they usually ran for three nights so
everybody would have a chance to see them. One guy
arrived later on who'd been shot down and he'd got a theatre
ticket in his pocket. It was for *Arsenic and Old Lace*. When he
mentioned this to someone in his room they said, "Oh, it's all
right. You can see it here next week."'

Diversion from boredom was, as we have seen, always the key factor in prison camp life. There was plenty of sporting activity. Some prisoners studied, and even took exams and degrees while they were in the camps, courtesy of the Swiss, who provided examination papers and examiners. Most of the tuition, however, was do-it-yourself.

Once the security system had been set up, and the locations for the tunnels had been decided on, it was time to start work. The first job was to select the best places in the chosen blocks to open the traps – the surface mouths of the shafts. As the blocks were raised on stilts, the only possibilities that offered decent camouflage were the places in each block where solid foundations reached down to the ground. This narrowed the field to the washrooms, which were set on concrete foundations, and the concrete-and-brick foundations beneath the stove chimneys. In Block 123, the location for Tom's trap was chosen by Wally Floody at the end of a short corridor which led to a room adjoining the kitchen, in a dark corner beside the kitchen stove's foundation. Three Polish officers, led by Jerzy Mondschein, took charge of the trap's construction. They used purloined cold chisels to cut out a sixty-centimetre square section of concrete, under which they found a layer of hardcore loosely mixed with sand. The concrete section was carefully removed and broken up, so that the pieces could be 'lost' around the camp, where there was still a lot of rubble and building materials lying around. The building materials provided them with the means of obtaining wood to make a frame, and in it they cast a new concrete section which perfectly fitted the piece they had removed. It was equipped with metal hooks, to which two strands of fine wire were attached. These could be slipped down into the narrow crack between the new section and the surrounding floor, and fished up in order to haul the section out when the diggers were working. Once in place, the crack was filled with cement and sand and carefully dusted over, making it impossible, in the dim light, to see any disturbance in the floor's surface. An officer – in this case Mike Casey – was appointed to take responsibility for the trap. He was known as the *Trapführer*.

Once that job was done, the Poles moved next door to Block 122 to work on Dick's trap, which was perhaps the most ingenious of the three, and owed its inspiration partly to the lavatory trap at Schubin and partly to Goldfinch's drainage trench trap in the old compound. Under the washroom, beneath a grille, there was a drain about forty-five centimetres square and a metre deep. The drain-off pipe was not at the bottom, but about thirty centimetres above it, so that the bottom third was always full of water. Once again, Mondschein cut a square of concrete out, this time out of the side of the drain, and replaced it with a specially cast replacement. Behind the concrete they found sand, so there was no other obstacle to digging a little way in before sinking the shaft. When the trap was in place, it was sealed with a waterproof mixture of clay, soap and cement. Water was let back in to the level of the drainage pipe, the grille was replaced, and the trap was as well concealed as it could possibly be. Dick's trap was never discovered. Its *Trapführer* was twenty-two-year-old Flying Officer Les Brodrick, a newcomer to the North Compound, having been shot down in mid-April (he was one of only two survivors of his Lancaster bomber), and arriving at Sagan in May, just in time for the start of the tunnelling operations.

Aircrew arriving as prisoners-of-war had always suffered the intense trauma of being shot down. Many had also just lost crew members and friends. Les Brodrick:

'I was twenty-one and this was my twentieth mission. It was all a series of misfortunes. The previous night we'd been on a very long trip to northern Italy. We'd arrived back at half past six the next morning after a ten-hour trip. It was into bed and up at three to be briefed for a raid on Stuttgart. Although the weather was very bad there were no problems as we crossed the coast, but when we got towards the target we could see the flak for miles and miles. We pressed on and as soon as we were in what we thought was the right position we dropped the bombs, dived down and came back low. We had been hit several times but everything seemed to be working all right. Then, somewhere near Amiens, I flew over a grass aerodrome and a machine gun opened up and hit the port engine and immediately it was in roaring flames, burning up the fuselage. I thought about climbing up so the guys could get out by parachute, but right then a straight, flat field opened up. I came in nicely and then, when I held off to land, the nose just fell and we crashed straight in and stopped dead. My harness held but everybody else in the forward cockpit was thrown through the roof. I managed to get loose and climb out and saw all these guys lying there. I checked round and found one, the navigator, still alive, bleeding badly and half unconscious, so I dragged him away. Then the mid upper gunner appeared, he'd stayed in his turret and he got out safely. So just three of us had survived.

'There wasn't a sound around the place and of course we were injured, and the navigator was in a terrible way by the look of him, so we blew our whistles, made as much noise as we could. Meanwhile the plane was burning up and the ammunition was exploding all the time. But there wasn't a reaction from anywhere. When it became light, the two of us who could walk went to the nearest village and asked for a doctor. Of course they said, "Oh, well, we can only get a doctor from the Germans," but that was fine because we wanted the navigator looked after. Then Jonesy, my mid upper gunner, was told to go and identify the bodies, which he did. I must say I was quite glad I didn't have to, by this time reaction was setting in, I suppose.

'Anyway there we were captured, taken to a nearby aerodrome where we got medical attention, and we were in the bag.'

Harry's trap in Block 104 was the last to be completed. This time it was decided to construct directly below a stove. This meant not only removable pipework, but taking the stove off its tiled-floor base, removing the tiles one by one and setting them aside, and then dismantling its 130-centimetre-square wooden base. The base was then reconstructed by the master carpenters of X-Organisation as fast as possible, for the stove could not be replaced without it. Then the tiles had to be fitted back together on their own frame, which could then be lifted off as a whole once the stove was removed. There was a panic then because, despite all the care that had been taken, several of the tiles had been broken, and it was discovered that none of the tiles beneath other stoves in the compound were a perfect match. Taking no chances, the escapers decided to scour the old compound for similar tiles, and after a frantic search the right number of suitable tiles was found. These were smuggled across by a kitchen orderly, who secreted them in his battledress. Seven hours later, the trap was complete. Once again, the cracks between it and the surrounding floor were disguised with a sprinkling of cement and dust. The stove was replaced and kept alight constantly. Dick's *Trapführer* was a Canadian, Flight Lieutenant Pat Langford.

Towards the end of May, as the spring sunshine at last

began to warm the desolate camp after the long winter, work on the shafts began. The shafts, which were to be deeper than any dug before, were crucial to the success of the operation, and the excavation of each was supervised by the three most experienced tunnellers: Johnny Marshall looked after Tom, Wally Floody managed Dick, and Harry was put into the hands of 'Crump' Ker-Ramsay. Dick, with its opening into sand, gave the diggers few problems, but the other two tunnels presented immediate obstacles. To reach the sandy soil beneath Harry's stove-trap, the escapers first had to cut their way through a solid foundation of brick and concrete. They managed to do this using a stolen pickaxe head, which they mounted onto a baseball bat, but apart from the fact that the work was slow and therefore time-consuming, as well as exhausting for men on a very low daily calorie intake, it was very noisy. To cover the noise of the pickaxe as it chipped away a man-sized hole in the floor in the middle of the foundations, X-Organisation detailed a group of prisoners outside Block 104. They busied themselves about making kitchen utensils, baking tins and saucepans, bashing them out of discarded tins and bits of sheet metal, and making more than enough racket to drown out the sound of the excavations.

Tom was an even tougher nut to crack. The rubble that had been removed beneath their new square of concrete had to be replaced by something else that would support it. There was also the question of making sure that the block's chimney foundations remained strong enough to hold it up. Travis, immaculate as ever – he was one of many prisoners throughout German captivity whose attention to his appearance not only formed part of a personal resistance but helped maintain his self-esteem – was called upon to design and make a frame which would support the block over the deepening hole in the sand below. Not only did he manage this, but he devised a wooden tray, filled with sand, to fit on top of the frame, between it and the concrete slab, so that there would be no risk of the trap making a hollow sound if a suspicious ferret might tap it with his heel. Travis' department was now equipped with a variety of tools – stolen, acquired or makeshift. Many of the smaller ones were kept concealed in the library in Block 110 in books, whose insides had been carefully cut out to fit the implements by Block 110's Little S, Ted Earngey. Every block wall was double, for insulation, with a ten-centimetre gap between the two skins. The carpenters were able to cut a concealed trap-door in the inner walls in rooms in Blocks 110 and 120, as well as, in time, other blocks throughout the compound, so that there was a wide choice of hidey-holes for larger implements, escape clothes, and so forth, scattered around the compound. In two rooms, one in Block 110 and one opposite Bushell's quarters in Block 120, one whole inner wall was brought forward about twenty-five centimetres, as much as was possible without changing the apparent dimensions of the little rooms, to provide extra storage space.

Once everything was in place, the diggers could start work on the actual shafts. They organised themselves into shifts, working from just after morning roll-call, at 8.00 a.m., until shortly before evening roll-call, which took place at about 5.30 p.m. There were four teams to each tunnel, each working all day, one day in four. To begin with there were no night shifts, since a tunnel had once been discovered through a German raid on a block at Barth at two in the morning, when the escapers had assumed that apart from the guards in the watch-towers, their guardians would have been battened down for the night.

The coal scoops they originally used soon wore out or broke in the heavy sand, so Travis devised iron hand-shovels made from stolen stove-plates. Every 150 centimetres or so they buttressed the shaft with lengths of the corner posts of dismantled bunks (space in the rooms thereby becoming more cramped), set into each corner of the shaft and shored between them with bedboards. On one side they constructed a ladder. Painstakingly, they worked their way ten metres down. Work on each tunnel progressed simultaneously.

The next job, which was to prove very tricky, was the construction of three small chambers at the base of the shaft: one to house the air-pump and its operator; a small store-room for bedboards and other materials; and a larger work-shop for cutting boards to size for shoring the tunnel. The pump chamber was about one and a half metres long, about 165 centimetres high, and some seventy-five centimetres wide. The storeroom was about seventy-five centimetres long and wide, and 165 centimetres high. The workshop was two and a half metres long, well over a metre high, and tapered in width from about seventy-five centimetres for the first metre and a bit to about sixty centimetres for the rest of its length.

There were near-disasters at this point in the digging of the tunnels. Ker-Ramsay, Floody and another expert tunneller, Norman Canton, had just started work on the chambers for Dick when one of them felt a small shower of sand on his head. Looking up, he could just see through the gloom to where sand was leaking steadily from between two boards near the top. He alerted his two companions, and they started up the ladder as fast as they could, and not before time, as the trickle very quickly became a flood as the weight of the sand rapidly pushed the boards further apart. Canton and Ker-Ramsay managed to get out before they were trapped, but Floody, who was last up the ladder, found himself with his legs stuck in the sand. The other two were able to haul him to safety, but when they looked down the shaft, they saw that it had filled almost to the top. There was nothing for it but to start digging again, cursing the wasted time and the additional quantity of sand that would now have to be 'lost' within the compound; but thanking God that no-one had been buried alive. A few days later, a similar disaster befell Harry's shaft. As re-excavation progressed, the tunnellers made sure that the shafts were more robustly shored. After that, the chambers below were hollowed out in relative safety. These, too, with ten metres of sand above them, had to be propped up with special care.

When the men were working below, the *Trapführer* or one of his assistants kept watch at the top. A tin can containing pebbles was lowered from there to the chambers on a length of string. If a guard or a ferret passed from the S to the D zone, the fact was relayed by a system of lookout stooges signalling to each other and finally to the man at the top of the trap. He would then agitate the string, the pebbles would rattle, and the men below would know to stop work until the danger was past. Noise was kept to a minimum. Even ten metres below the surface, the sound of digging, rising up the shaft, might be heard by some sharp-eared German. Security was always paramount in the escape committee's mind; and their job hadn't been made any easier by the recent arrival of a new young ferret who seemed potentially to possess all the instincts of Glemnitz and all the dogged application of Rubberneck: the kriegies nicknamed him 'Keen-Type'. 'He was a short man with blond hair, a long sharp nose, and a tight little mouth,' Brickhill remembered. His real name has not come down to us.

The next task was the installation of the air pumps. Prototype pumps had been developed before, but the ones for the three tunnels had to be large and robust enough to convey enough air down a ten-metre shaft and along a tunnel that would stretch for one hundred metres. The task of designing the new pumps was placed in the hands of Jens

Muller, a Norwegian flyer, and the Yorkshireman Robert Nelson.

Using the raw materials available, for each pump they sewed two kitbags together, after fitting them with wire hoops along their length, and sealed the join with the tar paper the builders had left lying around in rolls after using it to seal the roof joints of the blocks. The result looked like a giant concertina. Holes were cut in the middle of each end and intake and outlet valves made out of leather flaps were fitted. These were later refined, spring-loaded, and fitted with silencers. A by-pass valve was also attached to allow

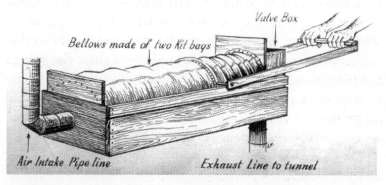

natural ventilation when the tunnel was closed and no operator was present. The concertina was mounted on a wooden frame, at one end of which a sliding seat for the operator was fitted, together with a handle whose push-pull mechanism expanded and deflated the bag. At one end an air intake pipe was attached, which led up to the surface, while the outlet pipe led into the tunnel and was lengthened as necessary. The pipes themselves were made of discarded powdered milk cans, their tops and bottoms removed, and fitted together (by luck the tops of the tins had a slightly smaller diameter than the bottoms), and sealed with tarred paper. The outlet pipe was laid along the floor of the tunnel in a very shallow gulley under the floorboards to protect it, its open end at the workface of the tunnel exposed and directed upwards towards the digger's face. Making the pumps, a job which was done in the library, was a noisy business, and one day early on the sound of sawing and hammering attracted the attention of three patrolling ferrets. Luckily the stooge-signalling system picked up on them in time, and well before they got to the library the alarm had been given. By the time they arrived, the tools were packed away in books and behind the concealed panels in the walls. There wasn't so much as a wood-shaving to be seen. From then on, Bushell got John Dodge to organise a choir. One hundred men practised community singing every day from then on just outside the library, to the accompaniment of an ancient accordion. The Germans never seemed to question whether or not the 'legitimate' users of the library would object to this disturbance. The singers themselves for the most part were innocent of the true purpose of their choir practice. Security was so tight that, of all the people involved in escape activity, only a dozen or so knew the whole picture.

There were further refinements, all planned in advance and put in place as the tunnels progressed. From the sophisticated tunnel at Schubin had come the idea of rigging up electric light in the tunnels, tapping into the camp's generator for their supply. Fat-lamps, which burned for about an hour before needing a refill, were sooty, smelly and dangerous, but they still had to be used for daytime digging, when the generator was switched off, and for emergencies; electric light was cleaner and, unlike the fat-lamps, required no oxygen. It was also less dangerous. Light was also an important weapon in the fight against claustrophobia, to which all but a very few were more or less vulnerable. Then there was the railway line.

As the tunnels lengthened, the escapers would be confronted increasingly by two problems: getting rid of the displaced sand, and getting it from the workface to the shaft with the maximum speed and the minimum effort. Wheeled trolleys were made by Travis and his department. They were flat-tops, and the flanges of the wheels were created by glueing together three wooden discs whose diameter decreased towards the centre. They were edged with strips of metal to protect them against wear, and their hubs were fixed to a wooden axle (the axles were the removed front rails of the stoves) that rotated on hardwood bearings lubricated with margarine. The tunnels themselves were boarded roof, sides and floor (it is a miracle that enough bedboards were available, and that their absence from the beds was never noticed), and the rails, made from battens removed from the blocks, were nailed firmly down. The gauge was about thirty-one centimetres. Each trolley had a hook at either end, to which a rope made by plaiting together several lengths of string was attached. By this means, the trolley could be pulled up and down the tunnel. Each trolley was strong enough to carry one man lying prone with his chest and thighs on it, or two boxes for excavated sand.

Les Brodrick:

'The longer things went on the more trouble they had with the tunnel – not with constructing it but with falls of sand. If the sand fell, as it very often did when they were digging, they'd just hear a sort of hissing sound and suddenly they were deluged with sand and they had to be dragged out very fast by the guy behind. No-one was ever suffocated, but some had nasty moments.'

As the shoring had to be secured without nails, the tunnel's cross section was trapezoid, the roof, at about forty-five centimetres, slightly narrower than the floor, at fifty centimetres. The tunnel was something under a metre high. The boards had tongue-and-groove slots, and once they were in place with the sand packed above and behind them, the weight of the sand kept them firmly in place. The problem that arose when there was a fall was that the tunnellers could only pack back about two-thirds of the sand that had been displaced, which meant that more sand had to be dispersed in the compound above. Carpenters kept the tunnellers supplied with shoring boards cut and trimmed and ready for use: it was a good system.

The first fifteen to twenty metres of each tunnel was dug and shored by experienced tunnellers, since the sandy soil of Sagan was so unstable that escapers new to digging had to be shown exactly what to do, and taught to proceed on the side of caution. There was a temptation to dig too quickly, and that could always lead to setback at best, disaster at worst. Before long, a routine had been established. After morning roll-call, two tunnellers, a pumper and two carpenters went below for the first shift and the trap was sealed over them. The first digger pulled himself onto the trolley and pushed his way up to the workface, taking a light with him. He climbed off and started work while the support digger hauled the trolley back and repeated the manoeuvre, hauled to the

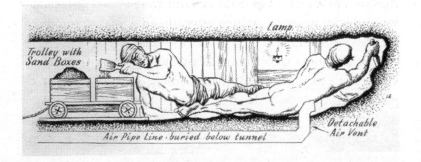

face by his comrade. The trolley was then pulled back to the base of the shaft again, and the empty sandboxes, shoring boards, and any other materials, such as milk tins and tar paper for extending the air pipe, were placed onto it. The number two digger pulled it back when it was ready. Signals between the base of the shaft and the workface were effected by pulls on the trolley rope. It was a very laborious business. The digger at the face scraped the sand away as he lay on his side, balanced painfully on one elbow, and passed the sand he'd dislodged back to the second digger, who cleared it away into the sandboxes. The second digger lay facing back towards the shaft in order to carry out his work. When the sandboxes were full, a tug on the rope told the carpenters at the shaft's base to pull the trolley back. There, one of them emptied the sand from the boxes into kitbags or sacks and stored them in the workshop for transporting to the surface later. The trolley with the empty boxes was then pulled back to the workface. Every so often, the front and rear digger crawled back to the shaft in order to change positions – there was no room to perform this manoeuvre in the narrow confines of the tunnel itself, unless the two tunnellers were very slightly built.

Falls of sand were not uncommon, and as these usually occurred at the face, it was the job of the number two digger to pull his comrade clear somehow by seizing his ankles and tugging hard. By a miracle, there were no fatalities on any of the digs. Falls of sand were usually preceded by a cracking sound, which gave the diggers a couple of seconds' warning.

This distribution of labour, all carefully planned in advance with great precision, meant that the diggers could concentrate purely on the work of lengthening the tunnel, and on a good day could clear nearly three metres. The work was mucky and the men stank; they were supposed to wear long underwear (supplied by the Red Cross) to protect their skin from tell-tale sand abrasions, but in practice many worked naked, for the scratchy underwear became so filthy and foul that they couldn't bear to wear it. Sand got everywhere, into the eyes and all the hair of the body, and clung there in the men's sweat. Skin rashes and other discomforts in the armpits, anus and groin had to be borne philosophically. Once a shift was over, the workers dressed in their uniforms, returned to the surface, and washed as much grime as possible off themselves.

After the evening roll-call, the first job was to haul the sacks and bags of sand up to the surface. Blankets were spread around the trap to catch any spilt sand. Then the engineering teams went down to check the shoring, do any maintenance necessary on the pump and air-lines, and extend the electric cable and lights. Every so often the surveying teams went down to check that the tunnels were running true and level, using a spirit level devised by Travis for the latter job, and stolen prismatic compasses for the former. The length was checked by the use of a cord which had been pre-measured using a ruler from a Red Cross Parcel.

At the end of every day's work, each tunnel yielded around 4,000 kilos of yellow sand. The dispersal of this around the camp was one of the hardest jobs the escapers faced. The chief ferret, Glemnitz, had once observed to Bushell that he would never succeed with a tunnel unless he found a way of destroying sand. By making it disappear, the escapers would be doing the next best thing. But how?

To begin with the men whose job it was to get rid of the stuff carried small bags hung around their necks. It was a slow job, but not impossible in the early days because they could take advantage of the upheaval of earth caused by the unfinished building works in the camp, uprooted tree trunks, and piles of builders' rubble. In time the prisoners started little gardens next to their blocks, and sand was mixed in with the turned-over earth in which grey little vegetable patches struggled. Sand could be lost along pathways, where the ground was always being disturbed, and along the edge of the warning wire, as so many prisoners took exercise and killed time in endless perambulations around it. But the little bags had a small capacity, and too many men wandering aimlessly around at all hours between reveille and lights-out would be bound to arouse suspicion. Furthermore, they had to wear their greatcoats to conceal the bags, and as spring gave way to summer it became difficult to justify wearing them. The problem increased with the amount of sand to get rid of.

It wasn't long, however, before Peter Fanshawe came up with an invention which solved it. This was the 'trouser-bag'. Each was made of the leg of a pair of long johns, cut off at the crutch. To the top a loop of string was attached, which went round your neck and under your arm under your tunic, long enough to suspend the long john leg inside your own trouser leg. The bottom end of the long john was closed with a pin, also attached to a string which ran up to your trouser pocket. The long john leg was filled with sand and a disperser carried one down each trouser leg. When he found a safe spot, he simply pulled the pin by means of the string held by its end in the trouser pocket. When the pin was withdrawn, the sand ran out. You could do it as you walked along and scuff it about as you did so. If you took adequate care, no guard would notice a thing; and the long john bags had a far greater capacity than their antecedents. Also cutting up long johns had a beneficial psychological side-effect. As Brickhill writes: 'They were the only things we had plenty of. It's bad enough to be rusting behind barbed wire thinking of Dorothy Lamour without the final degradation of long underpants. You feel so hopelessly celibate.'

About one hundred and fifty prisoners acted as dispersers. They came to be known as 'penguins', because the heavy sandbags down their legs made them waddle rather; and they were among the hardest-worked of all the escape team. In time, the system of loading them at the trap mouth became so streamlined that four penguins could be 'filled' every minute. If the alarm was raised, constant drilling and practice meant that a trap could be closed and disguised within two minutes. And because the wet sand had a strong odour, a tin of strong pipe tobacco was left smouldering in a corner. Though the smell of this turned some of the men green, at least it had the welcome side-effect of keeping the mosquitoes at bay.

The ability to close a trap and disguise it as fast as possible was of prime importance, however. Once, Keen-Type appeared in Block 123 completely unexpectedly, having for once got through the cordon of look-out stooges. Mike Casey had about seven seconds to cover the hole and wouldn't have managed it at all if George Harsh and another prisoner hadn't faked a fight and 'accidentally' knocked Keen-Type over. By the time they'd picked him up and apologised profusely, 'Tom' was covered.

Since Keen-Type was a real threat, Wally Valenta decided to give one of his German-speakers, Axel Zillessen, the job of 'taming' him. It worked surprisingly well. The war was going badly for Germany. Few rank-and-filers had any time for Hitler or the Party. Keen-Type was well aware that, when it was all over, Germans who'd behaved humanely to their charges would be treated better than those who had not. Slowly but surely, and it was a long and delicate process, Keen-Type was won round. In the end, over cups of tea, he was tipping the krie-gies off about planned raids. He wasn't the only ferret to be won round, and Valenta, trained in intelligence, was able to instruct his men on just how to extract all sorts of informa-tion from their German contacts. In time, he could pass on to Des Plunkett's mapmaking department all sorts of information about the camp: how far the forest reached, where the foot-paths through it were and where they led to. Similarly, Valenta's men found out about train times, and even managed to get hold of timetables with connections further down the line; the prices of tickets, what kind of food you could get without coupons, where Swedish ships docked at Danzig (Gdansk), how the borders with Czechoslovakia, Denmark and Switzerland were patrolled, and far more. Some railway information was collected directly by POWs themselves, as the prisoners who worked in the Red Cross parcel store were permitted to go (under guard) to Sagan station to collect the parcels. When they went, they kept their eyes and ears open.

Naturally, the men of the contact department couldn't suborn everyone, and there were always more loyal Germans than ones who could be 'turned', but Valenta's men always knew exactly when to withdraw if they were getting nowhere with a subject, so suspicions were never aroused. Those Germans who had been tamed found themselves in a lobster-trap: once caught, there was no going back.

Another major problem was the acquisition of wood. To counter the shortage, the tunnels were only partly shored after the first fifteen metres or so, but that in turn led to an increased risk of falls. To make up the number of bedboards, for not every single one could be taken, floorboards were taken up where possible, for some of the blocks had had two layers of floorboards laid, and the lower layer, stripped from beneath the block, was not missed.

Jack Lyon:

'Sometimes the escape activity was a damn nuisance when they came round stealing practically your last bed board. You thought, "Oh these people! Why don't they get on with the job and leave us in peace?" They weren't always entirely popular, the escapers. We had to live with them.'

By the end of May, all the tunnels were twenty metres long. Bushell appointed a wood-quartermaster, a New Zealander called John Williams, who organised a levy of two boards per bunk from all those who had not already contributed. This yielded a further seven hundred metres of board. Later on, when some bunks had no boards left at all, nets had to be woven from string to support the palliasses.

The tunnels continued to progress throughout the early summer undisturbed, while the day-to-day life of the camp was invigorated by a round of plays and revues in the theatre, which had just been completed, in which Roger Bushell frequently took leading roles, mock political debates, lectures on all manner of subjects (Valenta's talks on the progress of the war were always sellouts), and the occasional surface escape attempt, never successful, but always a welcome diversion, serving the additional purpose of keeping the Germans' attention diverted from suspicion of tunnelling activity. The ferrets did stage the occasional raid, but found nothing; and it is possible that they really did believe the sandy soil would put such an attempt out of the question. As the tunnels lengthened, so did the preparations in the blocks, as tailors, forgers, mapmakers and toolmakers all worked on, the various strands held together by Big X, with his almost superhuman capacity for organisation and administration.

One notable mass escape took place early in June. The Germans were always very nervous about possible outbreaks of lice in the camp. Lice could carry unpleasant diseases such as typhus, which ravaged the Russian POW camps, where conditions were considerably worse than elsewhere, and the concentration camps, where conditions were indescribable. But in the conventional prison camps precautionary delousing was a regular feature of life, and Stalag-Luft III had its own shower block a short distance through the forest from the North Compound. Trips to the shower block were welcomed by the prisoners, not just for the obvious reason, but because they meant a break in the monotonous routine of camp life, which could cast a pall over your mood even if you were actively engaged in escape activity; and a walk through the woods gave a fleeting impression of freedom.

Parties of prisoners for the showers were formed into sizeable groups and conducted there under a small armed guard. One afternoon, a party of twenty-four prisoners were lined up under two guards and, carrying bundles of clothes for washing too, marched to the gate. There, the escort showed their papers to the guard, and the party passed through. The gate guards' attention was already on a smaller group of British senior officers approaching in the company of a German corporal. It appeared that they were bound for a meeting with von Lindeiner at the camp's *Kommandatur* – the command centre. This time the guards looked at the escort's papers more closely. They carried an out-of-date identification mark. The corporal raised his arms. He was Bob van der Stok. The senior officers were equally spurious. It wasn't long before the guards realised that the escorts of the first, large party had also been disguised prisoners. All hell broke loose.

The blank gate passes had been provided by Sydney Dowse's tame contact, Corporal Hesse. Security in the North Compound wasn't yet as tight as it should be, and would become, and had it not been for the out-of-date identification mark, the second party would have got away as smoothly as the first. The German uniforms were the work of Tommy Guest's clothing factory, now becoming increasingly adept at faking them, and the fake weapons the guards carried had been the work of Jens Muller and two associates, Alex McIntosh and a Belgian officer called Henri Picard, who had a natural artistic talent and worked in Tim Walenn's forgery department. Picard managed to obtain the dimensions of a genuine German rifle. To make the fakes, Picard managed to get hold of some beechwood – a handful of bedboards in the compound were made of beechwood and not of pine. The boards were not thick enough to carve a rifle out of one in one piece, so the guns were roughly carved in two halves, and then stuck together using a glue made from boiling the grey ration-bread. When the glue was set, the rifles were carefully carved down to the last detail, and the parts supposed to be made of metal rubbed with graphite from pencils until they acquired the authentic dull shine of gunmetal. The wooden sections were rubbed with brown boot polish, and parts such as the trigger and the bolt were made from hammered down nails of various sizes. The muzzle, too, was made from metal – cast in a soap-mould from melted-down silver paper from cigarette packets. Melted-down silver paper and soap-moulds were also used for casting German military badges.

Reg Van Toen, who later helped build the memorial at Sagan, worked in the nutrition section:

'My room-mates and me started cooking first thing in the morning and went on to last thing at night . . . I was the chef who made the specialist escape cake food . . . I had inherited the recipe from a bloke called Van Rood. The nourishment would last you two days. My job and that of my colleagues in my room was to make enough for the mass breakout. This dreadful goo was put into cocoa tins to set. The ingredients came from Red Cross parcels and X-Organisation disposed of it round the camp.'

In the meantime, the nutrition section had come up with a form of concentrated energy-food which could be supplied in small bars: it consisted of oatmeal and breadcrumbs, powdered milk, chocolate and sugar, mixed together and baked. It was very hard to bite into, and tasted like synthetic toffee; but it had a high calorific value, and four days' supply could be stored in a pocket.

The overall preparation for the escape had taken about a week. The escapers were selected from among those who had worked especially hard for X-Organisation, but who could now be spared. The 'senior officers' had been chosen for their gravitas and generally imposing looks. The guards, of course, had been chosen for their perfect German. There had been one last-minute hitch. A German High Command order had suddenly decreed that NCO escorts should be issued with pistols instead of rifles. This was appalling luck, but the escape committee had been equal to the new challenge. Some of Tommy Guest's tailors made holsters out of cardboard, which were rubbed with black boot polish until they shone like leather. McIntosh carved some pistol butts out of wood, and they were also treated to the boot polish treatment. Sticking out from under the flap of the holster, they were indistinguishable from German military-issue Lugers.

After leaving the compound, the party of twenty-six escapers, whose bundles contained limited amounts of survival kit and food for their journey, walked in line for a couple of hundred metres before splitting into pre-arranged pairs and diving into the woods. They knew that most, if not all, of them would be recaptured, but they also knew that they would cause a major disruption in the camp and rattle the Germans. It was also important, as has been seen, to distract the Germans from the main escape work being done. If no-one had tried to escape, the Germans would have become very suspicious indeed, and that would have led to a greater tightening of security than a breakout would occasion. Besides, after successfully rounding up a bunch of would-be escapers, the Germans tended to become complacent, for a while at least.

Some of the escapers headed for the railway station at

Sagan to make use of their false passes and tickets. Others headed deeper into the woods, to try to cross the country-side on foot, navigating their way to a friendly or neutral frontier. These 'hardarsers' stood less of a chance than those taking the train. One member of this latter group got as far as Posen (Poznan) before being picked up, despite the fact that he was wearing RAF uniform trousers. Another was recaptured at Siegersdorf when the police found that the offi-cial who'd 'signed' his documents had died several weeks before the date of issue. Two others didn't get beyond Sagan station before they were recognised and arrested by the camp's doctor, who happened to be there.

Two others made for the nearby airfield in search of an aircraft in which they could fly to freedom. They made their way unchallenged to a two-seater trainer which appeared to be ready for take-off but was unattended. They managed to crank it up, but just then a German pilot appeared and started to talk to them in German, a language neither of them under-stood. All they could do was spring to attention and salute, which luckily satisfied the pilot, who climbed into the little aeroplane and flew off. Undeterred, the two cautiously approached another likely-looking aircraft. They gave it the once over, checked that it was fuelled up, and discovered that it lacked a starting-handle. They'd already noticed a nearby hangar, and cautiously made their way over to it in search of a crank. Still unmolested, they found one and returned to the plane, which they were just starting up when a Luftwaffe sergeant came running up, bawling at them. This time there was no escape. Because they were caught on an airfield, they were kept separately and subjected to ferocious interrogation, and no doubt whoever was in charge of security at the airfield was given a grilling too. Neither returned to Sagan: both were sent to Colditz.

Flying Officer John Stower had the worst luck of all.

Disguised as a Spanish worker, he made his way on foot towards Czechoslovakia, and covered the one hundred kilometres or so in a week. He'd been equipped with a contact address, and put himself in touch with the Czech underground through a friendly landlord who kept a bar near Prague airport. They tried to get him papers and tickets for a train journey into Switzerland, but when this plan failed, gave him a new identity and smuggled him back into Germany with a train ticket to carry him across the southern part of that country to the Swiss border. He disembarked about sixty kilometres short of the Bodensee (Lake Constance), where he skirted its north shore, heading west in the direction of Schaffhausen, where, as we have seen, a small pocket of Switzerland extends into Germany. X-Organisation had provided him with a detailed map of the area, but he misjudged his distances and actually wandered into Switzerland and out of it again, back into Germany, and into the arms of a border patrol. He was held by the Gestapo for a few weeks' interrogation, but ultimately returned to Sagan. 'I'm longing to see you all again,' he wrote home bleakly. 'So near, and yet so far . . .' But Stower's mistake would prove to be a fatal one. He would never see England again.

Everyone who returned to Sagan spent two weeks in the cooler, though there were so many prisoners in there that they had to share the tiny cells, so the object of solitary confinement was defeated. As soon as he heard of the escape, von Lindeiner ordered a roll-call which lasted seven hours, as Captain Pieber counted the prisoners twice over. Soon afterwards, all senior officers, and all airmen of British or American nationality, were classified as 'important prisoners', and were specially listed with photographs and fingerprints.

Roll-calls were doubled for a time, and supplies of Red Cross parcels suspended. No-one owned up to the serious charge of impersonating a German soldier. The head of security at Stalag-Luft III, Major Broili, was beside himself; but with such a vast camp to administer, North Compound was just one of his problems.

About 10 June, the prisoners became aware of another space being cleared in the forest to the south of their new compound. It was clear that the camp was being expanded once again. A few questions put to one of the tame goons quickly revealed that there was indeed going to be yet another new compound, to which the Americans would be moved. The Germans had decided that the Americans and the British and Colonial airmen were all getting on far too well. The good news was that none of the tunnels led in that direction, for in that case they would have been *kaputt*. The bad news, at least for the Americans, was that they would have left North Compound before they could benefit from the facilities of Tom, Dick or Harry. As they had put so much work into the tunnels, it seemed unfair.

Frank Tams:

    'We learned many things that were useful at the time. We had no fridge to keep food fresh in the summer, so instead a box was covered with cloth which was kept wet by having water dripped onto it and placed in the sun where it would keep items cooler than in the sweltering rooms, by using the cooling effect of evaporation. The technique was originally used by the Romans, and possibly even before that, but we found it very effective fifteen hundred years later. Washing machines were replaced by "dunkers": a small tin was fixed inside a large tin and secured to a pole to agitate one's washing, rather like the old "dolly", which was in use before the present-day washing machines.'

Bushell called a meeting of his escape committee and put it
to them that it might be possible to speed the work up.
Someone raised the question of security becoming stretched
if that were done, so a compromise was reached whereby
Dick and Harry would be shut down temporarily, and all
efforts concentrated on Tom, which was the farthest advanced
tunnel in any case. With any luck, they could get it finished
and used before the Americans were transferred. The best
tunnellers were put onto the job, together with some
Americans, who could at least gain experience of the business of tunnelling if the plan failed and they had to start their
own excavation in their own compound.

There was a brief break when the 4 July was riotously
celebrated with many flagons of what passed for rye whiskey;
but with all resources focused on it, Tom made rapid progress.
When it was about thirty metres long, having reached a point
below the warning wire, a 'halfway house' was constructed
to act as a relay station. It was about three metres long and
fifteen centimetres higher and wider than the rest of the
tunnel, so that men could just about pass each other in
comfort. This meant that the two diggers no longer needed
to crawl all the way back to the foot of the shaft to change
positions. There were no rails in the halfway house, so this
was a relay station for the trolleys as well. It was not possible
to manufacture rope strong enough to pull a heavy trolley
laden with sand for more than a certain distance. To act as
trolley-handlers, two extra men were stationed in the halfway
house; but even the mildest sufferer from claustrophobia was
unequal to protracted periods of inactivity so far underground
in the flickering light of a fat-lamp. Getting the extra air to
them was not an easy task, either. As work progressed, there
was a temptation to start sloping the tunnel upwards, to
obviate the need for another deep shaft at the escape end,
but the risk of a trolley breaking loose and careering back

down the slope, perhaps knocking out shoring boards and so collapsing the tunnel, was too great for this idea to be countenanced.

In the end, the accelerated activity did lead to a breakdown in security. One of the penguins jettisoned his load while watching a game of volleyball, but Glemnitz happened to be prowling nearby and spotted the yellow sand before it could be kicked into the grey soil. Luckily, he didn't notice quickly enough to see how it had got there, but he was quick to put two and two together. The ferrets donned their overalls (all but Glemnitz, who made it a point of honour always and only to wear his uniform) and started a search under his direction. They soon turned up sand where it shouldn't have been in the gardens, but then seemed to take no further action. Indeed, it was suspiciously quiet. Then, a couple of days later, someone noticed the guards in the watch-towers systematically scanning the compound with their field-glasses. They were clearly looking for patterns of activity, and to see if there was an undue amount of coming and going to and from any one block. As soon as Bushell learned of this, he restricted penguin activity around Block 123 and slowed progress, hoping things would cool off.

They didn't. Soon afterwards, a party of guards entered the compound one morning and started turning over the blocks on the west side of the camp, starting with 106 and moving on to 107. Luckily they didn't get to 123 before its *Trapführer* and his team had been able to close and completely camouflage the trap. The next day 'Rubberneck' and a team of guards entered 123 and spent five hours turning it over, but they found nothing. The following day, however, ferrets must have been concealed everywhere, as two were unearthed in one block alone.

Three full days after that were to elapse before Bushell

decided that it was safe to resume operations. They made three metres' progress that day – a near-record – but only dared disperse seventy-five per cent of the sand excavated.

The game of cat-and-mouse went on. Ferrets established 'hides' on the edge of the forest outside the camp from which to spy on the prisoners, and there were raids on blocks in the middle of the night. When Glemnitz found sand in the gardens outside Block 119, he called out the guard and had all three west-side blocks turned over once again, and had a 120-centimetre-deep trench dug parallel to 123, between it and the wire. They delved its bottom with their long metal probes in vain.

Glemnitz was experienced enough, however, to know that there was a tunnel somewhere, and X-Organisation knew equally that he would keep the pressure up. Block 123 had a disadvantage in that both its doors were in full view of watch-towers. Additionally, its trap was more vulnerable than the other two. It would have made sense to close down all operations on Tom until the Germans cooled down, but the tunnel had only about sixteen metres to go before its esti-mated exit point. Since the Germans were going to go on looking anyway, the escape committee decided to press ahead as cautiously as they could. They'd noticed a couple of plain-clothes policemen, who might have been regular Kripo, but could equally have been Gestapo. It was a sign of how seri-ously the Germans were taking their suspicions. Additionally, Glemnitz had the rest of the trees in the compound felled and cleared. The compound took on an ever bleaker aspect.

Security was stepped up. As a result Glemnitz was spotted hiding under a hut and had to withdraw. On another occa-sion, 'Rubberneck' Griese was marked into the compound by the duty pilot, but failed to return. He was run to earth hiding in the kitchen block, looking out of one of its west-facing windows. Bushell had all the outside shutters of the

windows closed. Soon afterwards, Rubberneck returned to
the guardhouse.

Reg Van Toen:

'Our daily ration of boiling water was used on Red Cross-
supplied tea early every morning. This had to be acquired by
the Duty Slave, queuing outside the kitchen block to await
his turn for one of the German cooks to pour boiling water
on the tea leaves already dropped into the jug, then hurrying
back to our room to serve us breakfast in bed: a slice of
black bread spread with marge and sometimes the luxury of
ersatz jam. We each took our turn at Duty Slave, unless you
had traded yourself out of it for a few fags or a bar of
chocolate. We made the pans from cocoa tins, carefully
unfolded, then joined by bending two edges together, and
riveting the result with a pointed tool, such as a nail or a
piece of broken fork. Trying to keep these crude pans clean
was, to the say the least, difficult. No wonder we all had
tummy troubles for much of our enforced residency.'

The duty pilot presented Glemnitz with a problem he was
never quite able to solve. Rubberneck encouraged him to
throw all the duty pilots into the cooler, but Glemnitz argued
that they'd be replaced with another system which might be
harder to keep an eye on. At least the duty pilots sat out in
the open. And he knew that they knew that he knew. A few
days after Rubberneck had been tracked down to the kitchen
block, Glemnitz entered the compound and said to the duty
pilot quite amiably, 'Mark me on your list. I'm coming in.'
The duty pilot duly did so. Glemnitz then asked him who
else was 'in'. He was told that he was the only one. Glemnitz
looked put out and demanded to see the list. After he'd

scanned it, he gave it back, told the duty pilot to mark him 'out' again, and marched off to the guards' quarters, where, the kriegies later learned, he found three ferrets who should have been on duty lounging around. One of them was Adolf, another, surprisingly, was Rubberneck. Adolf and the other junior ferret got four days each in the cooler. Rubberneck was confined to barracks with extra duties for two weeks.

Tom reached the edge of the woods successfully, and, with another six or seven metres to go, another halfway house was constructed. Only a few days more, and they would be ready for a break on the first moonless night that came along. Though they did their best to suppress it, tension and excitement mounted in the compound to nerve-stretching proportions.

Then came a major setback.

The kriegies woke up one morning to the sound of axes on wood. To the west of their compound, in the direction Tom and Dick were facing, a contingent of Russian POWs were felling trees for yet another new compound. In three days they cleared ten metres of forest, and went on clearing. This was a cruel blow, since it meant that Tom's length would have to be increased by some thirty metres, and Dick's eventually, by even more. There would also be the problem of additional dispersal. Plans had to be changed.

Digging continued, but Peter Fanshawe changed the dispersal system. Up until now, each penguin had been responsible for where he dropped his sand. Now, a dispersal officer was appointed to oversee where the stuff went, and the traffic of penguins to and from the block was broken up and staggered so that no discernible pattern of movement could be seen. When areas for dispersal ran out, sand was concealed in the Red Cross crates the prisoners had under their bunks for keeping personal bits and pieces that wouldn't fit into the lockers (there weren't enough lockers to go round anyway as the compound filled up). The crates in Block 123 couldn't be used, because that would have been tempting providence, so penguins still had to take the sand somewhere. Glemnitz managed to pick up a trail that led to Block 103, where a surprise raid yielded dozens of crates full of sand. Thereupon he ordered a couple of heavy horse-drawn waggons into the compound and had them drive around for a while, in the hope of collapsing the tunnel, but all three were too deep to be affected. Dispersal became a problem again, however, until Fanshawe came up with the idea of dumping sand from Tom into Dick. It was unlikely that Dick would be reactivated for some time, and the solution was a brilliant one.

Tom was about eighty-five metres long by now. It was still twelve metres from where the woods now began, but the escape committee deemed it safe enough to 'break' the tunnel where it was and crawl the exposed distance to the safety of the trees. With this in mind, Tom was closed down until the right moment came for the last push.

Meanwhile, Glemnitz had decided on another flash search. This time he concentrated on Block 104, where Harry was located, and 105. Harry, in disuse, was well disguised: there was ash and dust around the stove and the ventilation system which had been kept open was too small and too well hidden to attract attention. It was 8 September 1943 (some sources give 10 October, but this seems less likely). After his men had poked around in the two blocks for most of the morning, Glemnitz appeared to give up; but then he changed his mind and sent them over for another look at Block 123.

Everyone held his breath as the Germans once more turned everything in the block over. By late afternoon they had still found nothing, and the time for evening roll-call was only minutes away. The Germans prepared to leave the block. As they were doing so, one of the ferrets accidentally dropped his metal probe. It clattered down onto Tom's trap, dislodging the cement and sand that concealed the join between the concrete trap door and the surrounding floor. As he stooped to retrieve the probe, he noticed the join. He called his fellows back and one of them went to fetch Glemnitz as the others scraped around the edges of Tom's trap until the joins of the concrete slab were exposed.

When Glemnitz arrived he flexed some very underused muscles in his face, and grinned from ear to ear.

Chapter Six

THE DISCOVERY OF TOM WAS A BITTER BLOW, EVEN though everyone knew that its trap was the most vulnerable. It was hardest of all for the Americans, who would now have to start from scratch in their new compound, and for the British and Allied POWs who'd been in longest – men like Day, Dodge and Bushell himself. They could console themselves on the success of the achievement and the success of the planning – and they still had two tunnels the Germans knew nothing about. (Although there was a brief spurt of digging in Dick and Harry soon after Tom was discovered, the activity was shut down again almost immediately, for two months, because it was just too risky.)

On the day of the discovery, von Lindeiner was sent for immediately. He had the trap broken open, and sent over to the East Compound for the ferret 'Charlie' Pfelz, who was one of the few experts among the Germans who dared go down discovered tunnels, and who was quite a popular figure among the prisoners. Pfelz duly arrived and inspected Tom, crawling right to the workface and back again. His report impressed von Lindeiner. At close to one hundred metres long, Tom was one of the longest escape tunnels ever constructed, and its equipment impressed the Germans, who were worried that their own lax security could have made such a thing possible.

What was more, Tom had displaced getting on for 150 tonnes of sand, all of which had been successfully dispersed.

Tom had been a triumph of sorts, and scored a last point, even in death. The Germans didn't know how to destroy it: it was too big and well-built to flood with water and collapse it that way. Finally they sent for an army engineer who was supposed to be an explosives expert. He spent two days in the tunnel laying charges. When he was ready, he came out and set up his detonator. Everyone was cleared well away from the site. The explosives expert pushed down the plunger and there was, sure enough, a massive underground explosion. But this created such a rush of wind down the tunnel and up the shaft – a tribute to the strength of the shoring – that it blew the roof off Block 123, knocked its chimney askew, and caused the whole building to lurch to one side, like a listing ship.

Security may have been a prime question for the Germans, but that didn't prevent Glemnitz of all people from talking unguardedly to a ferret within earshot of a German-speaking prisoner, who overheard him say that there couldn't be another tunnel because the escapers on Tom must have used up all the wood, and he'd be keeping a check on bedboards from now on anyway. This news was relayed to Valenta, and when it was reported to Bushell, he had Williams organise the biggest bedboard levy yet, which yielded another two thousand. They were all stored either behind false walls or down Dick's remaining tunnel. When Glemnitz started his bedboard count, he wouldn't find any more missing – they'd all have gone.

Soon afterwards, the Americans were moved, and it was time to say goodbye to people like 'Junior' Clark, the USAAF colonel who'd been 'Big S'. George Harsh, however, because he'd joined the Canadian Air Force, stayed in the North Compound, and took over as head of security. During the lull occasioned by having to shut down work on Harry and the soon-to-be-abandoned Dick, there were plenty of other things to be getting on with.

Glemnitz was transferred with the Americans, but that was scarcely a help, since Rubberneck was left in charge, and, hungry for promotion, he brought the other ferrets quickly to heel. Fraternisation became much harder, and Keen-Type distanced himself from Zillessen. Adolf, protected from the cold weather by ear-muffs, though his nose was blue, kept an uncomfortably close eye on the forgers, who had already had to move their operation from an empty room in Block 123 to the library in Block 110. A new, more discreet system of stooges soon made it difficult for the forgers to be taken by surprise in any circumstances. This was important, as the forgers had to sit by a window to get sufficient light for their detailed work. In the end, as they worked in Block 110, three stooges – one at a window in the library facing west, one in the next block, 109, facing east, and a third in 110's northern neighbour, 103, facing south – were able to cover all possible approaches Adolf or any other ferret might make.

Forgery, as we have seen, was at the core of the escape operation. Tim Walenn now had a talented and experienced group around him, including Gordon Brettell, Alex Cassie and Henri Picard. Hand-lettering typeface was a painstaking job, yet they got so good at it that they even managed to fake typing mistakes, and the peculiarities and individual idiosyncrasies of type that all typewriters had in those days. Rubber stamps were carved from the heels of wellington boots. Paper was stained the right colour with cold tea, or diluted watercolour paint. Quality paper was obtained through contact Germans, or by ripping blank pages from library books. Official documents, such as a German soldier's pay-book, were borrowed under coercion from tamed goons. Once, they managed to 'borrow' the personal ID card of a captain who was standing in for Pieber and was unused to the ways of POWs. The wretched captain knew that it'd be better to ask for it back politely than confess to his commandant where he had lost it. Two days later, he got it back, after Walenn had made a copy of it.

To give an idea of the range of documents they worked on, 'Dean and Dawson' forged and supplied service IDs, which were printed on brown card and permitted the holder to be on military property; yellow leave passes, both for the military and foreign workers; pink repatriation passes, allowing foreign workers to return home; grey general identity cards, printed on buckram; French *cartes d'identité*; passport visas; various permanent and temporary passes; and police permits. A leave pass alone would take one forger, working many hours a day, four weeks to produce. And the daylight hours were few as autumn drifted into winter at Sagan, at the end of 1943. Some documents used ordinary typeface, some had headings in the German Gothic print – *Fraktur*. Most handwriting was in the Roman alphabet, but some officials still used old-fashioned *göthische Schrift*, which differs widely from conventional lettering. All of it had to be mastered.

It was a slow and painstaking business; signatures had to be copied and recopied, and checked to see that they were still valid. The Germans were also constantly changing the design and format of documents, and some of the papers on which they were printed had themselves printed designs on them, like a banknote's though mercifully not so complex; but they still had to be reproduced by hand. Embossing was a problem: originally the effect was achieved by laboriously, and very carefully, rubbing through with a pencil end; but later a small metal eagle-and-swastika stamp was made from melted-down silver paper cast in a soap-mould. Travis fixed it to a stamping machine of his own manufacture, and the problem was solved. Travis also made a little printing press, on which dozens of forms could be run off. Ink and pens and nibs were acquired from tame goons, but Brettell and

Cassie also manufactured ink from lampblack diluted with oil.

To add authenticity to an escaper's bundle of documents, the forgery department, 'Dean and Dawson', would also occasionally create a set of well-thumbed letters from a wife back home in Bordeaux, for example, or a typed letter on business letterhead confirming an appointment by a company in Nantes or Metz, or authorising the bearer to travel on company business. Favourite destinations were Stettin or Danzig because Swedish boats docked there.

It was hard-going, especially as, despite the demise of Tom, Walenn's men still needed to produce hundreds of documents for the Great Escape, which was still on. One of their number had befriended a guard called Fischer, who'd been a juggler in a circus in civilian life, and had no time at all for the war. Walenn had copied out a travel document on foolscap. This was given to Fischer, who smuggled it out of the camp tucked in his boot, and sent it to his wife in Hamburg. She had a typewriter, and typed stencils of the form, which she then sent back to her husband, who gave them to Walenn. This and similar operations lessened the time taken to produce documents considerably. In time, they acquired a small typewriter, and Captain Pieber, who always played an ambivalent role in the life of the camp, developed the films of 'passport photographs' for use on documents, which had been taken with a camera which Pieber had lent Valenta.

Valenta's intelligence section continued to gather and disseminate information. Bushell remained the authority on Germany, Tom Kirby-Green was responsible for Spain, while Bob van der Stok looked after the Netherlands still. Arnold Christensen stayed in charge of Denmark, and a Norwegian, Sergeant Halldor Espelid, looked after Scandinavia with his compatriot, Second Lieutenant Nils Fuglesang. Flying Officer Dennis Cochran, captured late in 1942, acted as a sort of minister without portfolio. Cochran was a complicated young man. Born in the East End of London, he lost two close friends in an early German air-raid. When he joined the RAF, the hatred of Germans that had grown within him as a result of the loss of his friends drove him to a high level of competitiveness, which resulted in his getting one of four commissions offered to an intake of 120 cadets. At the same time, he applied himself rigorously to learning German, in which he was fluent by the time he reached Sagan. Short-tempered and energetic, he was one of the keenest to get out and back into the fight. He was a good teacher of German, however, along with the Canadian Flying Officer, Gordon Kidder, and he was one of the best contact men in Valenta's group.

Because of snooping ferrets, John Travis had to move his department to the rather cramped, but very private, base of Dick's shaft. Des Plunkett's mapmakers were less troubled by Germans, perhaps because they were distributed around the camp, tracing maps which showed the surrounding countryside in detail, and broad routes towards Czechoslovakia, France, Switzerland and the Baltic. All maps were kept small, for ease of concealment, and divided into sets. Plunkett kept a careful note of which escapers required which sets in a notebook which he kept with him at all times.

The problem of mass-producing maps had been solved. Plunkett had managed to obtain some jelly from a hospital orderly – jelly was a delicacy reserved for the sick. He soaked the cubes in hot water and strained them through a handkerchief to extract the sugar. Left, finally, with pure gelatin, he melted it down and poured it onto flat trays beaten out of old food tins. When it was set, there was his mimeograph. He drew maps for reproduction on onionskin paper with ink made from the crushed leads of indelible pencils (obtained again from tame goons). Then he pressed the prepared map, its ink still wet, onto the warm gelatin, and could thereafter run off up to twenty copies per 'gel'. Tim

Walenn took advantage of this simple method of mass reproduction, too.

Such application was not in Plunkett's day-to-day nature.
Alex Cassie remembers him as amiable and clumsy, though
he and Cassie did an acrobatic double act in the theatre,
calling themselves the Royal Raviolis. (British and American
feature films began to arrive in the camp about this time and
were shown in the theatre, including the 1937 *Shall We Dance?*
with Fred Astaire and Ginger Rogers.)

Tommy Guest's tailoring department, armed with its
patterns cut out of old newspapers, was in full production,
keeping work-in-progress behind false walls, and hiding
finished goods, especially bulky items like greatcoats, in the
roof of the latrine block. A relatively new department was
also blossoming under an Australian POW, Al Hake. Hake
had set up a compass factory in a room in Block 103, since
evidently none of the MI9/IS9 compasses developed by
Clutty had reached the North Compound.

Hake's method was to make the compass casings out of bits
of broken gramophone records, heating the fragments until
they were soft and then pressing them into a mould. Artists in
Walenn's group painted the points of the compass on little
discs of card, and these were fitted to the bases of the casing.
A gramophone needle in the middle served as a pivot, and a
short segment of magnetised sewing needle was the pointer,
to which a minute pivot socket was soldered. The solder came
from the joints of food tins, and the resin from pine trees, or,
later, the pinewood the blocks were made of. Hake manufactured a little blow-lamp from a fat-lamp to which he attached
a thin metal tube, also recycled from food tins.

The pointer was given a dab of luminous paint (courtesy
of Valenta), so that the compasses could be used at night
without striking a match. The glass for the cover came from
broken window panes, cutting the little glass discs carefully

and then using the blow-lamp to melt the edges of the casing until the glass could be firmly held in place. To avoid the risk of any escaper being caught with one of these compasses and suspected of being a spy as a result, each was stamped on the bottom: 'Made in Stalag-Luft III'.

X-Organisation had all the materials being prepared deposited safely either behind false walls or down in Dick. Fake documents were kept dry by being stored in water-proof metal cans designed and made by Travis' engineers.

As clearance for the new compound to the west continued, it became obvious that Dick could never be finished, which left them with Harry, the longest tunnel to complete, as their last chance. The weather in late 1943 stayed fine, good for escaping, but the ferrets remained alert. A newcomer, nick-named 'Young 'Un', was successfully suborned, but the success was short-lived. Rubberneck smelt a rat, and had 'Young 'Un' transferred to the Eastern Front. That had a deleterious effect on prisoner/staff relations. Even the most coffee-thirsty guard preferred the thought of acorns and chicory to ending up freezing cold in inadequate winter kit, staring down the muzzles of Russian tanks.

Bushell, though he accepted the wisdom of the escape committee's decision, had to be restrained from ordering work on Harry to resume too soon. Both Herbert Massey and Harry Day knew that the Germans were keeping a partic-ular eye on him, and they were glad that Bushell found some outlet for his temporarily frustrated energies in acting, playing rugby, and learning languages – he was adding Czech, Danish and Russian to his German. As a natural man of action, the enforced confinement was driving him mad. He was given to fits of temper and long, brooding silences, and he made the force of his considerable personality felt when he thought anyone in the X-Organisation was not pulling their weight. A mood of gloom pervaded the compound, and it wasn't helped when one or two prisoners succumbed to cabin fever and had to be taken away to an asylum. Jack Lyon, an inmate at the time, recalled later how during his first days as a prisoner a similar feeling of doom had descended on him: 'I felt that it might be good to end it all on the wire. I think that a bit of music saved my life just at the time when I was considering doing this. Some people had gramophones in the camp and one had a record of Mozart's *Clarinet Concerto*, and he was actually playing the second movement, and I heard it and thought that it was written by a man in the last two or three months of his life, knowing full well that he hadn't got long to live. And he was living in abject poverty. I thought, well, if he could take it in those conditions, then I'd better rethink my own attitude.'

Frank Tams:
   'Eight guys occupying twelve feet by twelve with a table, chairs and three bunks, was a bit of a crush and living in such close proximity soon made one aware of the slightest idiosyncrasy in speech, gesture and behaviour which would probably never have been noticed in normal conditions. One knew what a fellow would do or say on any occasion and anticipated what would happen to such an extent that if for some unaccountable reason it did not, it became even more annoying. To alleviate the irritation we used various diversions, the principle one being circuit bashing.'

While the weather held, Bushell still helped organise individual efforts to get out 'over the wire', but he could not go himself. Bushell, too, belonged to the older generation in the camp, though he was still only thirty-three years old.

★ ★ ★

Though the inmates of the North Compound could not have known it, 1943 had been a good year for escaping. Ten days after Tom had been discovered, 132 French officers had got away, using a tunnel, from another camp, and in yet another camp, forty-seven Polish officers had tunnelled their way to freedom on the following night. At the end of October, one of the most famous and audacious – and completely successful – escapes was made from Stalag-Luft III's East Compound. Some time before, three men had started a tunnel near the wire, using a vaulting-horse as cover. The trap was simply concealed in the open compound, and the horse carried over to it every day with the three men hidden inside it. While other prisoners vaulted, the three dug. Michael Codner, Oliver Philpot and Eric Williams escaped on 29 October and successfully made their way to Sweden. Williams later wrote an account of the venture, *The Wooden Horse*.

Although there was still no sign of a Western Front opening up, that year also saw the fall of Italy, and Germany was robbed of its closest European ally. At the same time, POWs were becoming an increasing drain on German resources: nearly half a million men were involved in supervising them, and a further 100,000 needed to be mobilised (drawn from the Home Guard and the Home Army, as well as civilian police and the Gestapo) to cope with any mass breakout. Resultant changes in the German administration meant that Himmler's Reich State Security organisation took executive control of the Orpo, the regular uniformed police, and the Kripo. Himmler had been pressing for greater control of POWs for some time, and in October, the head of the Army High Command, Wilhelm Keitel, a man who was firmly in Hitler's pocket, issued the so-called *Igel* Order, which laid down that all POWs in transit henceforward should be chained. It was the beginning of a series of measures against POWs that ignored the Geneva Convention. And later, from the end of

July the following year, a German poster would declare:

> 'To all prisoners of War!
> The escape from prison camps is no longer a sport!'

The first snow arrived in November, along with the cold winds from the east, which swept the compound and kept the ferrets indoors for much of the time. Guards huddled in their inadequate greatcoats and thought of home, as did the kriegies, some of whom were looking forward to their fourth or even fifth Christmas in captivity. Bushell wrote home with a hint of desperation: 'It can't last much longer. This is definitely our last Christmas in the bag.' At least Christmas brought a brief variation to the diet, thanks to Red Cross parcels. As the war got worse for the Germans, so did the food they provided. Most of the kriegies thought they'd die if they ever saw another shred of sauerkraut.

Frank Tams:

   'Life as a POW is dull and frustrating. Christmas Eve was the only time of the year at which we really escaped. A bugler was allowed to open his hut door and play "Silent Night"; for once the camp was absolutely still. He was a very good bugler, but it would not have mattered if he had been appalling as we were all at home in England, New Zealand, Australia or, in his case, South Africa, thinking of our loved ones and hoping that next year we would be there in person. You could have heard a pin drop.

   'For many of us the cry as each Christmas arrived was "Home for Christmas", because to accept a period of longer than twelve months was too much to bear.'

New Year's Eve was celebrated with a moonshine whiskey party – Cookie Long's raisin and sugar concoction was getting better each time. However, this was to be the last such party in the compound. One young prisoner got very drunk and wasn't in his own block when lockup time came around. Later that night, he decided to climb out of a window and slip back to his own quarters. Unfortunately the dog patrol found him. After the German Shepherd had given his arm a good mauling, the handler emptied his pistol at him, missing completely except for one bullet in the stomach. The officer lived, but there was no more heavy drinking after that.

With the coming of New Year, the escape committee thought it was sufficiently safe to restart the excavation of Harry. The ground was hard and snow-covered on the surface, and the ferrets were relatively relaxed.

Harry had been left with a completed shaft and a tunnel already getting on for thirty metres long. Dick, at twenty metres but partly filled in with sand from Tom, would now, with the cleared compound to the west, have had to go about 160 metres to reach the safety of the trees. It was therefore decided to abandon Dick except as a storage facility, and to concentrate on Harry. If Harry were sprung, work could, at a pinch, be reactivated on Dick. Harry had a slightly less secure trap than Dick, set in the north-western corner of Block 104, but no German would think 104 could be chosen as the start of an escape route, as it was only a few metres from the main gate.

The weather had become warmer, and the ferrets were on patrol again. Nevertheless, on 10 January 1944, it was decided to reopen Harry. Pat Langford, its *Trapführer*, had done such a good job sealing it when it was shut down, that it took two hours to break into it again.

They found the tunnel in better condition than they might have hoped. The bypass valve on the airshaft to the pump had done its job well, and down below the air was relatively fresh. There were only a few leaks of sand and no falls, though some of the shoring boards needed replacing as they had warped. The trolley ropes had to be changed, and the kitbags that made the bellows of the pump had rotted, and had to be replaced. The ventilation system attached to it needed some attention, but in four days the tunnel had been over-hauled, and it was possible to start digging again.

By the end of January, Harry had passed the thirty-metre mark, and the first halfway house, known as Piccadilly, was carved out. It lay, ironically, just under the cooler, and if you listened carefully you could just hear the faint noise of guards' boots on the concrete above. But as the tunnel was under the *Vorlager*, work had to be conducted as quietly as possible.

The perennial problem of dispersal was even more acute at this time of year, with the whole compound covered in dirty snow. Also, penguins could scarcely shuffle around in the late afternoon, when the digging shifts ended, because by that time of day it was already dark in winter, and no excuse could be found for any prisoners to be outside, certainly not in numbers.

After considering the problem, the escape committee came to a conclusion that wasn't very popular: the theatre, unlike the other blocks, was built on solid brick foundations, and there was a gap of about a metre between its floor and the ground beneath. That space would provide a perfect dumping-ground for the sand from Harry. Those who ran the theatre argued, however, that if the Germans discovered that it was being used as part of an escape attempt, it would be closed, and an important, if not vital ingredient in the constant fight against boredom would be lost, dealing at the same time a serious blow to morale. The escape committee and the Senior British Officer took the argument on board, but overruled it. There was nowhere else for the sand to go, and to attempt to escape, in the absence of orders to the contrary (and none had yet been received from MI9 or any other outside source), remained a POW's first duty. The war still showed no sign of ending; there was still no Western Front, and the Germans were not only defending themselves well, but occasionally putting up extremely telling counter-attacks. Trained aircrew could still be of use to the war effort in action.

To prepare the theatre for its secret role as a sandpit, a trap was dug under one of the seats and the area beneath demarcated into dumping areas. Jimmy James and another officer, Ian Cross, were put in charge of directing the dispersal, which involved an overall team of eighty men, working between 6.00 p.m. and lights-out at 10.00 p.m. A constant stream of people from Block 104 to the theatre for four hours every night was obviously out of the question, so traffic was cautious and broken up, and there was none on nights of a full moon, when the snow reflected the moonlight back so well that the guards in the watch-towers scarcely had need of their searchlights. Luckily, Herbert Massey had persuaded von Lindeiner to permit prisoners to take exercise if they wished outside in the compound until lockup at 10.00 p.m.

As they worked, rehearsals and performances went on in the theatre as always. The pantomime that year opened at the beginning of February: *Treasure Island*.

With the re-opening of Harry, and the thought that freedom might once more not be too far away, the mood among the British, Colonial and West European officers lightened somewhat. That feeling wasn't shared by many of those from Eastern Europe. Reports of the Russian advance, gradual but inexorable, came to the camp via the BBC, and some of them wondered what their countries would be like in the post-war world. Most of them were aware of Stalin's ambitions, and weren't convinced that he'd let go of what he'd gained control over when the hostilities were at an end.

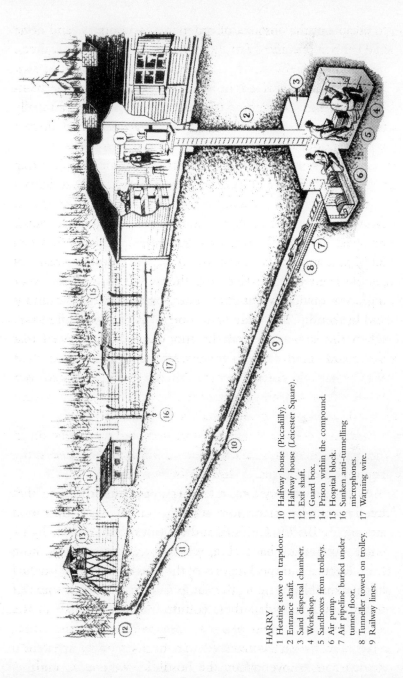

HARRY
1 Heating stove on trapdoor.
2 Entrance shaft.
3 Sand dispersal chamber.
4 Workshop.
5 Sandboxes from trolleys.
6 Air pump.
7 Air pipeline buried under
  tunnel floor.
8 Tunneller towed on trolley.
9 Railway lines.
10 Halfway house (Piccadilly).
11 Halfway house (Leicester Square).
12 Exit shaft.
13 Guard box.
14 Prison within the compound.
15 Hospital block.
16 Sunken anti-tunnelling
   microphones.
17 Warning wire.

They continued to contribute wholeheartedly to the escape effort, however, and Harry progressed so well (the experience of building Tom stood everyone in good stead) that by the middle of February it had doubled its length to sixty metres or more, and it was time to excavate a second halfway house: Leicester Square. Harry was two-thirds of the way to completion, and Leicester Square sat right under the outer *Vorlager* wire. There had been setbacks: at one point Harry had run out of true to the right, and it'd taken an extra ten metres of digging to put it straight; but on the whole everyone was pleased with what they had achieved.

Because it was full moon, operations were suspended, and the escapers took advantage of the lull to set about replenishing supplies. One of their problems was that their supply of electric cable was running out. Luckily, von Lindeiner had ordered loudspeakers to be set up in the camp so that the POWs could benefit from hearing German military music and the triumphant news from the front as broadcast by the Nazi radio. Two reels of wire, left lying around for too long by the electricians installing the loudspeakers, promptly disappeared. Then everyone waited with bated breath to see if there would be any reaction to the theft, but there was none, and the prisoners concluded that the workers had been too frightened of the consequences to report their loss.

As it was winter, the electricity supply in the compound was switched on for more hours than in the summer, and it was possible to work in Harry by electric light for the early and late hours of the daily shift. The cable was a godsend since electric light could now be extended right up to the workface, and there was enough left over to light the whole tunnel when it was completed. However, the diggers were working under enormous strain, because Rubberneck's ferrets were very much on the alert. There were spot checks on blocks at all hours, and the outer blocks – those nearest the wire – were especially targeted. In the meantime there were problems in the tunnel itself – Wally Floody was partially buried yet again, a bedboard fell from the top of the shaft and almost brained Cookie Long, and someone else dropped a metal jug, used for transferring sand from trolley-box to kitbag, down the shaft onto Floody's head, which put him out of action for a day or so. Down in Dick's shaft, the carpenters were suffering the effects of breathing in the smoke of fat-lamps all day – one or two developed minor breathing complaints, and another developed conjunctivitis and had to be taken to the hospital. His place was taken by the one coloured officer in the compound – a Maori, Flying Officer Porokoru Patapu Pohe.

Luckily the escape committee still had several tame goons – in fact, they seemed to be coming back as 1944 brought little good war news to the Germans. They were able to give warnings of ferret raids, and though Block 104 was turned over a couple of times, nothing was found, though the ferrets showed a disquieting interest in the tiled stove supports. Block 110 was also searched, though nothing was found in the library – the ferrets neglected to open the books – and one morning Bushell, Day and Floody were called out of roll-call and strip-searched. Extraordinarily, the Germans then brought in a dowser, an old man who wandered round the camp with his divining rod, followed by Rubberneck and the security officer, Broili, but turned up nothing at all. He'd walked past Block 104 without even pausing.

The dowser retreated to the sound of mocking laughter, but although the Germans in charge of the North Compound might often appear to be amiable incompetents at best and spinelessly disloyal to their country at worst (though to the great advantage of the kriegies), higher up the line of command, dark clouds were gathering. At the end of February, on an initiative from Himmler's office, Field Marshal Keitel issued the order named *Stufe Römisch III*. By this command, in future all escapers, other than those of British or American nationality, should be handed over on recapture not back to the prison camp system, but to the Gestapo. British and American escapers were to be held in police or military jails until High Command decided whether or not they should be returned to their camp, or sent to the Gestapo. Furthermore, the recapture of officers was henceforward to be treated as secret. Recaptured officers were officially to be reported as 'escaped and *not* recaptured'. As if this decree were not chilling enough, only a week or so later a further directive came from the desk of SS General Heinrich Müller in Berlin. Müller was Himmler's right-hand man, the co-author with his chief of the extermination programme for Jews in the concentration camps, and at the time head of the State Security Head Office Department IV, responsible for counter-intelligence and the extirpation of resistance and dissident groups within the Reich. The department's twenty-seven sub-departments had responsibility for everything from countering sabotage to dealing with the 'questions' of Jews, Catholics, Freemasons, Communists and others.

Müller's directive had yet another fanciful name, but more straightforward than its predecessors: the *Kugel* ('bullet') Order stated that recaptured officers, other than British and American nationals, were to be taken in chains to Mauthausen Concentration Camp. By that stage in the war, transfer to a concentration camp was a death sentence. The receiving camps – Mauthausen was in fact one of several – were given instructions to shoot the arriving officers before even entering them in the camp's books.

At about the same time, Gestapo officials visited Stalag-Luft III and intimated to von Lindeiner that any escapers would suffer harsher punishment than two weeks in the cooler from now on. Even lip-service to the Geneva Convention had been thrown out of the window, though it is difficult to this day to understand the workings of a mind as degenerate and criminal as Himmler's, who at the same time had SS staff in secret negotiation with the American secret service in Switzerland, in the hope of saving his own neck when the inevitable defeat came.

News of the decrees filtered through to the officer staff of the camp, and those who maintained friendly links with the prisoners went out of their way to warn them of what was going on, though they could only do so obliquely. Pieber mentioned to John Marshall that prisoners should avoid planning big breaks because that would provide the Gestapo with the excuse they were looking for to take over, and similar messages were received from other tame goons by their contacts. Von Lindeiner himself did his best to dissuade them from any more thoughts of escape. He summoned all the senior officers, doctors and chaplains in the camp and told them, 'The public temper outside is running very high, particularly against Allied Air Forces, and escapers may suffer harsh consequences. The war may be over in a year or two. It is not worth taking unnecessary risks now.' Many POWs refused to believe what they heard, though the news brought a certain disquiet.

The consensus was not to abandon the plan, whatever the risks, and teams of two began to form in anticipation of the escape, as Harry neared completion. Gordon Brettell and the Canadian Kingsley Brown decided to pair up again, travelling this time not as steel workers but as forestry students, which would give them good cover for marching through the woods. They would travel as Bulgarians again: there were many Bulgarian workers in Greater Germany, and as few Germans spoke Bulgarian, it was hoped, as before, that the assumed nationality would cover any faults in either Brettell's or Brown's German accents. Cookie Long decided to go with one of the youngest airmen in the camp, Tony Bethell. They planned to travel to the Baltic disguised as French workers, and there try to get to Sweden. Two of the Norwegians, Espelid and Fuglesang, were also aiming for Sweden, as were Arnold Christensen and his team-mate, Jimmy Catanach, a twenty-three-year-old squadron leader in the Royal Australian Air Force, who spoke fluent German. Two more Norwegians, Per Bergsland and Jens Muller (who had perfected the air pumps) aimed to reach Stettin, posing as Norwegian guest-workers for the industrial giant, Siemens.

The Lithuanian Flight Lieutenant Romas 'Rene' Marcinkus teamed up with Tim Walenn, who was leaving control of the forgery department to Alex Cassie. Walenn, who didn't speak a foreign language, was travelling as a Lithuanian. Marcinkus could only hope that if they were questioned, the Germans who did so would have no Lithuanian themselves.

Alex Cassie, who'd shared a room with Walenn, Plunkett, Brettell, Henri Picard and a mapmaker called Tony Hayter, all of whom were going out, stayed behind because he'd been down Harry's shaft and knew that his claustrophobia might freeze him up in the tunnel and impede the others' getaway. His room-mates left messages with him for their families, should they not make it. Harry Day, now almost forty-six years old and one of the most senior men involved, who was looking forward to yet another attempt at getting home (it would be his seventh), took as his running-mate another older officer, the thirty-eight-year-old Flight Lieutenant Pavel Tobolski. Tobolski was a German-speaking Pole, and for their cover they had decided that he would pose as a German NCO escorting Day, travelling as an Irish army officer working for the Germans. (The Republic of Eire was neutral during the war, but memories of British treatment of the Irish in the nineteenth and early twentieth centuries were fresh enough for many Irishmen to side with Germany against

Great Britain.) They had a contact in Berlin, an anti-fascist couple whose lodger, a young Dane, supposedly had Resistance contacts. Jimmy James intended to head down to Turkey via Greece, travelling with a Greek officer, Sotiris Skanziklas. Roger Bushell finally teamed up with an officer of the Free French forces, Lieutenant Bernard Scheidhauer, who'd worked in Valenta's intelligence group. Valenta was also making the escape attempt, having been given his *congé* by MI9. And John Dodge had no intention of being left behind.

Bushell and the escape committee intended that two hundred men should make the escape attempt through Harry; but over six hundred prisoners had been involved in the preparation of the escape, and there were just over five hundred applications for places to be considered. The only way to whittle this figure down to two hundred was by a series of ballots, which took place late in February 1944. The first one hundred names in the draw were those of men whose contribution to the work of the escape was outstanding, and/or those who, by virtue of their linguistic skills, or nationality, or knowledge of the territory, had the best chances of actually making it home. The remaining 410 names belonged to the rest of X-Organisation's workers. Eight additional names, belonging to the compound's administrative and entertainments staff, were put into the hat. These last had not contributed directly to the escape attempt, but without their contribution to the day-to-day running of the camp, the work could not have gone ahead so smoothly; and it was felt that this should be recognised. Once the two hundred had been selected, the exit order was decided by giving the first thirty places to train travellers with the best chances of successful escape, the next forty to the most prominent escape workers, and the last thirty to the next most important workers. The remaining places were determined by a general ballot among the rest of the applicants, and to the final two hundred Bushell added another twenty whom the escape committee thought deserved to be given a chance, but whose numbers in the ballot hadn't come up. Escape order also took into account pairs of men who had already formed teams.

There was still much organisation to do within the list. Experienced diggers who could put up with extended time underground were designated as 'haulers' – their job, acting in relays, would be to station themselves at Piccadilly and Leicester Square, and pull twenty escapers each through on the trolleys before leaving themselves. All those who had drawn a number successfully had to go into Harry to get a feeling for the place if they hadn't been down before. This meant a final revision of the people going as a handful, like Paul Brickhill, faced the fact that their sense of claustrophobia was too strong to allow them to go. Like Cassie, in the interest of the others, he withdrew.

Once the list of escapers had been established, a kind of euphoria swept through the camp, though clearly there were many disappointed POWs. It was, after all, nearly a year since the move to the North Compound, when preparations for the great day, now close, first began. For those who were on the list, this was a time when it was scarcely possible not to look forward to being reunited with loved ones, and to the chance of getting on with one's life at last. Neither Pavel Tobolski nor Wellington bomber pilot Jack Grisman had ever seen their infant children, born after they had been captured; Dennis Cochran, already one of the keenest to get out and back into the fight, heard that his mother had died suddenly in July 1943, aged only forty-three. After he'd received the news, his letters home indicated how urgently he felt the need to get home to his father and younger brother and sister to 'look after them'. Many missed sweethearts and fiancées, and were anxious about what such a long separation would have done to their relationships. Roger Bushell, still only a squadron leader in captivity, was shocked when another squadron leader arrived in Stalag-Luft III after Bushell had been a prisoner for over two years. Bushell knew him from his operational days: then, the man had been a lowly aircraftman engineer. But Bushell did not have time to brood on this. As escape-day drew inevitably closer, he became more aware of the eyes of the Germans on him. They had always paid particular attention to him, but he was not going to do anything to jeopardise the operation which now stood at the centre of his life. To his other 'cover' activities, he now took on the role of Henry Higgins in a production of *Pygmalion* which was just going into rehearsal. It was due to open at the end of March. Bushell's understudy was told to learn his lines carefully.

Harry was nearing completion. The surveyors assured the escape committee that it would soon reach its correct length. All that then remained would be for the exit shaft to be dug, and shored and sealed a short distance below the surface. The next thing to be decided on was the day – or rather, the night – of the escape itself. Once settled, it could not be altered, for many of the relevant documents would have to bear that date, and would be useless if not used then.

Before the escape committee could finalise the date, fate struck a couple of blows. The first was the news, through a tame goon, that Rubberneck was taking two weeks' leave from the beginning of March. This was good news: in his absence security was bound to lapse slightly and that would provide the opportunity to finish Harry except for the last bit, which would be broken through on the night of the escape. But the day before his departure, Rubberneck came into the compound at roll-call with a troop of guards and the security officer, Broili, and called out nineteen names. The designated prisoners were ordered to remain after roll-call had been dismissed. The number included Wally Floody, George Harsh, Peter Fanshawe, and several other mainstays of X-Organisation. They were searched, told to pack, and then marched off to the satellite camp of Belaria, five miles distant.

The loss of so many key members of the organisation could have been worse. Robert Ker-Ramsay took over from Floody as head of the tunnelling operation; but the re-organisation of escaping pairs, which had been disrupted by Rubberneck's selection, had to be achieved quickly, and the order of escapers duly rearranged. Gordon Brettell had lost his partner, and now paired with Henri Picard; Tom Kirby-Green paired with Canadian Flying Officer Gordon Kidder, and a handful of other regroupings took place, luckily with the minimum of fuss. For those removed to Belaria, it seemed a bitter blow. Had they known what was to come, they might have thanked their lucky stars.

Rubberneck's departure was a boon, and no sooner had he left than the tunnelling operation was reorganised and accelerated. The last thirty metres of Harry were dug out in the first nine days of March, and a chamber six metres long was prepared at the base of what was to be the exit shaft. The surveyors reckoned that the distance from the trap to the edge of the woods was 100.5 metres; Harry was now, by their reckoning, 104.5 metres long. The exit should therefore come up well within the forest.

The next job was to dig up to the surface. The risk of sandfalls now was very high indeed, so the work was undertaken only by the most experienced excavators. The excavation took until 14 March, and it was completed leaving an estimated sixty centimetres or so to the surface. The two diggers who finished the job just after roll-call that evening were Lester 'Johnny' Bull and 'Red' Noble. As they worked, they suddenly heard a loud rumbling which echoed through the tunnel below. It was the reverberations from a lorry driving along the road that ran between the outer northern fence of the compound and the forest. It sounded closer than it should. They worked on, and deciding that they'd dug far enough upwards, Bull pushed a broken length of fencing foil through the earth above his head to gauge how far they'd have to dig when they 'broke' the tunnel. To his surprise, and even horror, he saw from the markings he'd made on the foil that they weren't sixty, but only fifteen centimetres from the surface. Thanking God that he hadn't dug any further, for guards patrolled the outer perimeter of the camp and there were ferret 'hides' at the edge of the forest, he told Noble of his discovery. Luckily, the earth above didn't cave in, and they shored up the top of the exit shaft firmly.

The fact that the lorry had sounded so close was more serious. The escape committee would have to reckon with the possibility that Harry was not as long as had been estimated: it might come out short of the trees. But the calculations still seemed to check out. There was nothing to do but hope for the best.

After Bull and Noble had resurfaced in Block 104, Pat Langford sealed the trap with even more than his usual care, and washed the floor around it. Then, everything that was not essential to the escape, and superfluous tunnelling equipment, was either burned or hidden down the shaft of Dick.

The work had been completed in the nick of time. On the following day, Rubberneck returned from leave and immediately turned over Block 104 with a troop of ferrets; they found nothing, but the fact that he'd gone specifically for 104 was worrying. Did he have his own intelligence source? Or was he acting on a hunch? But with compounds now to the south and west, the only blocks which could contain tunnels were those on the north and east sides of the North Compound.

Excitement mounted. With the tunnel now complete, it

was logical that it should be used at the first possible opportunity, since every day that passed increased the risk of its
discovery, even though no-one would now go down it again,
except for one or two routine checks, until the night of the
break. Some kriegies were foolhardy enough to mention it
obliquely in their letters home, though luckily with enough
subtlety not to arouse the suspicions of the censors. Bushell
impressed on everyone the imperative need to keep up a
show of normality. With the grudgingly approaching spring,
some sporting activity resumed, and performances began in
the theatre of a production of *Arsenic and Old Lace*. Some of
the men started preparing their gardens for a spring planting
of vegetables, which they sincerely hoped they'd never see
grow.

Mingled with the excitement was tension. Tim Walenn
was keeping to his bunk, faking illness to avoid having to
turn up for roll-call. The reason for this was that he wanted
to keep an eye on the bag of rubber stamps that would be
needed for the documents the moment the date for the
escape had been decided on. The stamps, and much other
equipment which would be needed at a moment's notice,
would normally have been hidden securely down Dick's
shaft, but the time required to retrieve it from there was a
luxury they couldn't now afford. In the event, it was just
as well that Walenn didn't turn up for roll-call on the cold
morning of 20 March. All his other room-mates in Block
120 – Plunkett, Cassie, Picard and the others – had left.
Standing outside, Plunkett suddenly realised to his horror
that he'd left his notebook – the notebook containing all
the names of escapers with a note of which maps they'd
need – on his bunk. The situation wasn't helped when a
troop of guards suddenly appeared and surrounded Block
120: evidently there was going to be a raid. Thinking on
his feet, he passed the word to his friends. By now the

guards were entering 120. Plunkett and several others now asked the guards if they'd mind passing out their shower kits, which they'd left behind since they hadn't known that they were to be taken to the showers that morning. The guards agreed, and while they were busy doing this, Plunkett managed to speak to Walenn through the window and tell him what was up. Walenn quickly retrieved the notebook, stuck it into the bag of rubber stamps, and hid the whole lot in Plunkett's shower kit, which he gave to a guard, who gave it to Plunkett. The raid on Block 120 revealed nothing, but it had been a very close shave indeed. No-one told Bushell about it.

The escape committee had narrowed the night of the break down to one of two dates at the end of the month. Moonless nights would be between 23 and 25 March, but 25 March was no good because it was a Saturday. That would have meant catching trains on a Sunday, when the rail service was slower and fewer trains ran. So the break would be made, all other things being equal, on the night of Thursday 23 or Friday 24 March. Otherwise, they'd have to wait a month for the next new moon.

Ker-Ramsay and Marshall, as the chief tunnel experts, began to inspect escapers' kit, especially suitcases, to make sure that none was too big to go through the tunnel easily. They also instructed the escapers on how to lie completely flat on the trolleys, head down, kit in front, elbows tight to their sides. Above all, there was to be no panic. Panic cost time. If a trolley should spill, the directive was to get off it and push it to the nearest halfway house to get it back on the rails. There was no room in the tunnel itself for any manoeuvre which might risk knocking shoring loose and causing a fall of sand.

Everyone on the escape had to parade in the clothes he was escaping in, with his full escape kit. Anything not strictly necessary was removed. Each man's requirements for maps and documents were checked and double-checked.

Marshals were appointed and given special instructions in the lie of the land immediately around the compound. Their job was to lead escapers in groups of ten safely away from the camp, as far as the railway line that led to Sagan Station, before they split up. It was about 1.5 kilometres from the compound to the track. Travellers by rail had special instructions to make their own way through the woods to the station. To catch the correct trains and therefore make the right subsequent connections, their timing would have to be very exact.

Every escaper was briefed by one of the experts on the countries he would be passing through. Those travelling to Czechoslovakia Valenta taught to say in Czech: 'I swear by the death of my mother that I am a British officer.' They were assured that everyone they came across would believe this oath. Where possible, contact addresses for Resistance fighters and the owners of safe houses were distributed, and Des Plunkett handed out the maps necessary for each man. Nearly four thousand maps had been printed. Al Hake and his men had produced 250 compasses. Tommy Guest's tailoring department had made fifty complete hand-stitched suits for the escapers who were travelling as businessmen by train, and many more workmen's outfits and a handful of uniforms. Travis' department had manufactured water bottles for most of the escapers, especially the 'hardarsers' who would be making their way on foot. In Block 112, small cans of high-energy concentrated escape food, nicknamed 'fudge', had been prepared in their hundreds, mainly for use by the hardarsers. Train travellers tried to carry food bearing the labels of manufacturers within Greater Germany. Anything that might have come out of a Red Cross parcel would raise suspicions during a police search.

Jack Lyon was realistic about the real purpose of the 'hardarsers':

'My chances were virtually nil. In high summer, a walker could have done the distance. I could have probably walked to the Czech frontier or possibly even to the Swiss frontier, sleeping by day and walking at night. But you couldn't do that with temperatures going down to minus 10° Celsius and with snow to contend with. The clothing I had would not have protected me. We were not allowed to take greatcoats, bed rolls or blankets. You couldn't lie up in those temperatures and then there is the question of food. You couldn't take much food with you and you couldn't live off the country in midwinter.

'The chances would have been minimal in good conditions but absolutely impossible in those sorts. No-one really expected this category to make it, but that wasn't the objective, was it? It was just the fact that it was going to contribute to the success of the whole operation – the more people on the loose at the same time, the more confusion and difficulties for the Germans. The "hardarsers" were for the nuisance value. If they got home, good luck to them, but they were really just extras, shall we say. They were sacrificed like the slaves to save the patricians.'

Finally, Herbert Massey gave a brief talk to the escapers, wishing them god-speed but warning them, as von Lindeiner had earlier, not to expect too friendly a reception if caught. Allied air raids were exacting a heavy toll on Germany, and the civilian population was suffering from them too. Enemy aircrew were objects of hatred in Germany.

At last everything was ready. The cold snap had brought a snowfall with it, and on the morning of 23 March it lay fifteen centimetres deep, but the air was mild again, and the escape committee's meteorological adviser, Flying Officer Len Hall, forecast cloud-cover, lower temperatures and some wind over the next couple of days. The atmosphere at the escape committee meeting that morning was charged. Harry's trap was warping, and soon it would be obvious even to Dopey, the dimmest of the ferrets, that something was not quite right in Block 104. Even though the hardarsers would have a tough time ploughing through the snow in the woods, and leave very obvious tracks, if they risked leaving Harry unused any longer – let alone another month – it would certainly be discovered, and a year's work would have gone to waste. Bushell, as leader of the enterprise, also accepted that it was the act of escaping as much as the number of successful getaways achieved that counted. Anything that tied German manpower up was a blow for the Allied war effort.

He couldn't have known the degree of risk he and his fellow escapers would be taking. He couldn't have known how soon the Western front would finally open, with devastating consequences for Germany; nor that, in September 1944, MI9/IS9 would issue a directive to all POWs that escaping was no longer considered a duty. But even if he had, it's unlikely that he would have abandoned the project.

At the meeting, Ker-Ramsay said that he'd need half-a-day's notice to get Harry primed and ready. Walenn needed a similar amount of time to get all the documents date-stamped. Bushell said he'd let them know; they'd have another meeting in the morning. Most of them must have known anyway that if they weren't going that night, the following night would have to be the one. Few slept soundly that Thursday night, which passed in the deep silence of another heavy snowfall.

They reconvened at 11.30 a.m. on Friday in Block 101. Ten minutes later they'd made their decision. The big breakout was on for that night.

Chapter Seven

IT WAS A FINE MORNING, AN AUSPICIOUS MORNING. As
soon as the decision had been taken, Tim Walenn set the
team to work date-stamping all the papers and travel
documents and sorting them into piles for each individual
escaper. Meanwhile Ker-Ramsay, who wasn't going, as Massey
had decreed that some experienced tunnellers should remain
behind for the next shot, took his 'miners' and went down
Harry for the last time before the escape to check that all
was well and make the final preparations. He hung two blankets a metre apart across the mouth of the tunnel where it
debouched into the exit chamber, in order to muffle sound
and block light – the tunnel during the escape would have
escapers in it virtually nose-to-tail; it would be fully lit, and
the trolleys would be rumbling up and down it like tube
trains. The floors of both entrance and exit shafts were
carpeted with blankets to deaden sound, as were both halfway
houses, though here the principal purpose was to keep the
haulers' clothes as clean as possible. As it was, it would be
hard enough to look like a respectable businessman after
crawling through one hundred metres of narrow tunnel ten
metres underground. Sound was also deadened by nailing
thin strips of blanket to the rails for the first and last fifteen
metres or so. Additional lights were rigged to make the tunnel

as light as possible: the escape committee knew that there would be several escapers who would experience claustrophobia despite themselves: the lighter it was, the more their fear would be eased. The shoring was carefully checked and reinforced where necessary, and any warped boards were replaced. A special wooden shovel – designed to minimise noise – was taken to the exit end of the tunnel to use in making the final break out. The trolleys were strengthened and a stout rope attached to them, 'borrowed' from the compound's boxing ring.

The Little X in each block now had the duty of making individual final kit inspections, and of collecting and distributing travel documents, passports, and other papers. A large number of escapers would have to move to Block 104 after evening roll-call. To avoid drawing special attention to this, the normal traffic in and out of the block had been monitored for several days. This information had been used to work out a schedule whereby each escaper had a specific time given to him to leave his block and make his way to 104. Each Little X synchronised watches with his fellows in order to make this migration as precise as possible.

The tension was bad enough for those with plenty to do: if anything it was worse for those who simply had to pretend that this was just another normal day at the camp. By noon, every POW in the compound knew that the escape was on. Tension is a very easy thing to sense, and it was crucial that the Germans should get no hint of it. There were lectures and language classes as usual, but fewer people turned up for them than normal: a five-a-side football game took place, but the players seemed listless. One place that was busy as usual was the theatre, where the production of *Pygmalion* was about to take place. Bushell's understudy, Ian McIntosh, had someone read him through his lines as Henry Higgins twice. Bushell, travelling in the guise of a French businessman, would

Sonderausgabe

zum

Deutschen Kriminalpolizeiblatt

Herausgegeben vom Reichskriminalpolizeiamt in Berlin

Erscheint nach Bedarf	Zu beziehen durch die Geschäftsstelle Berlin C 2, Werderscher Markt 5—6

16. Jahrgang	Berlin, den 16. Juni 1943	Nummer 4610

Nur für deutsche Behörden bestimmt!
Die Sonderausgaben sind nach ihrer Auswertung sorgfältig zu sammeln und unter Verschluß zu halten.

A. Neuausschreibungen.

Entwichene kriegsgefangene Offiziere.

I. Flucht von britischen und amerikanischen Fliegeroffizieren aus dem Luftwaffenlager 3 in Sagan (Schlesien).

Von den aus dem Luftwaffenlager 3 in Sagan (Schlesien) entwichenen 26 britischen und amerikanischen Fliegeroffizieren sind **noch flüchtig:**

Hill, William, Ltn., 21. 9. 15 ?, Gef.-Nr. 1369/Stalag Luft 3;
Morison, Walter, Hptm., 26. 11. 19 London, Gef.-Nr. 476/Stalag Luft 3;

Stower, John Gifford, Obltn., 15. 9. 16 Ingenio La Esperanza (Argentinien), Gef.-Nr. 836/Stalag Luft 3;
Welch, Patrick, Obltn., 12. 8. 16 Dorset, Gef.-Nr. 610/Stalag Luft 3.

Morison, Stower und Welch sind hierunter abgebildet.
Weitere energische Fahndung! Festnahme!

16. 6. 43.   **KPLSt Breslau.**

Walter Morison   John Stower   Patrick Welch

A wanted poster issued by the Germans following the mass break-out in June 1943. John Stower made it to the Swiss border before being picked up.

German officers inspect the entrance to an escape tunnel at Stalag-Luft III. The attitude towards escaping prisoners changed dramatically during the course of the war.

Tom's discovery: the German guard Karl Griese, known as 'Rubberneck', was one of the keenest ferrets.

One of the lucky ones: Alex Cassie stayed behind because he suffered from claustrophobia.

Jack Lyon just missed going out in the Great Escape – and survived the war as a result.

Les Brodrick (right), pictured with his brother Stanley who served in the Navy, and (below) his Lancaster bomber after it had been shot down.

Arch-escaper Jimmy James, who ended up in Sachsenhausen concentration camp after being recaptured.

JIMMY JAMES

Bob van der Stok, one of only three prisoners not to be recaptured. He finally made his way through France and over the Pyrenees to Spain.

IAN LE SUEUR

The specially commissioned painting of the Great Escape, which is exhibited in the Royal Canadian Air Force Memorial Museum and

EVANS, B.
R.A.F. ENGLAND

FUGALSANG, N.
R.A.F. NORWAY

GOUWS, J.
S.A.A.F. SOUTH AFRICA

GRISMAN, W.
R.A.F. ENGLAND

GUNN, A.
R.A.F. ENGLAND

HAKE, A.
R.A.A.F. AUSTRALIA

HALL, C.
R.A.F. ENGLAND

HAYTER, A.
R.A.F. ENGLAND

HUMPHRIES, E.
R.A.F. ENGLAND

KIERATH, R.
R.A.A.F. AUSTRALIA

KIRBY-GREEN, T.
R.A.F. ENGLAND

KROL, S.Z.
R.A.F. POLAND

LEIGH, T.
R.A.F. ENGLAND

McGARR, A.
S.A.A.F. SOUTH AFRICA

MARCINKUS, R.
R.A.F. LITHUANIA

STOWER, J.
R.A.F. ENGLAND

STREET, D.
R.A.F. ENGLAND

TOBOLSKI, P.
R.A.F. POLAND

VALENTA, E.
R.A.F. CZECHOSLAVKIA

WALENN, G.W.
R.A.F. ENGLAND

WERNHAM, J.
R.C.A.F. CANADA

WILEY, G.
R.C.A.F. CANADA

WILLIAMS, J.F.
R.A.F. ENGLAND

WILLIAMS, J.E.A.
R.A.A.F. AUSTRALIA

features photos of the fifty men murdered on Hitler's direct orders.
RCAF MEMORIAL MUSEUM

Top: One of the crime-scene reconstructions that took place during the RAF's post-war investigation into the atrocity.

Above: Local Gestapo man Johannes Post during his trial. He was found guilty of murder and hanged in February 1948.

Left: Erich Zacharias, the man who shot Tom Kirby-Green. Zacharias was also hanged.

wear the grey suit he still had, which he'd smuggled in from Prague. It hung a little looser on him now.

Just before the escape, Tom Kirby-Green quickly scribbled his last letter home:

24th March 1944

My beloved adored darling,

I hope you are well and Colin too. My sweetheart, I am thinking so much of you now and I long so hard for you with every part of my soul and body. I am so lonely in my heart and a burning fire consumes my body longing to cool in the heat of yours, my darling lovely girl. I live only for the moment when I shall take you in my arms, arms which have been so sadly bereft of the softness of your waist and hips and thighs, as hungry have my lips been for yours and your lovely body. No love in the world can compare with ours, Maria. Darling love, how feeble are my words, how hard to express the wild tumult of my heart when I think of you. I feel so grateful for your love and tenderness and so humble, my girl, my darling love, and I shall be able to make the world a paradise for you with God's help, if love and adoring passion can bring joy for you and for Colin. God bless you and keep you Maria. I love you, darling, what more can I say?

Kisses to you,
Your Thomas

Most of the escapers hung around their rooms, smoking if they had cigarettes, or walked slowly round the perimeter of the compound. There was an occasional burst of too-hearty laughter when someone tried to crack a joke. Some attempted to lose themselves in a book, but found themselves reading the same sentence over and over again, unable to take anything in.

Just after six in the evening, Travis gave a last dinner party which he guaranteed would provide enough energy for days. It wasn't very appetising: fried corned beef and a concoction of boiled barley, dried milk, sugar and raisins. Several escapers joined him – Travis, on account of his claustrophobia, was not one of them – including Bushell and Bob van der Stok, but no-one ate or said much. All over the camp, those who were making the break were leaving letters and keepsakes behind with friends, to send to their families – just in case.

As the time for the migration approached, all the stooges took up their positions and tested their signalling system to one another. Soon afterwards, a Little X in one of the blocks gave the signal for the first man to go.

By the time Mike Casey reported to David Torrens, who was in charge of checking-in and room allocation in Block 104, the place was already filling up with escapers and the atmosphere was restive as everyone waited for the complement to be complete, so that the signal for the off could be given. Then Torrens and two assistants would call the escapers in order to ready themselves for the descent down Harry.

The place was crowded with an incongruous assortment of workers, railwaymen, and businessmen, sitting around clutching makeshift suitcases or bundles wrapped in blankets, checking and rechecking papers, passports and money, some chatting or trying to play cards, many smoking, others alone, staring into space. Casey found his berth and by the time he had another four or five men had arrived – the rate of flow was two a minute. So far all was going well. At about

7.45 p.m. Torrens got a shock when he looked up to see a Luftwaffe corporal approaching him down the corridor, but the man took off his cap and revealed himself to be Pavel Tobolski, who was travelling as Harry Day's German escort. If he can fool me, he can fool anybody, thought Torrens, checking him in.

Les Brodrick was among those waiting anxiously in hut 104:
'There was no room to sit on the beds or anything, we sat on the floor and people kept coming in and coming in and I was sitting there quietly and waiting and waiting and finally everybody was in. Then the Germans came round, shut the doors and put the barriers across. All the windows were open but all the lights were put out immediately inside the hut and we sat there all quiet and waited and waited and nothing seemed to be happening. It got so hot in there with all the bods that before long you could actually see steam coming out of the windows. We couldn't make out what was going on. Everyone was getting jittery asking "Why aren't we moving?", and it was obvious, of course, that there were all sorts of problems.

'I felt tired and fed up because there were so many delays. They didn't come and tell us what had happened, we just sat there and waited. We couldn't all chatter or anything; you just had to sit and think your thoughts. It was a hell of a long time to be sitting silently and just thinking. I felt a bit miserable, until the actual time came when my number was called ...'

At 8.30 p.m., exactly on schedule, Ker-Ramsay announced that the tunnel was ready. Torrens prepared to call the escapers in order and in groups, so that there would be no congestion. Another prisoner, Henry Lamond, took up a position

at the open trap to direct men down the shaft and regulate the flow in case of a hitch. Within ten minutes, the first batch were descending, led by Bull and Marshall, whose job it would be to break Harry at the far end. Then came Sydney Dowse, who would haul through the first twenty men to the bottom of the exit shaft, followed by Bushell and his partner Scheidhauer, then Valenta, and the men who would act as first haulers for Piccadilly and Leicester Square.

The first hitch was almost immediate. It took forty minutes for the tunnel to fill with the first batch of escapers, and it was only then that Bull could clamber up the exit shaft and break through the last fifteen centimetres of sandy soil that separated them from freedom. Once it was open, there had to be a steady stream of men from it out into the woods, and fast. To get two hundred men out (and they all knew that they'd be very lucky to achieve this), would take most of the night. Marshall remained in the chamber at the foot of the shaft as Bull climbed up the ladder into the darkness with the wooden shovel. Marshall expected to hear a whispered 'all clear' from Bull within a few minutes, but ten minutes passed, then another ten, before Bull came down again, sweat-stained and grubby. He was exhausted. The shoring boards at the top, which kept the earth from falling in, had swollen in the damp and were immovable. This was something no-one had expected. And precious time was passing. Back in the tunnel, crammed in the halfway house and at the base of each shaft, men waited and sweated, their clothes getting rumpled and dirty, their nerves fraying, and the sense of being buried alive beginning to creep up on some of them, especially when the lights flickered. The pump provided some air, and the open trap at one end helped, but with so many men down there the atmosphere was rapidly becoming fetid.

Marshall, who was travelling as a businessman and needed to keep clean, stripped off his suit carefully, thanking God they'd taken the time to construct an adequate chamber at the base of the escape shaft, though it was still cramped enough, and clambered up himself. Bull had not been exaggerating, but his efforts to loosen the boards, though in vain, had had some effect. Nevertheless it took Marshall another fifteen minutes to clear them, the job made more difficult by the fact that they had nothing except their hands to prise and lever the boards apart. The job done, he descended and let Bull climb up again to dig through the last few centimetres of soil.

It was now 10.15 p.m., but for the escapers at the base of the shaft panic soon gave way to relief as they felt a shower of earth and, soon afterwards, a breath of cold air which swept down and through the tunnel to the other end, bringing the good news to everyone that Harry was broken at last. The plan then was for Bull to get out, equipped with a blanket and a coil of rope, lie flat on the ground, make sure the coast was clear, and then give each man a tap on the head as he came up as the signal for the man to go. The blanket was for Bull to lie on. The rope he would give to the first man out, who would take one end and head a few metres into the wood. The rope would then act as a guide for the rest of the escapers to follow. The first of every ten men was a marshal: he'd make his way to a point in the trees where his group would meet him, then they'd disappear together. Bull's job would be taken over after ten men, and he'd then make his way into the woods to act as marshal for his group. His relief would then hand over after nine men, and become the next marshal, and so on. It should have gone like clockwork, but when Bull stuck his head out of the hole he'd made and gulped the keen night air that windy March night, he saw immediately that something had gone badly wrong.

He quickly descended again. Bushell, Marshall and the others could see from his expression that all was far from well. It emerged that the surveyors had miscalculated. Harry had broken between the road and the forest, in open snow-covered ground three metres short of the trees. The central watch-tower along the northern outer fence, which oversaw the main gate of the compound, was only fifteen metres south. The escapers had two things in their favour: the wind in the trees was very noisy; and the guards in the watch-tower would have their backs to them, as their job was to keep their eyes on the compound itself. Against that, the escapers would be badly exposed to regularly patrolling guards on the road for the short time it took for them to get from Harry's exit to the trees, and there could be no question of a man lying flat on the ground at the hole's mouth to control the departing escapers. But Bull had also noticed a ferret 'hide' nearby, just inside the trees, but luckily unoccupied at this time of night.

At the base of the shaft there was a fraught discussion, as everyone tried to keep control of his nerves. No-one wanted to abort an operation which was the culmination of a year's work for six hundred men. Some were for closing the hole and abandoning the escape until the extra few metres could be dug and a new exit created: there would be ample time for that between now and the next new moon. But would such favourable weather conditions coincide again? And what of Harry's trap, already so warped as to be now almost undis-guisable? And Rubberneck's clearly mounting suspicions? The clincher was that all the papers were date-stamped for use on Saturday 25 March. There was no way that Walenn's depart-ment could reproduce a new set of papers for everyone. So they decided to go ahead. The question remained, how to place a security man at the top without attracting the atten-tion of German patrols?

Then Bull had an idea: if they took up an extra length of rope, they could tie one end to the top of the exit ladder and run it across to the ferret-hide. The security man could shelter there and hold the other end. Escapers would wait at the top of the shaft with their hand on the rope. If they felt two tugs, they'd be clear to go, following the rope to the trees. There, Bull would have rigged the second rope leading into the trees for them to follow to the marshalling point. From the road, a thin rope across the snow wouldn't be visible. Bushell wrote the new instructions on a piece of paper and pinned it to the base of the exit ladder. The new instructions could be passed along by word of mouth, but they all knew what Chinese whispers could do, especially along a chain of two hundred men whose nerves were stretched to breaking point.

Jimmy James was one of the first 'hardarsers' to go through the tunnel:

'Finally the word came for us to go and it was a very exhilarating moment. Everybody was very excited. I had the feeling in the pit of my stomach that the guard might see me and shoot. You didn't know what was going to happen when you got out there. Climbing down the shaft was going thirty foot down, like down a ship's hold, then I was holding on to the trolley and being pulled up to the first halfway house. There I changed trolleys and was pulled up to the next one. Finally I was pulled up to the exit hole and I looked up and saw the stars. The RAF motto came to mind – *per ardua ad astra* – we had done a lot of work to get to this stage and now we were going up to the stars.'

The discussion had only taken fifteen minutes, but it was 10.30 p.m. by the time Bull went up the ladder again, closely followed by Marshall and the rest of the first group: two hours had passed already since Ker-Ramsay had officially declared Harry ready for action, and not a man was out yet.

In Block 104, some of the men with higher numbers were beginning to despair of getting out at all, though David Torrens sought to keep things calm by giving as adequate a report as he could as news was passed down the tunnel and up the entrance shaft to him. When the word came through that the first men were out and in the woods, the relief was almost as great as the previous tension, as at last a steady flow down through Harry's trap could begin. The men wished each other luck, promising to raise a glass to one another at the RAF Club in London in a couple of weeks' time. Alex Cassie was left alone in his room to reflect on the missed chance, though he knew in his heart that he had made the only decision open to him.

At the exit point, all was going well, though there was another hurdle to jump for those travelling by rail. Because of the delays, many of them had missed their trains, and faced a long wait at Sagan station. But there was nothing for it but to stick to their plans. They made it to the station in safety, though there was another problem there, because a subway entrance which should have been obvious had had a shelter built over it so recently that the intelligence unit had not heard of it. Consequently it took some of the escapers a while to locate it and make their way through it to the booking hall. There, they faced the added complication of seeing many of their number logjammed as they waited for trains. They had to pretend not to recognise each other. Luckily, there was quite a large number of other travellers despite the late hour, and they were able to mingle in the crowd. After what seemed an age, but was in fact barely half an hour, the express from Berlin to Breslau pulled in. The crowd at the station was thinner after that, and when the train pulled out, it had several escapers on board, including Des Plunkett, Roger Bushell and Bernard Scheidhauer.

Alex Cassie:

'Plunkett told me when I spoke to him years afterwards that he was in the train moving away from Sagan and Roger Bushell came along the corridor. As he went past he slipped his hand into Plunkett's and just gave it a slight squeeze. He didn't say anything, didn't look at him. Plunkett noticed that he was doing this to all the other kriegies who were standing in the train. This is Roger Bushell just saying, you know, he was still in charge and he wished them all the best and so on, thinking of them.'

They had been in the nick of time, as an Allied air-raid more or less coincided with their departure. The next arrivals at the station found it blacked-out, and Bob van der Stok, making his way alone through the woods, almost fell foul of a German soldier, who wanted to know what he was doing out in the open during a raid. Luckily van der Stok's German was fluent, and he passed himself off as a Dutch guest-worker who had got lost looking for shelter after the sirens had started. The German directed him to the subway entrance. Other escapers arrived to find the station in darkness, could not find the way to the subway, and watched helplessly from the edge of the woods as their trains came and went, slowing but not stopping at the station on account of the raid.

In the tunnel, new problems had arisen. The original estimate of one man through every three or four minutes had had to be revised. Some of the suitcases carried by the railway passengers were either too big, or, because their owners were nervous, they got jammed against the shoring as the trolleys were pulled through. This meant having to reverse the trolley to dislodge the case, but the only means of communication between the shafts and the halfway houses was to tug on the hauling rope. Inevitably there was confusion and more delay. If a trolley became derailed, as happened too frequently, the hauler next along had to crawl down the tunnel to reposition it on the rails, as its passenger lifted himself onto his toes and finger tips to make as much room for the manoeuvre as possible. Some plans had been settled on in advance for such contingencies, but others required instant improvisation. In the first hour, twenty-three men had got through, but the rate was slowing.

It was at about 11.30 p.m. that the air-raid sirens sounded. Air-raids meant blackouts, and instantly the electric power in the Stalag-Luft III was cut off. The tunnel was plunged into darkness. Down in the tunnel, Harry Day organised the lighting of the fat-lamps, which were there for just such an emergency, but several men panicked in the darkness, and it was a full half-hour before order was restored. Then a hauling rope snapped and had to be replaced. At the tunnel's entrance, Ker-Ramsay was beginning to make escapers shed some of their loads, for ease of passage, but it was clear now that the full two hundred wouldn't make it out. Privately, Ker-Ramsay wondered if they'd get even a hundred out. The only thing to do was to press on and get as many clear as possible. At least the escapers were helped by the fact that the whole camp, including the search-lights in the watch-towers, was also blacked out.

There was another setback soon afterwards when Tom Kirby-Green derailed his trolley between Piccadilly and Leicester Square. To save time, he decided to try to right it himself, but in his efforts he dislodged some shoring and brought down a metre of tunnel on top of him. The hauler in Leicester Square, Flying Officer Hank Birkland of the Royal Canadian Air Force, felt his rope tighten and looked down the tunnel towards Piccadilly. He couldn't see the line of fat-lamps all the way back, and knew there'd been a fall.

Leaving his position, he edged his way painfully down the track and reached the half-buried Kirby-Green, whom he carefully hauled clear. Then he pressed himself flat to the tunnel's floor while Kirby-Green crawled over him and on towards the exit shaft, cautiously pushing his kit ahead of him. After he'd gone, Birkland set about repairing the damage. No boards had snapped, so he was able to shovel back most of the sand and reshore, pummelling the excess sand as flat as he could between the rails. Then he righted the trolley and gave the signal for it to be pulled back to Piccadilly before working his way backwards to his own hauling station. He was exhausted. The job had taken a whole hour.

At least the air-raid was over and the lights now came back on. Then came two more falls, less serious, but still taking fifty minutes between them to fix. It was apparent that the falls were being caused by kit as much as nervous clumsiness. The hardarsers were going through now, and some of their blanket-rolls of kit were too thick, others too long. Ker-Ramsay noted that it was taking some of the men equipped with these rolls up to fifteen minutes to get through. He had a quick discussion with David Torrens and they decided that unless the blanket rolls were abandoned altogether, a realistic number of escapers would never get through. Although it would make life outside much harder for the hardarsers, it was decided to ditch the blanket-rolls. From now on escapers could only take what they could carry on them, and some, who'd put on too many layers of clothing, were obliged to take some off, in case they got wedged in the tunnel. Les Brodrick was the fifty-second man out. When he reached the base of the exit shaft, he found that he couldn't raise his legs to the rungs of the ladder, thirty centimetres or so above the ground, without becoming wedged in the shaft. He therefore had to haul himself up using only his arms. He was done in by the time he reached the surface, but had enough of an adrenalin charge left to make his way quickly to the shelter of the woods. He was followed by his travelling companion, Flying Officer Denys Street – the son of the British Permanent Under Secretary of State for Air – and they would be joined by Hank Birkland in their short-lived bid for freedom. The wind had dropped, and when he looked back from the woods, Brodrick saw a column of steam rising from Harry's exit. It seemed miraculous that no guard had spotted it.

Meanwhile, a fresh batch of escapers was beginning to gather at the station, waiting for the right trains to come in. One or two, including Bob van der Stok, had a close call when a female member of the camp's censor department showed a certain amount of suspicion and approached them, but they managed to allay her doubts. A number of camp guards about to go on leave were waiting for trains, which racked the nerves of the escapers further, but a group, including van der Stok, Dennis Cochran, Gordon Kidder and Tom Kirby-Green, managed to embark safely on the next Breslau train, which pulled out at 1.00 a.m. An hour later, Per Bergsland and Jens Muller, together with Rene Marcinkus, Walenn, now minus his huge RAF moustache, Picard and Brettell, boarded a train bound for Frankfurt-an-der-Oder. Harry Day and Pavel Tobolski had one of the longest waits, but finally caught their Berlin express at 3.15 a.m. Joining them were James Catanach, Arnold Christensen, Halldor Espelid and Nils Fuglesang.

At 4.00 a.m., Roy Langlois, number sixty to leave, was starting his turn at the ferret hide when he had to call a halt to the exit operation while the perimeter guard changed. Moments later, he had to crouch down and hold his breath while one of the guards in the watch-tower climbed down and wandered over to the edge of the trees to have a shit, not two metres from Harry's exit. Luckily, the wind had risen again and dispersed the steam, but the black hole against the snow seemed enormous to Langlois. But either the guard didn't look, or he was blinded by the glare of his searchlight, or the hole blended in with the shadows. Even so, it was another close shave.

As dawn approached, it grew colder. The escapers knew that very few more of them would manage to get out before daylight made an end of the operation. The guard made his way back to the watch-tower, and after waiting for a few minutes, Langlois gave two tugs on the rope.

Half an hour later, in Block 104, they decided that after 5.00 a.m. it would be too light to send any more men through. If everyone got clear, they'd have a few hours' start before morning roll-call. The last to go would therefore be number eighty-seven. In the meantime, still at his post in the ferret hide, Langlois could see the compound stirring to life, and felt that his nerves would snap at any moment. Lawrence Reavell-Carter was seventy-sixth out, followed by Flight Lieutenants Keith Ogilvie and Mick Shand. The seventy-ninth man, Squadron Leader Len Trent, waited at the top of the ladder in Harry's exit shaft. Behind him, the last eight men stood at the bottom, trying not to wonder if they weren't cutting it too fine.

Reavell-Carter had reached the trees when one of the perimeter guards left his route to relieve himself. He made straight for the tunnel mouth and, according to Len Trent, 'almost peed down the exit'. Langlois, Ogilvie and Shand, at the ferret hide, dropped to the ground, but the guard saw Shand and raised his rifle. Reavell-Carter stepped into the open and shouted to the guard in German not to shoot. This so startled the guard that he let fly anyway, but wildly. In the split-second confusion, Ogilvie and Shand plunged into the woods, but Reavell-Carter and Langlois raised their arms in surrender, as did Len Trent, already halfway out but too late to make a dash for it. The guard nearly jumped out of his skin, but quickly collected himself. Number eighty, Bob McBride, already in the mouth of the shaft, had no alternative but to haul himself out and join the others.

All around the camp, the prisoners not on the list waited, not knowing what was going on. Alex Cassie:

'There was no feedback from the 104. There must have been about two and a half thousand people in the same state – none knew what was happening and were just wondering what the outcome would be. Of course we heard an air-raid siren and we knew that would stop things. It was some time in the early hours of the morning that I heard a single shot and you could feel the shock of that shot quivering throughout the whole camp. Once the shot went off we just knew that was the end of the tunnel or the end of any movement, but we had no idea at that stage whether it was the first person out or the last person out or someone in the middle. We just didn't know.'

As soon as they heard the shot, the people in Block 104 knew it was all over. Ker-Ramsay went down the shaft to give orders that all the men in the tunnel should retreat back into the compound immediately. At the same time, the others were collecting their forged papers together and cramming them into stoves all over the block. Once the last man, Ken Rees, was out of the tunnel the trap was restored and sealed. Money and maps joined the documents in the stoves' fires, civilian buttons were ripped off converted uniforms. Some men tried to make a break for it back to their own blocks but the men in the watch-towers were on full alert now and a couple of bursts of machine-gun fire soon put a stop to that. Nevertheless, a handful made it. The first German to arrive in Block 104 was that night's duty dog-handler. Faced with the confusion all he could do was order everyone to

stay in their rooms. Then he gathered together a number of
abandoned greatcoats lying in the corridor and made a pile
of them. His dog climbed onto it, made itself comfortable,
and went to sleep. For the dog, it was the end of a long
night, and luckily for the prisoners, neither dog nor handler
were particularly aggressive types.

Jack Lyon was in hut 104 when the shot was heard:

'It was pandemonium in there. We knew immediately that
the balloon had gone up and I suppose two or three minutes
elapsed and then the general orders came. Someone shouted,
"The tunnel has been discovered! It won't be long before the
goons are here – you have got to destroy everything."

'We just set about destroying everything we could. We got
the stove going and everything was just piled into that, even
clothing. I didn't worry too much about my clothing because
you only really had to destroy it if it was a German uniform.
You could be accused of being a saboteur just by wearing a
German uniform. We also had to get rid of German money
and, above all, forged maps and passes. The forgery of
German documents was a very serious offence. So that was
how it went. After that was done we just awaited the arrival
of the Germans.'

The men caught at the edge of the forest were taken to the
guardhouse under escort, and there, in the general uproar,
managed to cram their papers into the stove. Soon afterwards,
von Lindeiner and Captain Pieber arrived, both displaying a
mixture of anger and panic. The recaptured airmen refused
to answer the torrent of questions fired at them, and were
sent to the cooler, where they spent two days without food,
heat, or the wherewithal to wash.

By 6.00 a.m. a guard troop had surrounded Block 104 and Ker-Ramsay could hear a desperate tapping from below Harry's trap. Taking his time, he removed the trap to reveal Charlie Pfelz, who'd entered at the other end and worked his way along the length of the tunnel. Now he was running out of air, and wouldn't have had enough to make the journey back to the exit. Von Lindeiner and Pieber had been joined in 104 by Broili and a very nervous Rubberneck, as Pfelz made his initial report to them there and then. Pfelz enjoyed his moment: he hated Rubberneck.

The four senior Germans had their pistols out and were waving them about dangerously. There was a bad moment when it looked as if Rubberneck might shoot Ken Rees and 'Red' Noble, but it passed. The damage was done and there was little the Germans could do but send the obvious leaders off to the cooler, which quickly filled to capacity, while rounding everyone else up for a head-count, which took two and a half hours as the one hundred and forty men found in Block 104 were made to stand outside in the snow. Von Lindeiner made his way to his office, where he faced the unenviable task of ringing the local police and Gestapo to report what he already knew had been a mass breakout. In all, he had to make forty-two telephone calls. By the end, he knew he'd be lucky to get out of the situation without facing a firing squad himself. Max Wielen, the head of the local Kripo and responsible for instigating the initial search and recapture procedure, ordered a *Kriegsfahndung*, or general alert. When the size of the escape became known, a *Großfahndung* was ordered: the highest level of security alert, which would have the effect of activating thousands of personnel. By that time there had been a general roll-call. When it was over, the Germans had established that seventy-six men had got clean away.

Chapter Eight

V ON LINDEINER WASN'T ONLY ANGRY AT THE PRISONERS whose escape had made a fool out of him and jeopardised his career, he was angry that their fate was now out of his hands. He had treated them as well as he could, and had been as lenient and relaxed in his regime as he could have been. But he had no control over the forces that now governed the prison camp system, and though he had tried obliquely to warn the men in his charge of the consequences of their actions if they attempted a mass escape, they had chosen to ignore him. Later, after the war, when serving as a witness at a war crimes trial in Hamburg, he was asked what he would do if presented with a 'Hitler-Order' to shoot recaptured POWs. A Hitler-Order was a direct command from the Nazi dictator, on no account to be disobeyed. 'In such a case I would take my own life,' he replied.

The reason why the Germans were so furious at the escape of so many airmen must be properly understood. By 1944, Göring's much vaunted Luftwaffe, owing to underinvestment and bad management, was beginning to fight a losing battle. The Allied air forces were pounding Germany day and night, hitting civilian targets as well as military ones, and consequently enemy aircrews were hated. It was for this reason as

much as anything that a *Großfahndung* was called so early.
Max Wielen, the local Kripo chief who had called the alert,
was about the same age as Lindeiner, an experienced
policeman in his early sixties, but he was also a canny enough
politician to play the Party game, and he was answerable
nowadays to Himmler's dreaded *Reichssicherheitshauptamt* in
Berlin. Within hours, news of the escape was being broadcast on German radio, so that civilians could also join in the
hunt for the 'terror-fliers' who brought death and destruction from the air. (As is usual in war, the Germans chose to
forget what they had handed out in England – in cities like
Coventry, Liverpool and London – and Hitler's planned so-
called 'Baedeker raids', never carried out, in which he targeted
cities of cultural and intellectual importance, such as Bath
and Oxford. To this should be added that the Allied air-raids
on Berlin, Dresden and Leipzig more than ensured that the
Germans reaped the whirlwind.) Official forces involved in
the manhunt included the Home Guard (the *Landwacht*,
reporting to Himmler), the Home Army, the Hitler Youth,
and *Waffen*-SS, Luftwaffe and Army barracks near Sagan.
Border police patrols were increased, all country lanes and
footpaths were watched, and messages were sent to Naval
stations at all ports, especially those of Danzig and Stettin, to
keep a sharp eye on all Swedish ships docking there. Tens of
thousands of people were involved in the operation, and at
its core lay the forces of the Gestapo.

Hitler had the Gestapo interim report of the escape on
his desk at Berchtesgaden, his retreat in western Austria, on
the morning of Sunday 26 March. After he had read it, he
fell into a violent rage and summoned Göring, Himmler and
Keitel to an immediate meeting. It was an unusual meeting
in that the Führer ordered that no record should be made
of it. He then demanded that all those recaptured should be
summarily shot.

Even Himmler saw that this would be an insane step to take, but it was left to Göring to point out that such a course of action would be political suicide. There would be no way of keeping it secret, the Swiss would ask questions, news of the atrocity would reach the foreign press, Germany would find itself in an untenable position politically, and the possibility existed that reprisals would be taken against German POWs in Allied hands. No-one there took into account the fact that the Allies were already aware of the existence of the concentration camps, but had taken no action in respect of them; however, Hitler, once he had calmed down, accepted the logic of Göring's argument and demurred – but not completely. He demanded that more than half, at least, of the number caught should be killed. Himmler suggested that, as seventy-six had got away, and as the average success rate of escapers was one per cent, most would be recaptured. Fifty of those apprehended should be executed.

Hitler agreed. So did Göring. His old attitude of gallantry towards fellow airmen, even if they were the enemy, had been dissipated by their success. He'd once sworn that the Luftwaffe would 'rub out' the air forces of the enemy. A joke going around Berlin at the time was that Göring had lost his eraser. Göring was a keen hunter. Berliners were already referring to the air-raid sirens as 'Göring's hunting horn'.

The business soon became a Gestapo matter, and Himmler referred it to Ernst Kaltenbrunner, the forty-year-old lawyer who had succeeded Reinhard Heydrich as head of the *Reichssicherheitshauptamt*. Owing, however, to the intricacies of German bureaucracy, the matter also had to be referred to the then Inspector of Prison Camps, General von Graevenitz. He objected strenuously to the plan, but was overruled. His successor, Major-General Adolf Westhoff, gave an account of the matter to the Allies after the war which throws an interesting light on German and Nazi thinking:

I was in charge of the General Department (*Abteilung Allgemein*) when the shooting of the escaped RAF POWs from Stalag-Luft III took place. It was the first occasion on which Feldmarschall Keitel had sent for me. I went with General von Graevenitz. . . . A certain number of officers had escaped from the Sagan camp. I don't remember how many, but I believe about eighty. When we entered, the Feldmarschall was very excited and nervous and said, 'Gentlemen, this is a bad business.' We were always blamed when POWs escaped – we couldn't tie them to our apron strings. 'This morning Göring reproached me in the presence of Himmler for having let some more POWs escape. It was unheard of!' Then they must have had a row because the camp didn't come under us, it was a Luftwaffe camp. All Luftwaffe camps came directly under the Luftwaffe itself, but the Inspector of POW camps was in charge of all camps for inspection purposes. I wasn't Inspector yet. General von Graevenitz was Inspector, and all camps came under him in matters concerning inspection and administration. Göring blamed Keitel for having let those men escape. These constant escapes were a bad show. Then Himmler interfered – I can only say what the Feldmarschall told us – and he complained that he'd have to provide another 60,000 or 70,000 men for the search.

Feldmarschall Keitel said to us, 'Gentlemen, these escapes must stop. We must set an example. We shall take very severe measures. I can only tell you that the men who have escaped will be shot . . .' We were amazed as that was a concept we had never come across before. . . . General von Graevenitz intervened at once and said, 'But, sir, that's out of the question. Escape isn't a dishonourable offence. That is specially laid down in the [Geneva] Convention.' . . . Keitel said, 'I don't care a damn; we discussed it in the Führer's presence and it cannot be altered . . .'

Camps only report to us after escapes have been made or else when the escapers have been caught. The camp reports: so-and-so many have been caught. But in this case none of our men had shot any of the POWs. I made enquiries at once. None of them had been shot by a soldier but by Gestapo men *only*, or else police sentries. . . . They weren't handed over to the police, they were caught by them. Usually when POWs were caught by the police they were returned to our camps and we passed sentence on them. But in this particular case only those caught by our own people were brought back to the camp, that is, those caught by soldiers.

Left virtually powerless, and unsupported by Keitel, all Graevenitz and Westhoff could do was try to limit the damage. Westhoff told his chief, 'Sir, the *only* thing we can do is to see that no dirty business is carried out where we are in charge.'

In fact, there was very little that they could do. The operation was out of their hands and the regular military forces involved in the manhunt were temporary and relatively small. Himmler contacted Kaltenbrunner soon after the meeting at Berchtesgaden, and on Monday 27 March 1944 Kaltenbrunner issued what is now known as the 'Sagan Order':

The increase of escapes by officer prisoners of war is a menace to internal security. I am indignant about the inefficient security measures. As a deterrent the Führer has ordered that more than half the escaped officers are to be shot. Therefore I order that the *Kriminalpolizei* are to hand over for interrogation to the Gestapo more than half of the recaptured officers. After interrogation the officers are to be taken in the direction of their original camp and shot en route. The shootings will be explained by the fact that the recaptured officers were shot while trying to escape, or because they offered resistance, so that nothing can be proved later. The Gestapo will report the shootings to the *Kriminalpolizei*, giving this reason. In the event of future escapes my decision will be awaited as to whether the same procedure is to be adopted. Prominent personalities will be excepted. Their names will be reported to me and my decision awaited.

Events then moved quickly. As he had expected, von Lindeiner was soon relieved of his post and arrested, confined to his quarters pending an investigation and court martial. In Breslau, Max Wielen sent an officer, Günther Absalon, to Stalag-Luft III to conduct an investigation. He was there for weeks.

In Berlin, Kaltenbrunner turned over the carrying-out of the Sagan Order, with the understanding that, where possible, US and British nationals should be spared, to Heinrich Müller, the head of Department IV of the *Reichssicherheitshauptamt (RSHA)*. Müller authorised the head of the Kripo and head of department V, Artur Nebe, to organise the operation.

Nebe deserves consideration. Born in Berlin in 1894, he was a career policeman, but joined the Nazi Party as early as 1931 (arguably to further his career). Less defensible was his command of one of the four *Einsatzgruppen*, or 'Task Forces' operating behind German lines in Russia between June and November 1941. The job of these Task Forces was to 'remove all elements hostile to the Reich and to Germany behind the fighting line'. In effect this meant intellectuals, journalists, teachers and Jews; women, and, in the last case, children, were not exempt. Nebe's force murdered 70,000 people – the smallest total of all four Task Forces. Nebe later claimed that he kept the number of killings down to a minimum and that, if anyone else had been in command, the rate would have been much higher. The number he himself claimed to be responsible for was 45,467, and one of his fellow Task Force commanders later claimed, rather disingenuously, at his trial after the war, that Nebe had in fact exaggerated to Himmler even the relatively low figures that he gave. The extraordinary thing about Nebe is that he was also part of the secret Resistance to Hitler which had its core in the Army General Staff and in the Counter-Intelligence department of the *RSHA* itself. Nebe claimed that he had never wanted the Task Force job, and had tried to get out of it, but that the Resistance had insisted that he stay within the *RSHA*, where he could be of most value to them. This may well be true, since those were the darkest of days, and extreme moral and ethical compromises were made in pursuit of an ultimate good. However, Nebe remains a shadowy figure whose usefulness to the State probably equalled his service to the Resistance. He was active within the Party machinery in investigating early attempts to oust or assassinate Hitler. Few papers have either been left behind or yet discovered about him, and the one eyewitness account of him, a biography, *Where's Nebe?*, was by his close friend and associate, Hans Bernd Gisevius, a lawyer not known for absolute accuracy or impartiality, who was for a time in the Gestapo himself and doubtless had to make compromises, and whose portrait of the hero of the German Resistance, Graf Claus von Stauffenberg, is a masterpiece of character assassination. But it has to be added that Nebe was arrested along with many, many other conspirators after von Stauffenberg's attempt to blow Hitler up and stage a *coup d'état* in July 1944 went disastrously wrong. He was tortured for two months before he was executed, but he betrayed no-one.

In this man's hands, then, lay the fate of the men who had got away from Stalag-Luft III.

Nebe summoned Max Wielen to Berlin and, according to Wielen's later deposition, gave him orders that any escapers captured by his police should be handed over to the Gestapo. He also showed Wielen an order signed by Kaltenbrunner but authorised by Himmler, addressed to the commander of the Breslau Gestapo, Wilhelm Scharpwinkel. It was a general order which stated that Scharpwinkel would receive precise instructions from Heinrich Müller. Nebe discussed the measures to be taken over his frequent business lunches with Kaltenbrunner and Müller.

In the early morning of Saturday 25 March the escapers were already beginning to fan out as they pursued their separate routes. Some of those travelling by train, especially those who had been among the first to make the break, were already well on their way. Others were still struggling through the snow-filled forest.

The first of the hardarsers emerged at about 1.30 a.m. A group of twelve of them, led by Jerzy Mondschein and posing as local workers on holiday from a local woodmill, were going to make their way to the little town of Tschiebsdorf, a short distance to the south-east of the camp, and there catch a train to Boberröhrsdorf, on the Czech border near Hirschberg. Among them were John Dodge, Bernard 'Pop' Green – at fifty-seven the 'father' of the camp, who really had no business to have been flying at all, but who'd wangled his way in for one raid and been shot down – Lester Bull, and Jimmy James and 'Nick' Skanziklas. After losing their way a couple of times, they reached the station without other incident, and Mondschein, whose German was perfect and accentless, went to the booking office, held his group travel document open for inspection, and ordered twelve tickets. The clerk was somewhat taken aback, but issued the tickets and took the money. They had to wait until 6.00 a.m. for the train, but the three-hour journey to Boberröhrsdorf was uneventful, and on arrival they split up with brief handshakes and wishes of good luck, and went their separate ways.

Skanziklas and James headed up into the mountains of the Riesengebirge. As they climbed, so the snow they were walking through became deeper, and by the afternoon they were slogging through waist-high drifts. Cold, hungry and wet, they found shelter for a short time in a lonely byre, where they lit a tiny fire and took it in turns to rest in the straw-filled manger. But it was no place to spend the night, so the two men pressed on towards the south, heading across valleys towards the Czech frontier, which they reckoned was about sixty kilometres distant. The temperature, James remembers, dropped to about −18 degrees Celsius.

James was used to the cold, having spent some time before the war in northern Canada, but it was too much for Skanziklas, so they made their way to a road, which took them to Hirschberg, where they decided to take the risk of catching a train to the border. The Greek wasn't going to make it on foot.

They arrived at the station, but they didn't even get as far as the ticket office. The hunt was already in full hue and cry, and the police stopped them and searched them as they crossed the hall. They were taken straight to a cell in the police station, where they were soon joined by most of the rest of their party. A 'very nasty-looking little man with glasses', as James remembers, interrogated them, asking all sorts of questions about the tunnel, mocking the enterprise, and finally trying to get them to sign 'confessions', which they, of course, refused to do. James was already considering ways to get out of the jail. Nobody had the faintest idea of what was really going on. Bushell had warned them that the Germans weren't above staging mock-executions to scare information out of a prisoner, but had said they would go no further than that.

Les Brodrick was 'hardarsing' it through the grim, snow-bound woods outside Stalag-Luft III with Denys Street and Hank Birkland:

'We were traipsing through the pine forest and it was cold and it was wet. We'd crossed a main road that we had been told about quite successfully. There was troop movement on it. But then we got into an area where the snow was quite deep. We laboured along and decided once it was light that we would have to settle down. We could hear voices nearly all day but luckily no-one came near. They were probably people who worked in the woods.

'When night came we got our little lamps out and used those to have a warm drink. We moved off at about five-ish. That was a bad night because we couldn't get out of this forested land and the trees seemed closer and the snow seemed deeper and pretty soon we were just struggling along, stopping every fifty yards. Occasionally we would find a ditch with some water in and we would drink that. It was absolutely wearing and I didn't think we were making much distance at all. We weren't as strong as we thought we were. I remembered all these stories of the Arctic that I read as a kid about whatever you do don't fall asleep in the snow because you won't wake up, so it was, "Come on, come on, let's go, let's go!" Then one would fall behind and the others would have to wait for him to catch up.

'When morning eventually came again we had reached a fairly open area with hardly any cover. But we did spot a bunch of bushes and made our way over to those and climbed inside and just sat there all day. We saw a couple of people in the distance going by who we thought might be other kriegies on their way too. By now it was so miserable and cold – everything was wet through, the blanket roll was as heavy as lead. We decided we weren't going to wait until it was dark because we were freezing, so off we went again and after a couple of hours it had got really dark and we were back in the forest again. We couldn't walk around it so we had to move along a bit and find another gap to go through. Then, in the middle of the night, old Henry Birkland started mumbling and talking to himself. We were all feeling pretty rough but when we stopped it was now difficult to get him on the move again, and he seemed to be wandering in his mind. Denys and I decided we had to get under cover tonight at least.

'We started looking around and eventually found some buildings in the woods. Denys, who spoke German, was going to tell them some story that we had missed the train and we were making our way from here to here. Denys approached this hut, knocked on the door and told his little story and the owner said, "Wait a minute," and went back inside. There were four German guards billeted there and they came out with their rifles and that was the end of our walk.

'In two and a half days we'd covered only two or three kilometres. I don't think we really thought we'd make it. I mean it's a bit stupid, isn't it, to walk down to Czechoslovakia? We were not going to get too far except with a tremendous amount of luck. By the time we did get caught it was a relief in some ways that it was over.'

Most of the other hardarsers were picked up quickly. Paul

Royle was travelling with Flight Lieutenant Edgar 'Hunk' Humphreys, as they'd drawn fifty-fourth and fifty-fifth places on the escape list. They'd got away at about 2.30 a.m. and headed south-east, making for an autobahn which they hoped to follow. It was bitterly cold and wet but they had a little portable stove (another invention of Travis) on which they tried to boil some water for tea. By dawn they still hadn't located the motorway so they decided to go to ground for the day and set off again at dusk. That night they found the road, but the snow in the fields to the side of it was too deep for them to skirt it, so they had to walk along the side, diving for cover if they spotted other people, and painfully aware of how exposed they were. At last their luck ran out, as they fell foul of three Home Guard soldiers. The Germans wouldn't listen to their story, and levelled their weapons at them. One of them went off and soon returned with a policeman and a regular soldier. The soldier was friendly enough, though the others were sour. They were taken to the jailhouse in nearby Tiefenfurt. They arrived there at 3.00 a.m. on Monday 27 March. They were soon joined, to their great surprise, by Johnny Marshall and Arnost Valenta. This was a serious blow, and everyone was worried for Valenta, though there was no reason for the Germans to suspect him of being anything more than just another escaped prisoner.

Valenta and Marshall should have been far away by now, since they were among the very first out. They were travelling disguised as Czech glass-workers, and the escape committee had issued them with two hundred *Reichsmark* to buy railway tickets from Sagan to Mittelwalde on the Czech frontier, where they'd planned to cross over on foot and make contact with Valenta's friends or, failing that, try to get across into Yugoslavia to join Tito's partisans. But at Sagan they had found the station in confusion due to the air-raid, and the next train they could catch wasn't due until

1.00 a.m. That would be too late for their Mittelwalde connection. Marshall's German was poor, so they decided that walking through the countryside was less risky than hanging around at stations. The Czech frontier was only about 120 kilometres distant, so they made up their minds to leg it. Unfortunately, they had had the same difficulties with the snowbound terrain as the others, and were forced to give themselves up after being stopped and questioned in a village near the autobahn.

The four men spent the rest of the night in a tiny cell in the Tiefenfurt jail, joined by another escaper, Albert Armstrong. Early in the morning they were packed into a police van and driven off in the direction of Sagan. They were almost relieved, but their relief soon turned to anxiety as they failed to take the turning to the camp and stopped instead at the police station. There they were searched and questioned (luckily they had managed to divest themselves of their most incriminating false papers, which could have led to spying charges), and bundled into yet another cramped cell. As the day passed, many other hardarsers, mainly picked up by the local Home Guard, were delivered to the police jail. Among them were Les Brodrick, Keith Ogilvie, Denys Street, Brian Evans and Hank Birkland. Most were suffering from exhaustion and mild exposure, Birkland more severely than the others. By the end of 27 March, there were nine-teen recaptured escapers in Sagan jail. It was overcrowded and smelly, and they had been given nothing to eat except for a hunk of dry bread and a mug of thin liquid that they were told was tea.

They were allowed little time for rest. In the middle of the night they were roused, again by police, and herded into a van, which, to their dismay, took them to the prison at the not-far-distant, much larger town of Görlitz. There was more room here, in the sense of capacity, but it was a grim place, and the fact that they were in the hands of the police, not the Luftwaffe, and that they were in a civilian jail, not a prison camp, gave many of them cause for concern. It was cold in the prison, the cells were small and spartan, and the prisoners were crammed four to each one. They were given an unvarying diet of bread with ersatz jam and coffee for breakfast, bread and thin soup for lunch, and bread for dinner. There was a bucket in each cell to use as a privy. Their shoes were taken away.

Over the next two days, the prison filled up with more recaptured escapers – among them were Mike Casey, Jack Grisman, Tony Bethell and Cookie Long. The group was soon joined by Mick Shand, Porokoru Pohe and the compass-maker, Al Hake. All were suffering from frostbite, Hake severely. No medical treatment was offered them. By the end of 29 March, there were thirty-five kriegies in the prison.

Meanwhile, the rail travellers, although many put a lot more distance between themselves and Sagan, were hardly experiencing better luck. They weren't necessarily surprised when they were caught: they knew that the scale of the escape would provoke a similarly sized hunt; but naturally they were disappointed when their freedom was curtailed yet again.

Roger Bushell and Bernard Scheidhauer were the first to be recaptured, early in the morning of 26 March, though they'd reached Saarbrücken without difficulty. So near and yet so far. Once again it was the police who arrested them: there was a tiny error in their travel documents. Two days later, the quartet of Jimmy Catanach, Arnold Christensen, Halldor Espelid and Nils Fuglesang were caught. They'd arrived in Berlin from Sagan early on 25 March, but their luck ran out near the Danish border at Flensburg, where a suspicious policeman inspected first their papers and then their adapted 'civilian' greatcoats, which failed to stand up to close scrutiny. The policeman handed them over to the Kripo. At about the same time, Gordon Brettell, Rene Marcinkus Henri Picard and Tim Walenn were picked up. They'd got as far as Küstrin (Kostrzyn, now in Poland) about sixty kilometres east of Berlin, by train, where they'd seen Jens Muller and his travelling companion, Per Bergsland, on another platform. They'd spent the night of 26 to 27 March at Willenberg and caught another train the following day, but they were taken off it after a document check at Schneidemühl, and escorted to a prison camp near Marienburg, where they were given battledress in exchange for their carefully dyed and tailored 'civilian' clothes, before being transferred to the prison at Danzig.

Muller and Bergsland, meanwhile, had caught a train to Stettin, where they arrived at lunchtime on the twenty-seventh. They had a contact address from Bushell, which they waited until the relative safety of evening to visit. It turned out to be a seamen's brothel. At first they drew a blank there, and panicked in case they would be betrayed, but as they were leaving they ran into a Pole who asked them in German if they had any black market goods to sell. They asked him if he could help them locate a Swedish sailor, as they wanted to find an old friend who was supposed to be arriving from Göteborg. The Pole obliged, and as soon as they were alone, the two revealed their true identities to the sailor, who promised he would help them. He arranged a rendezvous, which he kept, and then smuggled them onto the docks, leaving them near a pile of crates on the quay by his ship, and telling them to wait for his signal. Something must have gone wrong thereafter, however, for the seaman never reappeared and, after a long wait, the two Norwegians watched in despair as the ship cast off and sailed away.

It was now late and they were stranded on the dock, not knowing how to get away. If they were discovered, it would be all up with them. Luckily Bergsland had taken the precaution of memorising the name of another ship they'd passed, which was still tied up. They marched boldly to the gate of the dock, and managed to convince the guard that they were electricians on shore leave from that ship, helped by the fact that they spoke German with a Scandinavian accent. They spent the night nervously in a small hotel whose proprietor didn't ask questions, and spent the next day keeping out of sight until evening, when they returned to the brothel. There they met a pair of Swedish seamen, who immediately agreed to help them. In their company, they made it past the dock guards without difficulty – only the Swedes showed their papers, and the guards assumed that Muller and Bergsland were part of the same crew – and boarded the ship with them.

The sailors hid them in the chain locker, telling them that it'd be thirty-six hours before the ship sailed, but promising to bring them food, coffee, and a bucket for their personal needs. This they did, but the two Norwegians could barely relax for a moment. Early on the morning of 28 March they heard a German patrol come aboard. The Germans made a routine search of the ship, and there was one terrible moment when one soldier reached into the locker and almost poked Bergsland's eye out as he felt around. But Bergsland kept his nerve and bit his lip in pain, and the guard moved unsuspectingly away.

The ship sailed at 7.00 a.m., and at 11.00 p.m. on 29 March it entered Göteborg harbour, but the Norwegians stayed on board until she reached Stockholm, her final destination, the next day. There, they reported to the British Consul. It was six days – 144 hours – since they had emerged from Harry and bolted into the Silesian forest. Now they were free.

Meanwhile, in their cells at Görlitz, the POWs had little to do with their time and settled down to fight the usual battle with boredom, though there was a certain amount of tension in the air as they had no idea what they were doing spending so long in an ordinary jail. Once, Les Brodrick saw a small car draw up. Three men in black leather overcoats and black trilbys got out, but what happened then he didn't know, for the guard spotted him and shouted for him to get away from the window.

They were interrogated at regular intervals at the Gestapo headquarters across town. The interrogations varied in tone from mild to ugly. Some of the men were told that they wouldn't be returned to Stalag-Luft III because the Luftwaffe evidently couldn't hold them. Jack Grisman and another escaper were told flatly that they would never see their wives again. One, on telling his interrogator, in answer to a question, that his mother's first name was Rebecca, was immediately accused of being a Jew, and threatened with transportation to a concentration camp. One prisoner, Flight Lieutenant Max Ellis, had escaped independently from the satellite camp at Belaria and been rounded up with the men of the Great Escape. The fact that he didn't fit in with the others threw his interrogators into confusion.

At the police jail in Hirschberg, the POWs captured there were also being subjected to lengthy interrogations. The only mild relief in their dreary and frightening routine was that their meals, which were marginally better than the fare at Görlitz (there was a bit of fatty meat in the stew), were served by a pretty Polish girl.

Then John Dodge was taken away. On 29 March a Canadian, Jimmy Wernham, and Nick Skanziklas were ordered to pack, and left soon afterwards together with two Polish airmen, Pawluk and Kiewnarski. Later in the day two more, Doug Poynter and 'Pop' Green left. Mondschein and Bull had already been transferred to the civilian prison at Reichenberg, where they were joined by Flying Officer

John Stower after he was recaptured. Jimmy James was now the only one left at Hirschberg. He was alone for a week, and it wasn't a pleasant time. 'I was beginning to feel distinctly queasy now,' he remembers. 'After I'd been there a day or two I was transferred to a larger cell. The Gestapo arrived and I thought I was going to be in for it because the cell was large enough for rough stuff. But all they did was clear me out and bring in a French POW they wanted to interrogate. Later I was put back in the cell. At one point they let a large German Shepherd dog in, which was a bit alarming, and locked him in with me; but I've got a rapport with dogs and we made friends. After a bit, they let him out again.'

At the end of the week, at about 5.00 a.m. on 7 April, James was ordered to get his kit together by a Gestapo man brandishing a Luger. James thought for a moment that he was being taken out to be shot. He noticed the Polish girl waving goodbye to him. In fact he was taken to Hirschberg station and boarded a train under guard, which took him to Berlin. On arrival he was taken to Gestapo headquarters – 'which I am glad to say had been bombed and was looking distinctly tottery'. He was kept waiting for a couple of hours without being paid any particular attention apart from being asked a few desultory questions by an SS officer who finally took him downstairs to a waiting car which drove him out of the city. After an hour or so, they came to the edge of a dark wood.

At that time there were still escapers on the loose. Harry Day and Pavel Tobolski had made it to Berlin and successfully got in touch with their contacts there, but despite a warm welcome from the Germans, the Dane turned out to have feet of clay. Although he was no supporter of the regime, he was disinclined to help, and kept talking warmly about his

German girlfriend, who happened to be a Party member. Day and Tobolski decided to get out.

They left early on 26 March, and decided that they'd better try to make their way to Stettin. This wasn't too hard, and Tobolski's uniform and papers were so effective that he managed to get some genuine stamps on his forged paybook. There were three good reasons for them to go to Stettin: one was the brothel which Bergsland and Muller had already made good use of as a contact-source; another was Tobolski's sister, who lived there and might be able to help; and the third was the presence there of a number of French POWs whom the Germans were using as labour in the city. Once there, however, they were unable to make any contacts with Swedish sailors at the brothel, and Tobolski's sister was too scared to give them more than minimal help. That left the French POWs. Day managed to make contact with an unescorted party of them as they walked through the town, and, going for broke, explained to them in French who he was. They immediately and enthusiastically offered to give whatever help they could. Day was delighted, and made a rendezvous with them, explaining about his travelling companion, lest they took fright at a German uniform. The French honoured the rendezvous and smuggled the two escapers into their barracks, where they gave them food and a bunk each, and told them to get some sleep.

Their sleep was interrupted the next morning, the 29 March, by the arrival of a squad of German police. The officer in charge was friendly enough as he took them away, and confirmed what Day and Tobolski already knew: that they'd been betrayed by one of the Frenchmen. 'But don't worry,' the policeman told Day. 'These informers quickly outlive their usefulness. When that happens, we simply tell their comrades what they've been up to, and they do the rest. We usually find the bodies in the harbour.'

Day and Tobolski spent four days in the local prison, and on the fifth they were driven to Berlin. There, the two were immediately separated. Day knew the kind of fate that would be in store for Tobolski anyway – he was a Pole, he'd been caught wearing a German uniform. Day tried to persuade the Germans to let them stay together, to no avail. The two men saluted one another. As Jimmy James would be a short time later, Day was taken to Gestapo headquarters in the former School of Applied Arts at number 8, Prinz-Albrecht-Straße. There he was interviewed briefly by Artur Nebe himself. He had no idea that he was being treated as a 'prominent' prisoner. The encounter was brief. Nebe merely said, 'As the Luftwaffe appears incapable of keeping you, I am sending you to a place from where there will be no eighth escape.' Two Gestapo officers then escorted Day to a car and drove him northwards, out of town.

As for Gordon Kidder and Tom Kirby-Green, they got as far as Breslau, and made a connection with a train bound for Czechoslovakia; but they were arrested at Hodonin in southern Moravia on 28 March and taken to the prison at Zlín. There they were interrogated and – uniquely among the recaptured POWs – tortured. It is almost certain that one of the prisoners had his handcuffs torn off one wrist without their having been opened.

Few remained at liberty. Dennis Cochran, travelling alone, was picked up only seven kilometres from the Swiss border on 30 March. He was taken to the prison at Ettlingen. On 4 April Tony Hayter was arrested in Mulhouse, France, just across the border from Basel in Switzerland.

It wasn't long before all but a handful of the escapers had been recaptured. Indeed, the *Großfahndung* had been so thorough that as well as the escaped POWs, it had turned up a large number of deserters and forced-labourers who were also on the run. In Berlin, Artur Nebe sat at his desk. In front of him was a pile of index cards, one for each of the POWs who'd got away from Sagan on the night of 24 March, with their names, dates of birth, rank, and personal details. They had been prepared for him by his assistant, Hans Wilhelm Merten, as a result of several teleprint messages between Berlin and Breslau, Görlitz, and Hirschberg, and other prisons where the recaptured airmen were being held. Nebe shuffled and stacked the cards, and called Merten in. He handed his assistant a selected handful of cards and asked him to sort them out according to which men were married, which had children, and also by age.

When he'd completed the job, Merten, who had severe misgivings about what he was involved in, handed the cards back to Nebe. Merten later recalled that Nebe then 'looked at each card individually. He would take the first card, look at it, and he would say, for instance, "Oh, this man is still very young; he can stay alive." He then looked at a second card and he would say, "This man is married but has no children. He will be one of them." ' In this way, Nebe made his selection, ending up with one pile of fifty cards, and another of twenty-three. He stared at them for a moment, looked through them again, and exchanged one or two cards from one pile to the other. Finally he handed the larger pile to Merten with the words, 'Make a list of those, and do it quickly.' Merten, a lawyer by training and no fool, knew exactly what was going on. As he compiled the list, he made a desperate effort to sabotage it, by putting incorrect places of recapture against at least some of the names, in the hope that orders to shoot officers would be misdirected and there would therefore at least be a delay, perhaps even a stay of execution, if the paperwork got sufficiently snarled up in the massive Nazi bureaucracy. But the mistake was noticed before the teleprint messages were sent out. Nebe reprimanded him and dismissed him from his post, sending him to a college in Fürstenberg to teach criminology, and giving as his reason that Merten was suffering from nervous exhaustion.

On the day that Cochran was recaptured, the first prisoners were taken away from Görlitz. At dawn three large Gestapo cars drew up in the prison yard. Minutes later, six men were taken out of the cells, including Casey, Hake and Pohe. They were driven away. Either the guards wouldn't say where they were going, or didn't know. The men left behind hoped they were being returned to Sagan. But if that were the case, why hadn't Luftwaffe personnel collected them?

On 31 March, the procedure was repeated. Ten more men were removed, among them Birkland, Brian Evans, Ed Humphreys, Langford and Valenta. They were also escorted by Gestapo. But two days after that, a quartet of Luftwaffe guards appeared, two of whom the prisoners recognised, and took away Keith Ogilvie and Paul Royle, with two others. One of the prison guards told the group that they were 'lucky' they were going back to Stalag-Luft III. The others who'd gone, he explained, hadn't been recognised as military prisoners and had been taken away for 'civilian investigation'.

On 6 April six more prisoners left Görlitz. Jack Grisman and Denys Street were among them. As they apparently had a Luftwaffe guard (though no-one recognised the men), Mick Shand, desperate to get back to Sagan, asked Street if he'd mind swapping places and offered him a square of chocolate in return. But Street was just as keen to get back to the relative security of the camp, and refused. Given the Nazi love of paperwork, it'd been a long shot anyway. Shand settled down to wait, but he and those remaining in the prison were growing more and more uneasy with every day that passed. What were the Germans up to? Soon after the last contingent had left, as the guard came in with the evening meal, John Marshall noticed that the letter 'S' had been chalked on the outside of the cell door. 'Must mean Sagan,' one of the inmates said, and there was a little ripple of relief before another pointed out that it could just as well stand for *schiessen* (shoot [them]). The mood dampened after that, but the next morning another Luftwaffe patrol came into the prison and called out the names of Albert Armstrong, Tony Bethell, Les Brodrick, Dick Churchill, John Marshall and two others. They were all taken downstairs and loaded into a Luftwaffe truck.

Only Cookie Long and Max Ellis were left. On 11 April they were moved into separate cells. Later that day, Ellis met Long outside the cells – there was a bucket in the corridor for them to relieve themselves – and asked if he could borrow Long's comb. Long sent the guard over with it, and Ellis borrowed it a couple of times again over the next two days. On 13 April, a civilian entered Ellis' cell and asked if he were Long. When Ellis told him, 'No', the man smiled politely and withdrew. The following day, the guard failed to bring Long's comb over. 'Your friend left yesterday,' he said. Only years later did one of Long's fellow escapers reflect that his swarthy looks may have encouraged the Gestapo to think that he had either Jewish or Slav blood.

On 6 April, seven escapers were still at large. Sydney Dowse was travelling with his Polish comrade, Stanislav Krol. They'd been stymied by the air-raid at Sagan station, and decided that they'd better start off on foot. Dowse was posing as a Dane, and Krol as a Slav worker. Their plan was to head east towards Poland, following the railway line, where they hoped to make contact with friends of Krol. It would be quite a trek, but they were both in good shape, and Dowse had got three-weeks' worth of real food vouchers, all courtesy of the tame goon, Corporal Hesse. They looked a bit odd: Dowse was dressed in a real suit (also courtesy of Hesse) and a great-coat dyed plum red to make it look less military. Krol was wearing ordinary RAF officer's trousers, several pullovers, and another greatcoat.

The journey took them twelve days, following the railway track. On 6 April they were three kilometres from the Polish border and planned to make the crossing that night. They were sheltering in a barn during the day when the owner surprised them and threatened them with a pitchfork. They managed to convince him that they were Polish migrant workers returning home, and he even brought them coffee. But that might have been to put them off their guard, for soon afterwards, as they were settling down to drink it, a member of the Hitler Youth turned up, swiftly followed by two soldiers of the Home Guard. Dowse and Krol were taken to the jail at Oels, where they were interrogated by men from the Breslau Gestapo. Dowse was told that he'd be sent to Berlin for further questioning. Krol, the Gestapo said, would be returned to Sagan. When Dowse broke this news to Krol, however, the Pole looked at him in terror. 'We mustn't separate,' he pleaded. 'If you leave me, I'm finished.' But then a policeman grabbed Dowse and hauled him away.

Des Plunkett and his Czech travelling companion, Freddie Dvorak, caught a train successfully from Sagan station at about 5.00 a.m. on the morning of 25 March. They got as far as Bad Reinerz by train, about twenty kilometres from the Czech border, planning to cover the rest of the way on foot. Unfortunately they arrived in the middle of a heavy snowstorm, and even worse, after relieving himself at the station lavatory, Plunkett said loudly to Dvorak, 'That's better!' in English. A German soldier was within earshot, but though he stared at Plunkett for a moment in bewilderment, took no action. Perhaps he'd thought he was hearing things; perhaps he was off duty and simply couldn't be bothered with the palaver of making an arrest. At all events, their luck held, and the snowstorm abated. As they set out, the sun began to shine.

They were making for the village of Novi Hradek, just inside Czechoslovakia; but first they had to cross a pass where the snow was up to their waists. This slowed their progress considerably. Late in the afternoon, they met a uniformed man on skis, who greeted them pleasantly enough, but seemed suspicious that they were not on skis – any local out here would have been using them to travel in such weather. They told him they were on their way to Grunshubel, the next village along the valley. The man seemed satisfied and told them it was about three kilometres farther. Then he went on his way.

Worried that the man might have been a border patrolman, Plunkett and Dvorak did their best to hurry, but they were sodden, and getting tired. Worse, the darkness was falling swiftly. They reached Grunshubel without further difficulty however, where Dvorak, ready to speak German, was pleasantly surprised to hear everyone speaking Czech. Plunkett, who spoke only a little Czech and German, had to pretend to be dim-witted. There was no inn or *pension* in Grunshubel, but fifteen kilometres down the road, in Novi Hradek, just across the border in Czechoslovakia, they'd be bound to find one.

The small hotel they found was warm and comfortable, and after Dvorak had explained to the owner who they were, he agreed to help them, though he couldn't shelter them for long, on account of the *Großfahndung*. They subsequently took shelter in a nearby barn belonging to a friendly farmer, while they tried to figure out a way of getting to Prague; but in such a small community their presence could not be kept a secret for long, and soon they were obliged to move on.

On the morning of 1 April, after a narrow escape – they had been closely questioned by a Czech policeman who then inexplicably decided to let them go – they were en route by train for Prague, tired and dirty but still looking respectable enough to pass muster. They reached the capital without further incident and made their way to the suburb of Gbeli. Dvorak had the address of a hotelier there who was in the Resistance and had helped escapers before. Then their luck let them down: they discovered that the man was out of town and wouldn't be back for five days. They killed the time as best they could, moving out of town and staying in third-class hotels, where security was not so tight, and praying that during this enforced wait they would not be picked up by the police. At last the hotelier returned, gave them a warm welcome, and helped them plan a route by train across Germany to Switzerland. They left on 7 April – Good Friday, taking advantage of the holiday crowds.

They spent the first night at Domazlice, but became so convinced they'd aroused the suspicions of the innkeeper there that in the hope of throwing any pursuer off the scent, they decided to double back to Klatovy, rather than continue their journey to Fürth, in Germany.

It was the wrong decision. At Klatovy, Dvorak passed through the police check unhindered, but Plunkett did not: he didn't have the correct travel pass, it appeared. Rather than abandon his friend, Dvorak went back to help, and very soon afterwards they were both in a cell in the local prison. They spent the rest of the month there, alternately being interrogated and threatened. As the days passed, Dvorak came to wonder more and more what their likely fate would be, and Plunkett knew that this was scarcely standard treatment for recaptured POWs. At last, on 4 May, a car came to collect them, and they were driven away by the Gestapo.

After he'd got away from Sagan, Bob van der Stok travelled alone. He managed to get to Breslau by rail without difficulty, and there he cut through unnecessary difficulties by simply buying a through ticket to Alkmaar in the Netherlands. The journey involved changes of train. The first leg was to Dresden, which he reached at 10.00 a.m. on 25 March. Having a day to kill, he resisted sightseeing in the historic city, which had not yet been flattened by the Allies, and spent it instead lying low in a cinema, before returning to the station to snatch a meal of bread and bratwurst, washed down with beer, before his next train left at 8.00 p.m. If all went well, he would soon be home in the Netherlands – an occupied country, of course; but home anyway.

At Hanover the train stopped for an hour, but no-one disturbed him and he feigned sleep. As they approached the Dutch border, his heart started to race. The train slowed and stopped, and all the passengers disembarked in order to go through the customs control and police checkpoint. The security policeman glanced at his papers and asked him his final destination. Speaking German with a Dutch accent helped van der Stok, who was waved through. He rejoined his train and resumed his seat, breathing deeply to slow his heart down. It was now 6.00 a.m. on the morning of 26 March. He'd been free for just over twenty-four hours.

He reasoned that by now the tunnel would have been discovered, and that it was possible that the Germans would have found out that someone bought a ticket at Breslau for Alkmaar in the small hours of Sunday morning. If they had, the police might well be waiting for him at the station. He therefore decided to get off at Utrecht, the stop before Alkmaar. He was familiar with the city because he'd passed his student days there, and it was possible that he could make contact with old friends who could help him. It was a risk, and he didn't want to jeopardise anyone else's safety, but he made his way to the home of a former professor and rang the bell. He was made welcome and fed, and given the address of a safe house in Amersfoort, where he spent the next three weeks, while making contact with the Resistance. They were not helpful, either because they suspected van der Stok of being an *agent provocateur*, or simply because they hadn't the resources. Either way, van der Stok decided to continue under his own steam, and, not wanting to put the family he was staying with to any further risk, he made his way into Belgium. There, he rang an uncle in Antwerp, who had some cash transferred to the local bank for him, and also gave him the address of a place where he could stay in Brussels, where he spent another three weeks. Once again, however, the local Resistance was suspicious, though he was given an address in St Gaudens, in south-western France. It was possible, he was told, that from there he might find a way across the Pyrenees into Spain.

It was frustrating to be so close to England and not have the means of getting there, but van der Stok resigned himself to a long and dangerous roundabout route. He crossed into France, and embarked on a long and wearisome journey by rail across the country to Toulouse, and thence to St Gaudens. He'd forgotten the name of the café he'd been directed to there, but remembered that it had a Dutch connection. The town wasn't large, but it wasn't that small either, so he wandered the streets in some despair until he finally came across what he was looking for: a little bar called L'Orangerie.

From then on, it was relatively plain sailing. Van der Stok was introduced to the local Resistance cell, and moved to a remote farmhouse, where he joined a motley assortment of fugitives and refugees, including thirteen frightened German Jews. They all faced an exhausting trek across the mountains, and there was a terrifying moment when there was a shoot-out between the *maquisards* of the Resistance and a German patrol, but within a few days they crossed from the rainy to the sunny side of the mountains. They were in Spain.

Van der Stok was the last man accounted for; but only the third to make a clean getaway.

Chapter Nine

AT STALAG-LUFT III, THE ENTRY SHAFT OF HARRY WAS filled with sand except for the last metre or so, which was sealed to the top with concrete. There was to be no repeat of the disaster when the Germans had blown up Tom. Instead, the rest of the tunnel was pumped full of sewage, while the exit shaft was filled with sand. Although Absalon and a party of other Gestapo officers prowled round the compound and the camp generally, conducting their enquiry, no further punishments were meted out. Having served their term in the cooler, the escapers who'd been captured immediately rejoined the life of the camp unhindered. However, extra roll-calls became a regular feature of daily life, spot searches were more frequent, Red Cross parcel delivery was stopped for a while, and the theatre was closed for a period except for meetings. The fact that punishment measures were so light after a major escape was in itself, however, a cause for concern.

The Gestapo conducted searches of their own, but being unused to the ways of POWs, were relieved of the occasional item, lifted from their greatcoats which they left unattended as they rummaged through a block. A trilby hat went missing, and a couple of pairs of gloves, together with two scarves and a torch. One young POW even nicked a small pistol, but when he showed it triumphantly to Norman Canton, the veteran member of X-Organisation sharply told him to replace it immediately, which by the grace of God he was able to do before its loss was noticed. The Gestapo also lost some papers, which, however, didn't look all that important, and it was just as well. They never mentioned these depredations, presumably unwilling to lose face before the Luftwaffe.

On 29 March the first two recaptured escapers reappeared in the camp: 'Pop' Green and Doug Poynter, returning from Hirschberg. At first the new commandant, who had only just arrived, a Colonel Braune, thought there'd been some mistake, and packed them off back to the police at Sagan. They cooled their heels there for the better part of a day, very nervous, until an SS officer arrived, confirmed that they were indeed due to return to the prison camp, and escorted them there himself, telling Braune that he had better not question SS or Gestapo orders again. After a fortnight in the cooler for good measure, Green and Poynter were reintegrated into the life of the camp, but the story they had to tell, slight as it was – for it was only later that anyone could understand the full picture – nevertheless caused deep disquiet.

During the next few days, several more men, this time from the prison at Görlitz, reappeared. Among them were Albert Armstrong, Tony Bethell, Les Brodrick, Dick Churchill, Johnny Marshall, Keith Ogilvie, Paul Royle and Mick Shand. Shand looked in vain for Denys Street. They were kept in the cooler for the regulation fortnight, but they took their exercise in an area next to the parcels store, so that their stories were communicated to the rest of the compound in dribs and drabs. The overriding concern in the compound was that so few had returned – only fifteen. The weather had closed in again, and it seemed incredible that the others – especially the hardarsers – had all got away. And the men

who had returned were anxious about the fate of their fellow
escapers who'd been in civilian jails with them, but who'd
been taken away before them. Had they been sent to Colditz
or other camps, so as not to unite all the escapers in one
place again? Rumours were rife, and they were not helped
by the bits of unconfirmed information that filtered through
from friendly camp staff. One German officer mentioned to
John Casson that he was glad that Casson hadn't been picked
for the escape, because a dire fate awaited those who had.
But he could not, or would not, elaborate.

Then things started to happen. On 6 April, shortly before
lunch, the Senior British Officer, Herbert Massey, who had
recently heard that he was to be repatriated via Switzerland
on account of his damaged leg, which was getting no better
in the camp, was called to a meeting with Kommandant
Braune. The officer who brought the message was Hans
Pieber, and Massey noticed that he was looking grim. Clearly
something serious was up. Massey sent for his interpreter,
Squadron Leader Philip Murray, and set off for the
Kommandatur with him.

Braune had with him Pieber and his adjutant, Gustav
Simoleit. He invited the officer prisoners to sit down, but
remained standing himself. He held a communiqué in his
hand, which trembled slightly. He looked more than embar-
rassed; he looked strained, even guilty. Massey braced himself
for bad news. Even before Murray had interpreted for him,
he could tell from Braune's stiff, deliberately impersonal tone
that his intuition wasn't wrong.

Braune stopped talking, and placed the communiqué carefully on his desk. Murray, thinking that he had misunder-
stood one detail, asked Braune:

'How many were shot?'

'Forty-one,' replied Braune, not meeting his eye.

Murray translated, his own voice disbelieving: 'I am

instructed by a Higher Authority to pass on certain information to you. With reference to the recent escape from the North Compound of Stammlager-Luftwaffe III at Sagan, I am ordered to notify you that forty-one of the escapers were shot while resisting arrest or in their attempt to escape again after having been recaptured.'

Massey repeated to Murray the question Murray had already asked Braune.

'*How* many?'

'Forty-one.'

For a moment there was total silence in the room. Then Massey said, 'Ask him how many were wounded.'

Murray translated the question, and the answer came back from an increasingly stiff and uncomfortable Braune that he was only authorised to give them the contents of the communiqué, not to elaborate or answer questions. Massey remained seated, and told Murray to repeat the question nevertheless. There was another deeply uncomfortable pause before Braune said, 'I think none were wounded.'

'How could forty-one men be shot at in those circumstances and all be killed, none just wounded?'

'I can only tell you what is in the communiqué.'

'Have you a list of their names?'

'I do not have that information.'

Massey rose. 'I expect you to provide it as soon as possible.'

'Of course.' Braune hesitated, and then added: 'I am acting under orders. I am unable to say more than I have been ordered to communicate by the Higher Authority.'

'What is this Higher Authority?'

'Just a Higher Authority,' said Braune weakly.

Massey had been among Germans for long enough to have formed a shrewd idea of what that meant. Only the SS and the Gestapo, with Hitler and Himmler pulling the strings, could be behind this. Through Murray he registered a request that he be informed of the whereabouts of the bodies so that he could arrange for their burial and the proper disposal of their effects. He also demanded that the Protecting Power be informed. To these matters Braune agreed conciliatorily, adding, however, that all his actions would be circumscribed by any future orders from the 'Higher Authority'.

Pieber escorted Massey and Murray out of the office. Before they parted, he turned to Massey and said: 'Please do not think that the Luftwaffe was involved in any way in this dreadful affair. It is terrible.' He was clearly genuinely moved, and shaken to the core. An awkward silence followed. Pieber bowed slightly, and returned to the *Kommandatur*.

Massey immediately ordered a meeting of the three hundred senior officers in the compound – the head man of each room in each block – and when they had gathered in the theatre, he told them every detail of his interview with Braune. The meeting didn't take long, and there were few questions – people were too stunned. Within ten minutes the news was known to every POW in the camp, let alone the compound. The events of two weeks earlier seemed a lifetime away.

There were some who simply could not believe what had happened, but it was confirmed by the attitude of the Luftwaffe staff at the camp, from whom further details filtered through. It appeared that neither Army High Command, the Prison Camp Inspectorate, nor the Luftwaffe Prison Camp Authority had been informed by the Gestapo or the Kripo of any of the recaptures effected by them. General Westhoff went so far as to lodge a formal complaint with Kaltenbrunner – in itself a very brave act, given that the totalitarian state, in the last eighteen months of its power, was becoming as dangerous as a dying tiger. Kaltenbrunner brushed him off. Westhoff knew better than to insist. Justice would clearly not be done; nor would its cause be helped if he were ordered to the Eastern Front, or placed under arrest. MI6 reports later confirmed 'deep disquiet' among regular German Luftwaffe personnel at the atrocity.

On 15 April the escapers in the cooler began to return to the camp, to learn the news of the killings. The same evening, a senior guard walked quietly to the bulletin board and pinned a sheet of paper to it. This was nothing unusual, and no-one bothered to go and read it at first, but when someone finally did, he realised that it was the promised list of those who had been 'shot while trying to escape'.

He quickly spread the word, and within minutes the bulletin board was surrounded. The POWs read the list again and again. They found there not forty-one names, but forty-seven. Alex Cassie read the names of all his former room-mates, except for Des Plunkett's. Mick Shand read the name of Denys Street, with whom he'd offered to change places in the prison at Görlitz. In all, twenty-two of the names on the list belonged to men who'd been held in the Görlitz prison. The names on the list included those of Hank Birkland, Gordon Brettell, Lester Bull, Roger Bushell, Mike Casey, James Catanach, Arnold Christensen, Dennis Cochran, Halldor Espelid, Brian Evans, Nils Fuglesang, William 'Jack' Grisman, Al Hake, Tony Hayter, Edgar Humphreys, Gordon Kidder, Tom Kirby-Green, Pat Langford, Rene Marcinkus, Jerzy Mondschein, Henri Picard, Porokoru Pohe, Bernard Scheidhauer, Sotiris Skanziklas, Rupert John Stevens, John Stower, Denys Street, Arnost Valenta, Tim Walenn, James Wernham and George Wiley.

Some time later, an additional, very short list was posted, with three names on it: those of Cookie Long, Stanislav Krol, and Pavel Tobolski. The total killed accorded with Hitler's wish: fifty.

On 11 April, Massey, together with a small number of other prisoners who had been seriously wounded when they were shot down, left the compound under escort. They were bound for Switzerland, from where they would be repatriated to England. The new Senior British Officer was Group Captain D. E. L. Wilson of the RAAF.

Russell Cochran, seven years younger than his brother Dennis, was still at school when he heard the news:

'I can remember quite clearly listening to the one o'clock news and being told about this event – there'd been a mass breakout from a prisoner-of-war camp, it didn't say how many. A number of officers had been shot afterwards. I can say, hand on heart, that I knew then that Dennis would have been among that lot. He just really wanted to come home and take care of us all.

'I've always been told time is a great healer . . . but that's not true.'

Almost immediately, the Germans took away the kitbags containing all the kit of the fifty men who had been executed. Then they brought them back, with the suggestion that the possessions should be auctioned off to the other POWs. Bids were made in sterling, and successful bidders wrote 'cheques' on pieces on paper which were held by appointed 'treasurers', to be redeemed after the war, the money to go to the families of the victims. Jack Lyon bought Kirby-Green's wooden suitcase and some of his books. Alex Cassie got Tim Walenn's green neckscarf, and was later asked to return a gold watch, which had been a twenty-first birthday present (Walenn was twenty-eight when he died), to Walenn's parents. After the war, Cassie fulfilled his promise.

On 17 April the camp was visited by Gabriel Naville, who was a representative of the Protecting Power, to whom Wilson gave a full report, which Naville later communicated to the

Eden Tells Full Story of Stalag Shootings; says, "These Foul Criminals Shall Be Tracked Down to the Last Man"

FIFTY OFFICERS MURDERED; "COLD ACT OF BUTCHERY"

JUSTICE AFTER THE WAR

Mr. Eden, Foreign Secretary, after making a statement in the House of Commons to-day on the shooting of R.A.F. prisoners of war who were at Stalag Luft III., said:

"FROM THESE FACTS THERE IS ONLY ONE POSSIBLE CONCLUSION: THESE PRISONERS OF WAR WERE MURDERED —AT SOME INDEFINITE PLACE, OR PLACES, IN THEIR REMOVAL FROM THE GESTAPO PRISON AT GORLITZ ON SOME DATE OR DATES UNKNOWN.

Foreign Office in London. The Foreign Secretary was Anthony Eden, who incidentally took no action when presented with positive proof of the existence and nature of Auschwitz, and turned a deaf ear to pleas from escapers from there to bomb its railway links. On 19 May 1944 Eden addressed the House of Commons, giving his fellow politicians the news of the escape and the atrocity following it. Just over two months later, he augmented his first statement, ending it with the words, 'It is abundantly clear that none of these officers met his death in the course of making his escape from Stalag-Luft III or while resisting capture. The Gestapo's contention that the wearing of civilian clothes by an escaping prisoner of war deprives him of the protection of the Prisoners of War Convention is entirely without foundation in international law and practice. From these facts there is, in H. M. Government's view, only one possible conclusion. These prisoners of war were murdered at some undefined place or places after their removal from . . . prison . . . at some date or dates unknown. H. M. Government must therefore record their [*sic*] solemn protest against these cold-blooded acts of butchery. They will never cease in their efforts to collect the evidence to identify all those responsible. They are firmly resolved that these foul criminals shall be tracked down to the last man, wherever they may take refuge. When the war is over they will be brought to exemplary justice.'

The fifty dead men thus became a *cause célèbre*. Far more airmen were being killed in the average bombing raid, and today many of the survivors of Stalag-Luft III take the view that the deaths of their comrades were an accident of war. But the manner of their deaths constituted a war crime, and the British authorities were right to pursue an investigation. Even though the resources of the men who undertook it were limited, they were experienced and dogged policemen. The investigation began in 1946. The last conviction was obtained in 1968.

Les Brodrick was one of the returnees scanning the list of the men killed for the names of friends and comrades on the escape:

'We couldn't believe that it had happened at first. I thought about it and just couldn't make out how it could have happened. At this stage I suppose I felt lucky, lucky to have survived. I felt shock mainly, then some relief, then I wondered what could have caused me to be left out. I hadn't the faintest idea.

'The main thing I wonder about now was whether it was worth it. They say that hundreds of thousands of troops were involved in searching but they would all have been troops who were on leave or probably not front line troops anyway. I suppose we did cause a certain amount of disruption, but was it worth it? I don't think so.'

A month after Eden's second statement, on 22 July, only two days after the attempt on his life by Stauffenberg, Hitler sent for the cover-up statement which his Foreign Minister, Joachim von Ribbentrop, had busily been preparing with regard to the Great Escape. Having read it, he tore it up. He viewed Eden's statement, in which the British Foreign Secretary had impugned the Gestapo's view that the wearing of civilian clothes robbed escaping POWs to their right to protection under the Geneva Convention, as 'insolent'. Germany therefore made no further statement on the subject.

Jack Lyon:

'We didn't believe it first of all. There was still this idea that it was just propaganda, that they had been sent to another camp. But when the ashes were returned you had to accept that it was true. But I still maintain that we'd seen what war could do and a lot of people had seen their own relatives killed in the bombing, so there was a certain spirit of resignation, that whatever they hand out we can take it. After the initial shock we said, "Well, I'm afraid this is war." They knew the risks when they were escaping. They could have been shot by a guard as they were coming out of the tunnel. In fact one nearly was. And it reinforced our opinion that the only good German was a dead one. I'm afraid we were a hard lot, you know, we didn't give way to emotion a lot. We just carried on grimly, determined not to let things get us down, saying "These Germans have got to be beaten absolutely as soon as we can."'

Over the two months following the escape, forty-six urns and four boxes containing the ashes of the cremated POWs who had been shot by the Gestapo were delivered to Stalag-

Luft III. Kommandant Braune handed them over to the Senior British Officer, and arranged for building materials to be given to the prisoners. so that they could construct a memorial tomb for their fallen comrades.

Fifteen of the escapers had been returned to the North Compound. In time, through coded letters, those remaining in the camp learned of the successful escapes of Bergsland, Muller and van der Stok. The fate of the remaining eight did not become generally known until after the war.

Des Plunkett and Freddie Dvorak were taken from Klatovy (then known by its German name of Klattau) to Prague, where they were placed in separate cells in Pankrac Prison. There, they discovered by chance another of the escapers, a Czech called Ivo Tonder, who'd made an earlier escape attempt with Plunkett. Tonder had been one of the tailors in X-Organisation. The three of them remained in Pankrac until November, whence Dvorak and Tonder were transferred via Hradcin military prison to Stalag-Luft I at Barth. They were only there for two weeks before they were rearrested by the Gestapo and sent to Leipzig, where they were given a show-trial and sentenced to death. They were then transferred to Colditz to await execution, but Colditz was liberated on 16 April 1945 (which happened to be Tonder's thirty-second birthday), and the two were freed.

Plunkett was left alone at Pankrac for a few weeks longer, then he followed the others from Hradcin to Barth, arriving there at the end of January 1945. He had a rough time in the camp. No-one knew him, and one fellow officer suspected him of being a German stool pigeon. When he learned of the Sagan killings, he had a breakdown and came close to committing suicide. Two Canadians talked him round. He was liberated from Barth. Many years later, he and Alex Cassie were reunited, and drank too much whisky together.

When Jimmy James approached the dark pine forest in the

car with his SS driver, who'd chatted quite amiably along the way, he thought that his last hour had come. But the car drove on until the forest cleared to reveal what was clearly another camp, with a high wall topped with what looked like electrified wire, and watch-towers. After about a quarter of a mile the car stopped beside a small door in the camp wall. It opened and, as James was handed over, the SS officer assured him that this was one place he'd be certain not to escape from. He was taken to a small compound containing two wooden barrack blocks within an inner fence of electrified wire. Between this and the outer wall was a pass for patrolling sentries and dogs. The compound adjoined the wall of the main camp and was called *Sonderlager A*.

To his intense surprise the first fellow inmate he met was Harry Day, who greeted him warmly. James assumed he had arrived at Colditz, but Day told him that it was in fact Sachsenhausen concentration camp, near Oranienburg to the north of Berlin. Day, the senior British officer, was not alone in the compound, James discovered. Also in residence was Major John Dodge. The three of them were joined soon afterwards by Sydney Dowse, who, after being parted from Krol, had been taken to the Gestapo in Berlin for interrogation, and subsequently transferred to the concentration camp.

Sachsenhausen housed a brickworks, and is chiefly known for its infamous clay-pit, where inmates who were the victims of the Nazis' 'positive annihilation' programme were worked to death. Hitler had classed male homosexuals as degenerate, and it was here that most of those arrested in that category under his laws were systematically killed. The death rate was thirty men a day. The camp's population also contained a large number of common criminals, resistance fighters, and Jehovah's Witnesses, a sect regarded by Hitler as anti-social, largely because it had from the first been firmly resolved against Nazism. One French Resistance fighter imprisoned there, Robert Deneri, remembers that 'there were seven [*sic*] British officers there – airmen, I think. They would obey only the orders of their senior officer. If they were being marched anywhere, they wouldn't obey the camp guards when ordered to halt; they'd only stop on the orders of their senior officer. Then they would cheer. They inspired the rest of us enormously.'

In fact the POWs, who shared their compound with several Irishmen who may or may not have been double agents, a handful of White Russians, and some resistance fighters, were segregated from the main compound, where the vile work of the concentration camp took place, and from another prison block, where some of the members of the German Resistance to Hitler were kept, pending their execution. Four separate houses held, for a time, prominent Germans and Austrians who were enemies of the regime, but who were being kept alive, according to curious Nazi logic, as bargaining counters with the Allies, should the need arise.

There were no ferrets in Sachsenhausen, and the guards here had no experience of POWs. If the POWs had had experience of concentration camps, or even had an inkling of what was going on elsewhere in the camp, they might not have been so foolhardy as to start to dig a tunnel, with its trap under James's bed; but start one they did, motivated as they were by a sense of duty and desire to escape. They were soon joined in the enterprise by another British officer, a commando colonel called Jack Churchill, who'd been transferred to the camp after capture. They sank a shaft about 150 centimetres deep, and pushed the tunnel from there towards an empty, uncompleted compound about forty metres distant. Within the compound, unbelievably, a three-metre ladder had been abandoned – and it was just the height of the surrounding wall. The plans was simply to dig a basic tunnel and use it to get out as fast as possible. The soil was firm, so there was no need of shoring. James and Dowse did the excavation, hiding the displaced soil under the corridor of their block.

By now it was late July. Harry Day was leafing through the Nazi newspaper, the *Völkischer Beobachter*, one afternoon, when he came across a condemnation of Eden's second statement to the House of Commons. It was from this that the men in Sachsenhausen learned the fate of their comrades, but as no names were printed, they had no idea who had died. There was a brief moment during which they considered the wisdom of their latest escape attempt, but then they got on with it. The tunnel was ready by September, and on the twenty-third, the five men made their way through the hole. Soon they were free again.

Dowse and Day hoped to hitch a lift on a lorry, arranged through a contact made in the camp, and get to France that way; but they were spotted and reported to the police. Soon they were returned to Sachsenhausen and chained to the floor in cells in the punishment block. Dodge, travelling alone, followed the railway track in the direction of Rostock, and with the help of some French workers managed to stay free for a month; but he couldn't get far without papers and as soon as he broke cover he was recaptured and returned to Sachsenhausen. A similar fate befell the last two, James and Churchill, who'd covered 100 miles by foot and freight train trying to make their way to Stettin.

Back in the concentration camp, although Himmler had ordered their execution they instead spent five months in solitary confinement. Then in February 1945 the Germans began to make curious overtures to the British prisoners. Dowse was approached with the proposition that he be allowed to 'escape' again, in order to carry a conciliatory peace proposition to England. Fearing a trap, Dowse refused. He and the others were released from their harsh captivity nevertheless, and returned to their original compound, where they ran into the last escaper from Stalag-Luft III to have survived, a Frenchman called Raymond van Wymeersch, who'd arrived via the infamous Berlin prisons of Alexanderplatz and Plötzensee. At about the same time, John Dodge was separated from them.

The Thousand-Year-Reich was, by now, on the verge of collapse, and the Germans resorted to desperate measures. Long 'death-marches' of prisoners had already started west-wards and northwards from the concentration camps in the east, and huge movements of prisoners were now taking place as the Nazis sought to rationalise their vast and complex prison system. On 3 April, the British officers together with most of the men in their compound were transported south to the concentration camp at Flossenburg, where they stayed for ten or eleven days before being moved on to Dachau, just to the north of Munich. There they were joined with a large group of 'prominent' prisoners who had been kept at that camp, including Martin Niemöller and a handful of other survivors of the German Resistance movement; and major German political figures who had either opposed Hitler before the war, or supported him for a time and then either grown disaffected, or been cast aside by him. Among them were General Franz Halder, former Chief of the German Army General Staff, the former Austrian Chan-cellor, Kurt von Schuschnigg, and the French statesman, Léon Blum.

The large contingent moved on two days later with their increasingly nervous SS escort, first to a camp near Innsbruck, and thence across the Brenner Pass to a village in the South Tyrol by bus. It was now the end of April. The American forces were not far away. Italian partisans were in the woods. Graf Otto-Philipp von Stauffenberg, a nephew of the conspir-ator, who was a teenaged member of the group, recalls what happened next:

233

I think the Nazis were keeping us as hostages to buy their liberty or at least clemency. There were over one hundred of us as we arrived at the village on about 1 May. There was a rumour started that orders had been given to kill us rather than let us fall into enemy hands. Our ordinary guards were scared, but their officers were fanatics, and the SS men would have carried out their orders. Against orders, we disembarked from the buses and followed the officers who had gone into the village to sort out billets. We wanted to find out what our fate would be. Our guards didn't dare fire at us, and so they escorted us. Among us was the General Staff Colonel Bogislav von Bonin, who had been arrested for retreating on the Eastern Front in defiance of a Führer Order, but he still had his full uniform with decorations and the General Staff red stripe on his trousers. He found a German Army radio post in the village, and went there without the knowledge of the SS. The regular soldiers there didn't know he was a prisoner and obeyed him when he ordered them to put him in touch with the Commander-in-Chief, Italy – General Vietinghof, whom he knew well. He spoke to Vietinghof and explained the situation candidly, requesting help. He then rejoined the rest of us in the schoolhouse where we had been billeted. That night there was a great clamour, though no shots were fired. An army major appeared in the school and told us that his unit had arrived, disarmed the SS, and sent them off in one of the buses – they were killed later by Italian partisans. The unit had been sent by Vietinghof and we were now under the army's protection. They took us to a hotel nearby, where they left us. We were liberated by the Americans a day or two later.

After he had been separated from his companions, John Dodge, to his amazement, found himself in the company of a personable young SS officer who escorted him unhandcuffed to a comfortable staff car in which they drove back to Berlin. Once there, the officer took him shopping for a complete civilian wardrobe, assuring him that he would not be compromised by wearing them, and took him to the grand apartment of an SS major and his family, with whom Dodge was to stay.

Dodge had hardly got over this treatment when he was introduced to a visitor, Dr Hans Thost, of the Foreign Ministry. Thost took him by car to the Adlon, the best hotel in Berlin, still serving the finest food in Germany despite bomb damage. In a private room Thost introduced him to another man, Paul Schmidt, who was Hitler's interpreter. Schmidt shook hands – Dodge was too bewildered not to – and poured him a large whisky. Then he smiled and came straight to the point:

'We are sending you home, Major Dodge. We'd like you to be reunited with your kinsman, Mr Churchill.' Dodge began to see what was up as Schmidt continued. 'We would ask you to remember three things: first, no unconditional surrender. Second, the restoration of Germany's prewar frontiers. Third, the balance of power in Europe must be maintained, for all our sakes. I am sure you understand.'

Dodge understood perfectly. Germany wasn't to suffer as a result of her bid for world supremacy and the destruction of millions of people; she was to retain her old frontiers, and in return she would be a powerful ally against Russia, whose Soviet armies were already in full possession of most of the fertile east of the country. And he was to be sent back to England as a peace emissary to his distant relative, Churchill. They must be desperate, he thought.

A few days after the meeting with Schmidt, Thost drove Dodge down to Dresden, where they narrowly escaped death during the Allied carpet-bombing of that city. They moved on to Weimar, and then to Regensburg, where someone overheard them speaking English and called the police, who duly arrived and arrested them. Thost was livid, and pulled out his identity card. The police baulked, but ironically it wasn't until the Gestapo arrived that the misunderstanding was fully sorted out.

Thost got Dodge to the Swiss border on 25 April and wished him luck. Two days later he was being debriefed by MI6 officers in Bern, and a week later he was home. He didn't get to meet Churchill until a day or two before the war officially ended, and then the prime minister listened to his story with profound amusement.

Despite the warnings about what would happen to future escapers – it was by now an open secret that if they were caught they would be shot – the escape committee at Stalag-Luft III reorganised itself after the debacle of the Great Escape, and planned further attempts. In the North Compound Norman Canton and Robert Ker-Ramsay took control of tunnelling operations and started a new one, codenamed 'George', which ran east from a trap under one of the seats in the now-reopened theatre, where productions resumed and costumes were supplied from theatres in Berlin. As before, sand from George was dispersed under the theatre's floor. The tunnel was not connected to a specific escape plan: it was, in a sense, a morale-booster, and everyone involved thought it might come in handy. The war was clearly heading towards its end, but there was no knowing what the Germans, particularly the Gestapo and the SS, would do to prisoners once they'd lost. George made good progress, and before work was abandoned on it for the winter, it reached to just beyond the outer eastern fence. Security in those last days was less ferocious. The ferrets had lost a lot of their edge. It's possible that they felt the fate of the men killed on the Great Escape would act as sufficient deterrent. Certainly the

Germans can hardly have dreamed that another tunnel would be started so soon.

On the morning of 27 January 1945, soon after the Russians had started what was to be their last great winter offensive, and as their tanks swept over the flat Polish plain from the east, the Luftwaffe staff began to evacuate the entire Sagan complex – a massive operation, since the camp complex held over two thousand men. Formed into six columns, the prisoners were marched seventy-five kilometres westwards, in freezing, stormy weather, to Spremberg. They were accompanied by their old friends Pieber and Glemnitz. Glemnitz kept asking them if they'd brought their radio receiver along with them, but he was only half-serious. In fact, they had. It was secreted in Pieber's staff car.

Len Hall:

'Glemnitz was a very human man – very determined, very good at his job. At the end of the war when he was taken prisoner I saw him and he said, "Hello, I've made two escape attempts already!"'

At Spremberg, the POWs were divided up and loaded onto goods waggons. The Americans were taken to Moosberg, near Munich. The men of the North Compound were taken to a broken-down naval camp near Bremen, where they stayed until 9 April. Then they were marched again, 150 kilometres north-east to Lübeck. Fortunately by now, though the prisoners were weakened, and many were suffering from dysentery, the weather was much improved, and they had had access to Red Cross parcels at Bremen. Knowing that the end was in sight, and aware of the panic in their guards, their morale

was high, too. When they arrived at the designated impro-
vised camp fifteen kilometres short of Lübeck, the buildings
were so verminous as to be unfit for human habitation, and
the prisoners were billeted instead on two large farms nearby,
where they spent their last days in captivity. The guards abandoned them.

On 2 May two tanks appeared through the trees to the
south. The prisoners had heard gunfire from that direction
earlier, and now waited the arrival of the tanks nervously.
They were still too far away to see if they belonged to the
Allies or the Wehrmacht. It was still possible that the tanks
had been sent to liquidate them.

But as the tanks drew closer, they could see that they had
no black crosses on their sides. Then the hatch of one of
them opened and a man in a black beret and brown battledress appeared. He surveyed the bedraggled kriegies, all
waiting anxiously.

'Fucking hell,' he said.

Chapter Ten

I N THE CHAOS THAT WAS EUROPE IMMEDIATELY AFTER THE
war, with millions of displaced persons engaged in a
massive migration between ruined cities across devastated
countryside, it was easy for anyone so inclined to disappear,
especially as half the continent – Poland, the eastern part of
Germany, Czechoslovakia, Hungary, Romania, Bulgaria and
Albania – had now fallen into the sphere of influence of the
Soviet Union. Amid the confusion, new battle-lines were
being drawn for what was to be a forty-year-long Cold War.
One of the investigators into the killing of the escaped prisoners from Sagan remarked that 'It is probably true that
neither the Poles nor the Russians really believed our motives
in conducting this investigation. To them the murder of fifty
officers was a matter of such triviality, when compared with
their own civilian and military casualties, that that they simply
could not see why we were making such a fuss about it. I
believe they thought we were spies, using the investigation
as a pretext for our presence, and this accounts for their
complete lack of cooperation.' Sagan itself was now well
within the Russian sector.

Looking for Nazi war criminals, especially the relatively
minor officials who had carried out the murders of the fifty
escapers from Stalag-Luft III, would be, on the face of it,

harder than looking for the ghost of a needle in a haystack as big as a castle.

The Special Investigation Branch (SIB) of the RAF was given the go-ahead to start work soon after the end of the war, but fully seventeen months after the killings. By then, many trails had gone cold, and the detachment of men delegated to do the job numbered only five officers and fourteen NCOs. Demobilisation in the months following the war reduced this team, by May 1946, to three officers and four NCOs. Their achievement was all the more remarkable.

Colin Kirby-Green remembers being told the news of his father's death. He was eight years old:

'One evening after prayers the headmaster asked me to go to his study and I thought, Oh gosh, what have I done? Captain Fenn, the headmaster, had been a soldier in the First World War. He was very aloof, but kind. He told me my father was dead, that he had been shot while trying to escape. That was all he told me and I remember bursting into tears and he let me do that; I think he might have handed me a handkerchief. After I don't know how long I was able to go out of the room and upstairs to bed. The headmaster's wife, who had talked to the other boys while I was in with the headmaster, had said that if Kirby-Green was crying in the night they weren't to tease him or say anything about it. I had the most desolate night. I don't know if I fell asleep. I was in a room full of other people that I was probably keeping awake and they said nothing. Somehow the night passed and we all got dressed and washed our faces and went down to breakfast and it was as though nothing had happened and nobody said anything, no one at all.

'I just wanted my mother so badly then.

'I found out later that the Germans decided by looking at

a list of the seventy-six who would be shot and there were things like, Oh he is too young, he's got children. Well my father had a child.'

They were, however, exceptional men. In charge was Wing Commander Wilfred Bowes, a career officer in the RAF Police and one of the founder members of the Special Investigation Branch. Working closely with him was Squadron Leader F. P. McKenna, a thirty-eight-year-old former detective sergeant with the Blackpool police. Flight Lieutenant Arthur Lyon had been an inspector in London before joining RAF Intelligence in the early years of the war, and spoke fluent German. The rest of the team was no less gifted.

Working sometimes together, sometimes alone, they covered Europe over the next three years, doggedly following every lead they could find. In the end they identified seventy-two culprits, and accounted for sixty-nine of them, though not all could be brought to justice. Many had died, among them some by their own hand; others had disappeared into what had become Eastern Europe. But there was a trail to follow of paperwork, wronged wives, abandoned mistresses, and former colleagues so appalled by what had taken place that they were willing to provide leads. Two Gestapo officials implicated in the killing of Kidder and Kirby-Green were identified from their portraits in a pornographic mural on the wall of their favourite bar in Brno. Others were already in Allied prisons – the various 'cages' set up to hold suspected former Gestapo and SS-men, and other Nazi Party officials, pending their investigation.

Additionally, not all the governments in what was soon to become the Eastern Bloc were unfriendly in the early days. The Czechs were helpful, for example. The investigation was also considerably aided by the relative stupidity of some of the perpetrators. After only a short time, some began to come out of the woodwork; and they had covered their deeds so unimaginatively that even while the war was still on, Gestapo high command had to order them to change their cover stories somewhat: all had adhered rigidly to the general guide-line that the prisoners were shot while let out of the car that was carrying them to relieve themselves by the side of the road – a situation, so the reports went on, which the pris-oners took advantage of in order to flee. This was precisely the cover story the *RSHA* had suggested to its various regional offices; but Müller and Co. hadn't expected it to be followed in each case virtually to the letter.

Beryl Fitch, Dennis Cochran's sister, remembers the day the dreaded telegram arrived:

'The telegram just contained the bland statement "Shot trying to escape. Details to follow". They didn't have anything else to say at the time. There was disbelief at first, one couldn't take it in. He'd been away from the war, he'd been safe from the war in a prison camp. Some people looked at it and said, "It can't be true, they've made a mistake, it's not true," and I didn't know how but I knew it was true. The fact that it said "trying to escape" – one could accept that that's what he would do.

'I suppose when anybody loses his life, it is just a terrible thing for the relatives, but this was really something rather different. They were not defending themselves, they were not fighting, they didn't have a gun, they were completely vulner-able and just gunned down.

'It was awfully difficult for the family to deal with. It's not like a death where you have got a funeral to arrange, which in a way helps you through, draws a line. There was none of that, and the war was still on and it wasn't really until people started being repatriated and the war was over and plane after plane was coming with prisoners of war returning and general jubilation – I think that's when it hit really that he wasn't coming back.'

There were dangers. The RAF uniform was not popular in post-war Germany. On at least one occasion, driving at night in an open jeep, two of the investigators stopped just in time to avoid having a wire, which had been stretched across the road, slice their heads off. But despite all the difficulties in their way, the investigators managed to bring several of the murderers to justice. At their trials, none of those accused pleaded 'guilty'.

The investigation into the death of Dennis Cochran turned up two names, Josef Gmeiner, head of the Karlsruhe Gestapo, and Walter Herberg, a member of his staff. They had received a secret teleprint message from Berlin with their instructions, and reconstructed its contents for the SIB. In outline, the message proved to be similar to the others sent out to the relevant Gestapo offices ordered to carry out the various 'executions':

Reich Top Secret. RSHA to Chief of the Gestapo Office, Karlsruhe, or his deputy: By order of the Führer, the Reichsführer SS [Himmler] has ordered that the British airman Cochran who escaped from Sagan and is now held by the Kripo at Ettlingen, Karlsruhe, will be taken over by officials of your office and during transport in the direction of Breslau will be shot while trying to escape. The shooting will be done in such a way that the prisoner concerned will be unaware of what is going to happen. The corpse is to remain on the spot until inspected by the local gendarmerie and a death certificate has been issued. The body is to be cremated in the nearest crematorium. The urn is to be kept by the Gestapo Office. Further instructions about the urn will be issued at a given time.

The death certificate is to be returned to me with a description of the spot where the shooting took place. Only persons strictly concerned with this matter will be allowed to know of this teleprint. These persons must be pledged to special secrecy. The teleprint must be destroyed after the order is carried out. Destruction of the teleprint must be notified to me by teleprint. The Kripo, Karlsruhe, have been given relevant instructions.'

The order was signed by Heinrich Müller, head of *RSHA* Department IV. Once the order had been received, two police officers, Wilhelm Boschert and Otto Preiss, were deputed to act as driver and executioner respectively. Herberg, despite his objections, was ordered to go along too, to smooth over the bureaucratic end of things – the death certificate and the crematorium orders. At his trial, Herberg told the court that he had considered 'the possibility of letting the prisoner escape or helping him across the Swiss border, but this too was out of the question because nobody would have accepted any excuses in this direction, and I must say I even thought of committing suicide and shooting a bullet through my head, but this would not have saved the life of the prisoner, so I did not see any way out to avoid the carrying out of the order to save the life of the prisoner'.

The following morning, Cochran was picked up, hand-cuffed, and put in the back of a green Mercedes. Herberg asked him his rank, and then asked what the equivalent of a Flying Officer was in the American Air Force. 'Never mind that,' Cochran replied humorously, suspecting nothing. 'The important thing is that he gets paid four times as much as I do.' As they drove, Herberg told him that he was being taken to a transit camp before being returned to Sagan. Preiss gave Cochran a sandwich and a cigarette. Near Natzweiler concentration camp, they drew up by the side of the road, and Herberg told Cochran that he needed to take a piss, and invited him to do the same. Cochran accepted, and climbed out of the car with Herberg. Preiss and Boschert did the same.

During his interrogation by McKenna, Herberg then described what happened next: 'I walked another twenty metres along the road . . . I could not possibly watch what was coming, and I turned my back. Shortly afterwards I heard a shot, and then another. I walked back and saw the officer lying on the ground, face down, about three metres from the car. Preiss stood beside him with a pistol in his hand, and Boschert was standing near the car. I could see that the officer was dead. He had been shot in the back near the heart, and through the back of the head. The second bullet had come out through the left eye. None of us spoke a word. Boschert took off the handcuffs.' Herberg later said that he'd told Preiss to fire the second shot, as the first hadn't killed Cochran. Preiss later personally delivered the urn with Cochran's ashes to Sagan. It emerged later that he, too, had been unwilling to carry out the killing.

Preiss and Boschert were tracked down, interviewed and arrested.

Almost all the urns returned to Sagan had written on them the place of cremation. Those of Gordon Kidder and Tom Kirby-Green were marked 'Mährisch Ostrau' (now Moravská Ostrava, in the Czech Republic). A number of Czechs had been killed following the Sagan breakout, and the authorities were inclined to help the investigation. In autumn 1945 they had picked up a driver called Friedrich Kiowsky, who had worked for the Gestapo, and he had been interrogated.

It emerged that Kiowsky had driven Kirby-Green from Zlín, where he had been held with Kidder, in the direction of Breslau via Moravská Ostrava, together with a Gestapo official called Erich Zacharias. Kidder travelled with them in another car. About ten kilometres before Moravská, both cars drew over to the side of the road. The excuse of stopping to have a break to urinate was used again, and Zacharias shot Kirby-Green, while a Gestapo colleague, Adolf Knüppelberg, travelling with Kidder, shot him. A Czech lawyer, F. V. van der Bijl, who had served with Kirby-Green early in the war, alerted the British ambassador in Prague to the case, who referred it to SIB. Following a prolonged search, Zacharias was apprehended and later brought to trial. Taken to London and placed there in the London 'Cage', as many German suspects were, he accused the commander of the cage, Lieutenant-Colonel A. P. Scotland, of torture. He subsequently escaped twice from captivity, but was recaptured. Van der Bijl noted that Zacharias was involved in two other murders. and had been implicated in the rape and murder of an eighteen-year-old Czech secretary at Zlín.

Four of the escapers – Brettell, Marcinkus, Picard and Walenn – had been murdered near Danzig, in an area from which the British were now barred. However, a former member of the Danzig Gestapo, Kurt Achterburg, made contact with Flight Lieutenant Arthur Lyon at a holding camp for suspects at Esterwegen, near the Dutch frontier, where Achterburg was himself being held. Lyon already knew from other sources that the head of the Danzig Gestapo, Günther Venediger, had been involved in the killings, but Achterburg was able to give him the name of the actual executioner – a police officer called Reinhold Bruchardt, a dangerous brute of a man whom Achterburg felt justified in betraying as Bruchardt was having an affair with Achterburg's wife. SIB traced the man to Kempten and ambushed him in bed. It took four of them to hold the big man down – the hand-cuffs weren't wide enough to go round his wrists – but they overpowered him before he could reach his revolver. Venediger himself wasn't caught until 1952, when he emerged from the Russian zone. He was finally sentenced to two years in prison in 1955.

Meanwhile, two other members of the SIB team, Sergeants Stuart Greet and J. W. Venselaar, were on the track of Dr Leopold Spann, head of the Saarbrücken Gestapo, whom they knew to have written a report on the deaths of Roger Bushell and Bernard Scheidhauer, 'shot while trying to escape'. It appeared that Spann was the only local Gestapo head man apart from Wilhelm Scharpwinkel, the chief of the Breslau Gestapo, to have actually done the killings himself, rather than delegate. Greet and Venselaar learned that Spann was assisted by a Gestapo colleague called Emil Schulz. Their driver was Walter Breithaupt. It emerged that Spann had been killed in an air-raid on Linz towards the end of April, 1945, but with the help of the Americans the two SIB investiga-tors managed to find Breithaupt, who was living with his parents in a suburb of Frankfurt-am-Main, and, subsequently, Schulz, a married man with two young daughters, whom they traced through his wife to a French holding camp for suspects near Saarbrücken.

Breithaupt's confession had a depressingly familiar ring to it. He'd fetched the two prisoners from the Kripo jail and they got into the car with Schulz and Spann. They'd driven about forty kilometres when Spann ordered him to pull over. 'The prisoners were told they could come out of the car to relieve themselves. One of them pointed to his handcuffs, but I do not remember if they were taken off. The two pris-oners went into the bushes a few metres to the right and rear of the car, and Spann and Schulz followed, each with their pistol in their hand . . . I stood next to the car, and could see everything. Both prisoners were just unbuttoning their trousers with Spann and Schulz standing a metre behind them. Spann gave a sign, and Spann and Schulz each fired one shot at the same time into the necks of the prisoners.' At his trial, Schulz later said that he had knelt down by one of the prisoners and shot him again, on Spann's order, 'although I was of the opinion that the man was already dead'. This contradicted an earlier statement he had made: 'Scheidhauer fell on his face. I think Bushell crumpled up, fell somewhat on his right side and was lying there turned on his back. On approaching closer I noticed the dying man was in convulsions. I lay on the ground and shot him in the left temple, whereupon death took place immediately.' Crucially, if a man had been wounded while trying to escape, under the Geneva Convention his captors should have arranged to take him to hospital, not finish the job.

On his way to London to be interrogated, incarcerated and ultimately tried for his crime Emil Schulz, 38-year-old husband and father of two little girls, asked a favour of Frank McKenna – to write a letter home. McKenna unlocked the handcuffs and Schulz wrote:

'Dear Angela, dear Ingeborg, dear Helga you dears of mine!

I am already in England now, and, alas, could not say goodbye to you.

I am here as a prisoner because of carrying out an official order in the spring of 1944.

I never on my own initiative acted against the laws of humanity . . . I am waiting for justice. I only ask to be treated as I deserve and judged according to my position . . . you dear Angela have courage and live only for the children. The snaps of Ingeborg and Helga are my faithful companions.

How easier it would be to suffer death three times in order to prevent all this happening to you and especially to the children . . .

Ever your faithful husband, your Daddy and your Emil.'

One suspect who continued to elude them was the Breslau Gestapo head, Wilhelm Scharpwinkel. SIB knew that he was in Moscow. They suspected that he might now be working for the Russian Secret Police. They never got him. On 17 October 1947, the Russians told them that he'd died in Moscow. But they did at least manage to interview him, under Russian supervision, in Moscow in the late summer of 1946. The interview was conducted by a British Intelligence Officer, Captain Maurice Cornish. Scharpwinkel gave Cornish a statement which led the SIB men to Kiel, where they discovered what had happened to James Catanach, Arnold Christensen, Halldor Espelid and Nils Fuglesang. They interviewed the director of the Kiel crematorium, a man who'd been at his post for many years. He showed them an entry for 29 March 1944 where, instead of names, there were just four Roman numerals: I, II, III and IV; and he remembered that on the evening of that day, at about 6.30 p.m., four members of the Kiel Gestapo arrived with an undertaker and two large coffins, each containing the corpses of two men. Further investigation, including questioning of the undertaker and of two former Gestapo typists, revealed that the corpses were allegedly those of 'agents' captured and shot by the Gestapo. By degrees, SIB tracked down the Gestapo officials involved in the murders. Most of them were already in an internment camp at Neuengamme, which during the war had been a concentration camp so foul that inmates there had been fed pieces of their fellows' corpses in the soup.

Interrogation of the men revealed that two cars had been used for the operation, which had been led by the deputy chief of the local Gestapo, Johannes Post. They'd collected the prisoners from the Flensburg Kripo, where they were being held, and driven them back through Kiel to a point about sixteen kilometres south of the town where there was a small hamlet called Roter Hahn. The first car was driven by Artur Denkmann, and the passengers were Post, Catanach, and a police inspector called Hans Kähler. On their way through Kiel, Post ordered Denkmann to make a small diversion so that he could deliver some theatre tickets for that evening to his mistress, in case he was delayed. All the Gestapo men interviewed swore that they were convinced that they had been detailed to execute spies or saboteurs, not POWs. They did admit that they were ordered to do the job by the local Gestapo chief, Fritz Schmidt.

Further enquiries failed to turn up Schmidt, but McKenna did manage to trace Post to a holding prison at Minden. Post turned out to be an unregenerate Nazi, who gave a full and detailed account of the operation with absolutely no remorse and even with a note of pride in his voice, as one describing a job well done. Kiel Gestapo had received the usual instructions from Berlin, and made the arrangements for the pickup and place of execution of the prisoners. They even determined upon the kind of pistol to be used, a Walther 7.65mm service automatic, and took a rifle along too in case any of the prisoners should genuinely try to escape and get out of range of the handguns.

Post, in the first car, reached Roter Hahn first, at about 4.45 p.m. He'd been talking to Catanach quite amiably up until then, but just before they arrived, he explained that they would be stopping shortly so that he could shoot him. This was a ploy Post had used before, and it seemed to divert him. Catanach thought it was merely a tasteless joke. Then the car drew up, and Post, Catanach and Kähler got out, Post making the usual excuse. They walked a short way, during which the nervous Kähler drew his pistol, cocked it, managed to jam its mechanism, and then fired it by accident. Afraid that Kähler would bodge the execution if left to his own devices, Post drew his own weapon and coolly shot Catanach through the heart from the back.

At that point the second car arrived and stopped, disgorging Christensen, Espelid and Fuglesang, with the other Gestapo men. Seeing Catanach dead on the ground, the prisoners shouted in fear and tried to make a break for it. The Gestapo officers started firing wildly, killing two of them but only wounding the third. Post fetched the rifle and delivered the *coup de grâce*. The other Germans also fired into the bodies of the prisoners. 'Whether it was necessary or not I cannot say,' said Post at his trial. Post, who, unlike his fellow accused, refused to have affidavits lodged in his favour at his trial, despite the fact that earlier in the war, at Altona, Hamburg, he had saved the life of a British pilot, gave as his reason: 'Because I could not have been a National Socialist for so many years and suddenly put in affidavits from Communists or Jews or Freethinkers.'

The search for Fritz Schmidt lasted until January 1967, when he was arrested and put on trial. He pleaded that he was only obeying orders. In May 1968, he was given a two-year sentence. The seven officers directly involved in the murder were tried soon after their arrest, except for one of their number, who hanged himself in jail.

The majority of those escapers shot had been held in the Görlitz prison, and those in command of the operation were Wilhelm Scharpwinkel and Max Wielen. In his interview in Moscow, Scharpwinkel tried to shift the bulk of the responsibility onto Wielen, which provoked an angry response from the Kripo chief. Wielen had been more deeply involved than any other ordinary senior policeman, and had been in direct contact with Nebe; but he claimed the usual excuse of having only been obeying orders. He did not, however, know the details of how the shootings had been carried out. These came from Scharpwinkel, who told Cornish that, with the prisoners being taken away from Görlitz in small groups, a death-squad was created under a Gestapo officer by the name of Lux. In Scharpwinkel's words, with reference to the killing of Casey, Hake, Pohe, Wiley and two others: 'The British were brought to the headquarters. As I speak English, I put one or two questions while they were being interrogated: were they married? had they children? and so on. Lux explained to the prisoners that by order of the Supreme Military Commander [Hitler] they had been sentenced to death. Then we drove away. When the Reichsautobahn was reached the summary shootings were carried out. The prisoners showed considerable calm, which surprised me very much. The six prisoners stood next to one another in the wood. Lux gave the order to fire and the detachment fired. By the second salvo the prisoners were dead.' It is clear from the way he phrases his description that Scharpwinkel was trying to give a veneer of legitimacy to this particular shooting. He stressed that this was the only one he attended, and that he himself did not fire. He went on to imply that he had little or nothing to do with the rest of the Görlitz operation, suggesting that Lux and his associates were chiefly responsible. Lux had been killed at Breslau; one of the associates, Erwin Wieczorek, was arrested, and sentenced to death in November 1948, though the sentence was quashed on review. Wieczorek told his SIB interrogators that Lux's team had also earlier been responsible for 'executing' some prisoners at Hirschberg – two Polish officers, and Sotiris Skanziklas and Jimmy Wernham. Wieczorek said that he'd been present, but had not fired. He also told them that Scharpwinkel was there.

Scharpwinkel's driver, Robert Schröder, was never charged, but appeared as a witness. He was present at the shooting of a group of ten officers, including Birkland, Evans, Humphreys, Langford and Valenta. He asserted that Scharpwinkel was present, along with Lux and five Gestapo associates. The prisoners were transported in the back of a lorry. 'It was the Sagan road. About halfway there was a halt to let the prisoners and the guards relieve themselves and also warm themselves up a bit. It was freezing cold. The lorry was about forty metres behind my car. I was sitting alone in the car when I suddenly heard shouts, followed immediately by a mad firing of machine pistols. I jumped out of the car and ran to the rear. Behind the lorry lay the prisoners scattered on the ground. Some of them were right on the road, others were on a slope nearby, but they were all close together. When I asked one of the officials what had happened, he said that some of the fellows had tried to escape and that they had all bought it.'

The inscriptions on the urns of Jack Grisman, Denys Street and four others were marked 'Breslau' when they were returned to Sagan; but no-one was ever found who could throw light on how they met their end – it seems reasonable to assume that Lux's gang took care of the matter. Nor do we know how Krol, Long and Topolski met their isolated ends, though their urns were also marked 'Breslau'. Tony Hayter became the responsibility of the Strasbourg Gestapo, whose head was Alfred Schimmel, a lawyer, assisted by an official called Heinrich Hilke. Schimmel was already in American custody at Dachau when SIB tracked him down. At first Schimmel denied any connection with Hayter's death, but when his assertions were checked, they let him down. He was a weak man, and finally confessed that he had ordered the airman's arrest because if he hadn't obeyed orders he would himself have been shot. Hilke and another Gestapo man called Max Dissner carried out the action, in the usual manner. Schimmel told his SIB interrogators that at first he had toyed with the idea of taking Hayter to the Swiss border and letting him go, before crossing to safety himself, but the thought of what reprisals might be taken on his family prevented him. He gave the order to shoot Hayter, but told McKenna, 'Müller's order was to shoot him the following day. That was Good Friday, the holiest day of the year. I could not have this man killed on Good Friday. I could not go to church knowing that that was happening.'

'How did you resolve that?' asked McKenna.

'I had him shot that very day. On Maundy Thursday.'

Schimmel received the death sentence and was executed at Hameln (Hamelin) on 27 February 1948. Dissner hanged himself in his cell on 11 May the same year. Hilke was finally caught and charged in 1966, but the case was dismissed. He died peacefully on 11 April 1968.

The first trials of those brought to justice by SIB – there were eighteen accused in all – began on 1 July 1947 before Number 1 Court in the Kurio Haus in Hamburg. Verdicts and sentences were handed down on 3 September. Among those sentenced to death were Boschert, Gmeiner, Herberg, Kähler, Post, Preiss, Schimmel, Schulz and Zacharias. They were hanged on 26 February 1948. Breithaupt and Wielen were sentenced to life imprisonment. Denkmann was given ten years.

Flight Lieutenant Brian Evans, born on 14 February 1920, shot dead on the Sagan road by Lux's Gestapo team some time in late March or early April 1944, wrote to his fiancée, Joan Cook, five days before the Great Escape. She still has the letter. It ends:

You know darling I still haven't got over the idea that we're going to spend the rest of our lives together. We're going to have even better times too, than we've yet had. In one of your letters you said you were going to spoil me when I get home. I'm very anxious to know how you're going to spoil me. I think you deserve a lot of spoiling too, dearest, in fact I've got a terrific lot to repay to you. If it weren't for your letters I don't know what I'd do for they've helped me tremendously, Joan. I've got such a lot of things to say to you but somehow they just can't be written; they wouldn't make sense, in fact I don't think this letter reads too well. Hope you can understand what I mean. Letters are unsatisfactory things, aren't they? Remember I'm coming back home to you soon to look after you darling. Until then, remember I'll always love you.

Marie Brochin, Jack Grisman's widow, gave an interview to the London *Daily Mail* on the fiftieth anniversary of the Great Escape. She told them, 'I've never forgotten him. I still see Jack in my dreams. I had a dream the other night and I said to him, "We're all so old now," and he said simply, "It doesn't matter. We still love one another." It was as plain as if he was in the room.'

Jack Lyon drew Number 88 or 89 in the Great Escape, so he just missed going out. Looking back, he says: 'As far as the cost is concerned you must look upon it in perspective. Only a week later, we lost ninety aircraft and up to five hundred aircrew on a raid on Nuremberg. We lost in total 58,000 members of Bomber Command during the war. You could say that the Great Escape was a successful but costly operation, and I think I've never really altered that opinion, and I still hold to it.'

And that is the story.

The Great Escapers

★ Executed by the Gestapo following the escape

Flight Lieutenant Albert Armstrong Royal Air Force (RAF)
Sergeant Per Bergsland RAF
Flight Lieutenant R. A. Bethell RAF
★Flying Officer Henry J. Birkland Royal Canadian Air Force (RCAF)
★Flight Lieutenant E. Gordon Brettell RAF
Flight Lieutenant Les G. J. Brodrick RAF
★Flight Lieutenant Lester J. Bull RAF
★Squadron Leader Roger J. Bushell RAF
Flight Lieutenant Bill Cameron RCAF
★Flight Lieutenant Michael J. Casey RAF
★Squadron Leader James Catanach Royal Australian Air Force (RAAF)
★Flying Officer Arnold G. Christensen Royal New Zealand Air Force (RNZAF)
Pilot Officer Dick S. A. Churchill RAF
★Flying Officer Dennis H. Cochran RAF
★Squadron Leader Ian K. P. Cross RAF
Wing Commander Harry M. A. Day RAF
Major John B. Dodge Territorial Army
Flight Lieutenant Sydney H. Dowse RAF
Flight Lieutenant Freddie Dvorak RAF

*Sergeant Halldor Espelid Royal Norwegian Air Force
*Flight Lieutenant Brian H. Evans RAF
*Lieutenant Nils Fuglesang Royal Norwegian Air Force
*Lieutenant Johannes S. Gouws South African Air Force (SAAF)
Flight Lieutenant Bernard Green RAF
*Flight Lieutenant William J. Grisman RAF
*Flight Lieutenant Alastair D. M. Gunn RAF
*Flight Lieutenant Albert H. Hake RAAF
*Flight Lieutenant Charles P. Hall RAF
*Flight Lieutenant Anthony R. H. Hayter RAF
*Flight Lieutenant Edgar S. Humphreys RAF
Pilot Officer B. A. James RAF
*Flying Officer Gordon A. Kidder RCAF
*Flight Lieutenant Reginald V. Kierath RAAF
*Flight Lieutenant Antoni Kiewnarski RAF
*Squadron Leader Thomas G. Kirby-Green RAF
*Flying Officer A. Wlodzimierz Kolanowski RAF
*Flying Officer Stanislav Z. Krol RAF
*Flight Lieutenant Patrick W. Langford RCAF
Flight Lieutenant Roy B. Langlois RAF (caught at mouth of tunnel)
*Flight Lieutenant Thomas B. Leigh RAF
*Flight Lieutenant James L. R. Long RAF
*Flight Lieutenant Romas Marcinkus RAF
Flight Lieutenant H. C. 'Johnny' Marshall RAF
Flight Lieutenant Alastair T. McDonald RAF
*Lieutenant Clement A. N. McGarr SAAF
*Flight Lieutenant George E. McGill RCAF
*Flight Lieutenant Harold J. Milford RAF
*Flying Officer Jerzy T. Mondschein RAF
Second Lieutenant J. E. Muller RAF
Lieutenant Alastair D. Neely Royal Navy (RN)
Flight Lieutenant T. R. Nelson RAF
Flight Lieutenant A. Keith Ogilvie RAF
*Flying Officer Kazimierz Pawluk RAF

*Flight Lieutenant Henri A. Picard RAF
Flight Lieutenant Des L. Plunkett RAF
*Flying Officer John (Porokoru Patapu) Pohe RAF
Lieutenant Doug A. Poynter RN
Squadron Leader Lawrence Reavell-Carter RAF (caught at mouth
    of tunnel)
Pilot Officer Paul G. Royle RAF
*Lieutenant Bernard W. M. Scheidhauer Free French Air Force
Flight Lieutenant Michael M. Shand RNZAF
*Pilot Officer Sotiris Skanziklas Royal Hellenic Air Force
*Lieutenant Rupert J. Stevens SAAF
*Flying Officer Robert C. Stewart RAF
*Flying Officer John G. Stower RAF
*Flying Officer Denys O. Street RAF
*Flight Lieutenant Cyril D. Swain RAF
Flight Lieutenant Alfred B. Thompson RCAF
*Flying Officer Pavel Tobolski RAF
Flight Lieutenant Ivo P. Tonder RAF
Squadron Leader Len Trent RNZAF (caught at mouth of tunnel)
*Flight Lieutenant Arnost Valenta RAF
Flight Lieutenant Robert van der Stok RAF
Flight Lieutenant Raymond L. N. van Wymeersch RAF
*Flight Lieutenant Gilbert W. Walenn RAF
*Flight Lieutenant James C. Wernham RCAF
*Flight Lieutenant George W. Wiley RCAF
*Squadron Leader John E. A. Williams RAAF
*Flight Lieutenant John F. Williams RAF

Bibliography and Sources

Books consulted include:

Otl Aicher: *Innenseiten des Kriegs* (Fischer, Frankfurt-am-Main, 1985)
Allen Andrews: *Exemplary Justice* (Harrap, London, 1976)
Paul Brickhill: *The Great Escape* (Faber and Faber, London, 1951)
Martin Broszat and Helmut Krausnik: *Anatomy of the SS State* (Paladin, London, 1970)
Matthew Cooper: *The German Army 1933–1945* (Macdonald and Jane's, London, 1978)
Distel und Jakusch (eds.): *Konzentrationslager Dachau 1933–1945* (Comité International de Dachau, Dachau, 1978)
Alexander Drozdzynski (ed.): *Das verspottete Tausendjährige Reich* (Droste, Berlin, 1978)
Joachim Fest: *The Face of the Third Reich* (trans. Michael Bullock) (Penguin, Harmondsworth, 1983)
Joachim Fest: *Hitler* (trans. Richard and Clara Winston) (Penguin, Harmondsworth, 1983)
Burghard Freudenfeld (ed.): *Stationen der deutschen Geschichte 1919–1945* (DVA, Stuttgart, 1962)
Hans-Jochen Gamm: *Der Flüsterwitz im Dritten Reich* (List, Munich, 1990)
Anton Gill: *An Honourable Defeat* (Henry Holt, New York, 1994)
Anton Gill: *The Journey Back from Hell* (HarperCollins, 2001 edition)
Hans Bernd Gisevius: *Wo ist Nebe?* (Deutscher Bücherbund, Stuttgart, 1966)
Yvan Goll: *Sodom Berlin* (Fischer, Frankfurt-am-Main, 1988)
Heinz Heger: *The Men with the Pink Triangle* (Alyson/Gay Men's Press, NYC, 1980)
Horst Hildebrandt (ed.): *Die deutschen Verfassungen des 19. und 20. Jahrhunderts* (Schöningh, Paderborn, 1975)
Reinhard Rürup (ed.): *Topographie des Terrors* (Arenhövel, Berlin, 1989 edition)
A. P. Scotland: *The London Cage* (Evans Brothers, London, 1957)
Louis L. Snyder: *Encyclopaedia of the Third Reich* (Wordsworth, Ware, 1998)
F. A. B. Tams: *A Trenchard 'Brat'* (The Pentland Press, Bishop Auckland, 2000)

Jonathan F. Vance: *A Gallant Company* (Pacifica Military History, Pacifica, 2000)

John Wheeler-Bennett: *The Nemesis of Power* (Macmillan, London, 1952)

Elizabeth Wiskemann: *Europe of the Dictators* (Collins, London, 1966)

Sources consulted in the Public Record Office include two important sets of documents:

The Official History of the North Compound, Stalag-Luft III (AIR 40/2645 [82475])

Hamburg Trial of Gestapo agents and testimonies (WO 235/425,426,427 and 429).

Sources consulted in the Imperial War Museum include (document summaries from which further documentary evidence was derived):

Miscellaneous 77/1175.

Index

categories of 68
German 237, 246
'over the wire' 66, 94
by plane 132
from prisoner transport 43–4, 55, 69
punishment for 58, 159–61, 220
successful 45, 47, 151–2, 205–6, 216–18
'through the wire' 45–6, 50, 58, 104,
129–32
'under the wire,' *see* Great Escape; tunnels
escape cake food ('fudge') 130–1, 170
escape committees (X-Organisation)
Dulag-Luft 30, 32, 40, 41, 42, 45, 50
members of the 2–3, 32, 68
Oflag XXIB, Schubin 69
Stalag-Luft I 38
Stalag-Luft III 58–9, 67–8, 73, 75, 92, 93,
95, 149–50, 155
Espelid, Sergeant Halldor 147, 162, 186,
204, 224, 249, 251
espionage 17, 81–7
Ettlingen prison 210
Evans, Flight Lieutenant Brian 40, 44, 50,
108, 203, 212, 224, 253, 254–5
executions
of German civilians 17–18
of Great Escapers 224, 240, 242, 243–5,
246, 247–8, 249–51, 252–3, 254
Kugel Order 160
'Sagan Order' 196, 243–4
SBO informed of 221–3
'shot while trying to escape' 5–6, 50, 70

false documents 42, 50, 60, 66, 129, 150
burned 188, 189
date stamping 173, 180
error leading to capture 204
range of 146–7
Fanshawe, Lieutenant-Commander Peter
'Hornblower' 38, 58, 60, 69, 106, 125,
139, 140, 166
fat-burning lamps 33, 67, 120, 150, 184
Fenn, Captain 240
Filmer (POW) 44
First World War 12, 16, 21–2
Fischer (guard) 147
Fitch, Beryl 242–3
Floody, Wally 60, 75, 89, 111, 115, 117,
159, 166
floorboards 127
Flossenburg concentration camp 233
food section 68
Foot, M. R. D. 85
forced-labourers 16, 89, 98, 209
Foreign Office 226
Forester, C. S. 38

forgery unit 50, 59, 60, 75, 91, 97, 129,
145–7
France 15, 78–9, 82, 218
Frankfurt-an-der-Oder 66
fraternisation 32, 80–1, 126, 145, 147, 150,
159
French prisoners-of-war 151, 209
Fuglesang, Second Lieutenant Nils 147,
162, 186, 204, 224, 249, 251
Führer-Order 191, 234
furniture 102–3

gardens 136, 137
Geneva Convention 1, 2, 4, 5, 20, 56, 86,
152, 160, 195, 228, 248
George (tunnel codename) 236
German currency 42, 85
German–Soviet Pact of Non-Aggression
(1939–41) 15
Germany
constantly changing official documents
146–7
invasions of Czechoslovakia and Poland
77–8
Nazism 10, 16–21, 31
reason for fury at Great Escape
191–2
treatment of POWs 29–30
verge of collapse 233–6
Gestapo 5, 10, 12, 16, 18, 73–4, 105–6, 133,
137
investigated for war crimes 241, 243–7
manhunt for escapers 160–1, 190, 192,
198, 208, 210, 212, 214, 216, 229
shooting prisoners after interrogation
196
at Stalag-Luft III 220
Gisevius, Hans Bernd 197
Glemnitz, Sergeant Hermann 'Dimwits' 62,
66, 124, 136, 137, 138–9, 140–1, 144,
145, 237
Glorious, HMS 28
Gmeiner, Josef 243, 254
Goebbels, Josef 19
Goldfinch, Bill 63–5
'goonskins' (German uniforms) 50
Göring, Hermann 21, 22, 191, 192–3, 194
Görlitz prison 203–4, 206–7, 212, 224,
251–2
Graevenitz, General von 193, 194–5
Great Escape (24 March 1944)
British Government's response to deaths
226–7, 232
discovery by guards 187–8
estimate of men out revised 183–4
final checks 174